THE COMPLETE IDIOT'S GUIDE® TO

Making Money in the New Millennium

*by Christy Heady
and Janet Bigham Bernstel*

alpha
books

A Division of Macmillan General Reference
A Pearson Education Macmillan Company
1633 Broadway, New York, NY 10019-6785

Copyright © 1999 by Christy Heady

THE COMPLETE IDIOT'S GUIDE TO & Design are registered trademarks of Macmillan, Inc.

Macmillan General Reference books may be purchased for business or sales promotional use. For information please write: Special Markets Department, Macmillan Publishing USA, 1633 Broadway, New York, NY 10019.

International Standard Book Number: 0-02-862932-9
Library of Congress Catalog Card Number: 99-63130

01 00 99   8 7 6 5 4 3 2 1

Interpretation of the printing code: the rightmost number of the first series of numbers is the year of the book's printing; the rightmost number of the second series of numbers is the number of the book's printing. For example, a printing code of 99-1 shows that the first printing occurred in 1999.

Printed in the United States of America

Note: This publication contains the opinions and ideas of its authors. It is intended to provide helpful and informative material on the subject matter covered. It is sold with the understanding that the authors and publisher are not engaged in rendering professional services in the book. If the reader requires personal assistance or advice, a competent professional should be consulted.

The authors and publisher specifically disclaim any responsibility for any liability, loss or risk, personal or otherwise, which is incurred as a consequence, directly or indirectly, of the use and application of any of the contents of this book.

Alpha Development Team

Publisher
Kathy Nebenhaus

Editorial Director
Gary M. Krebs

Managing Editor
Bob Shuman

Marketing Brand Manager
Felice Primeau

Acquisitions Editor
Jessica Faust

Development Editor
Phil Kitchel
Amy Zavatto

Assistant Editor
Georgette Blau

Production Team

Development Editor
Nancy D. Warner

Production Editor
Mark Enochs

Cover Designer
Mike Freeland

Photo Editor
Richard H. Fox

Illustrator
Jody P. Schaeffer

Book Designers
Scott Cook and Amy Adams of DesignLab

Indexer
Angie Bess
Ginny Bess

Layout/Proofreading
Angela Calvert
Mary Hunt
Julie Trippetti

Contents at a Glance

Contents

Introduction

The dawn of a new millennium—it's nearly impossible not to be profoundly affected by celebrating and moving forward into a new century. The key ingredient in this new age is *change*, be it technological, economical, or financial—and you are at the very core of it all.

One thing you can count on in the new millennium is change, and it goes beyond any computer date problems that could take place. Nothing can ever be the same one minute from now as it was a minute ago, whether it's your outlook on life, your to-do list at work, or the percentage return on your mutual fund portfolio.

Your mission in the new millennium is to use your observation toolkit: your eyes. Keep them open to the constant transformations before you. The secret to this book—and making money in the year 2000 and beyond—is being able to recognize change and adjust your personal and financial objectives accordingly.

What You'll Learn in This Book

In creating this book for you, we've made the following assumptions:

➤ You have the drive and motivation to make the new millennium profitable but are unsure how to develop the right investment strategy.

➤ You have logged on to the Internet and have searched the World Wide Web, but it's unclear how you can profit from all the information you've found.

➤ You are ready to take the next step toward financial and economic freedom by using your talents and skills in a career that fits with your aspirations and hectic schedule.

Whatever your situation and whatever type of plan you set aside for you and your family, the *clean slate* of this next century that we are embarking on allows for anything to happen to anyone. So let's prepare for these times by first getting an education and here's how to do it.

Part 1: The Internet, Your Money, and You grounds you in some basics on how to do more than just surf the Web. It gives you information to help you select the right Internet tools you need to begin your financial journey, as well as provides you with some facts on banking and trading online.

Part 2: Making Money in the Millennium Marketplace devises key investment strategies for you to create and complete your investment portfolio. From learning simple wealth-building strategies to deciphering which stocks and mutual funds will not only be hot in the 21st century but work with your objectives—you can find it here.

Part 3: The Future of Your Money On and Offline picks apart the retirement icon that most Americans call the panacea to the future, Social Security, and whether it will still be here. Important information on developing the right 401(k) strategies, helpful real estate information, and key tidbits to buying and selling your way online are also available.

Part 4: Thriving in Tomorrow's Workplace enables you to do just that! It deciphers which jobs will be hot for the future, how to set up an online store, and ways to get your work done and balance your family life through telecommuting.

Plus, you get appendices on how to plan for the Y2K Bug, information about small business-friendly banks, lists of online discount brokers, and a glossary of terms to help you with all the jargon.

Extras

Along the way you'll find these helpful boxes offering definitions, online resources, and some interesting asides:

Click Here

Boot up and log on because the Internet is where it's at. These boxes contain helpful online resources that take you from the book to your computer all with the touch of a few keystrokes.

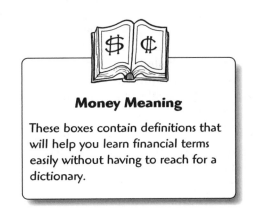

Money Meaning

These boxes contain definitions that will help you learn financial terms easily without having to reach for a dictionary.

Bet You Didn't Know

These boxes contain interesting or useful background information about investment opportunities or the fascinating worlds of Wall Street and cyberspace. They show better ways to get things done—ways to save money or time. Think of them as a friendly word in your ear.

Acknowledgments and Dedications

Christy Heady would like to dedicate this book to her mother, Diane, whose wondrous devotion, divine spirit, and pure faith for her four children will certainly leave an indelible mark on their souls no matter what century it is.

Christy Heady would like to especially acknowledge the outstanding Macmillan team for their guidance and faith in producing her third book, in particular: Kathy Nebenhaus, for her tireless efforts of encouragement and loyalty to this author; Robert Shuman, for his knack of accomplishing so many tasks in an ever-changing industry; Nancy Warner, for her ability to polish sentences and paragraphs with great finesse; and Mark Enochs, for his expertise in putting everything together seamlessly and effortlessly.

Christy Heady would also like to acknowledge the countless number of people in the financial services industry who make it their jobs to provide journalists with data and information at the drop of a hat. This book would not be possible without the help of the staff at the Employee Benefits Research Institute, the American Bankers Association, the Consumers Bankers Association, Morningstar, Inc., Hewitt Associates, the Securities Exchange Commission, NASDAQ, Weiss Research, the Federal Reserve, the Social Security Administration, editors at the *Online Banking Report*, Spectrum, Inc., CDA Investment Technologies, Challenger, Gray & Christmas, and the Congressional Budget Office. And to all the online pioneers who blazed the Internet trail, you've made covering the worlds of personal finance and investing such an exciting medium to work in.

Janet Bigham Bernstel would like to thank the many editors and assistants at Macmillan Publishing who helped bring this book to completion, in particular Kathy Nebenhaus, the Publisher, for the opportunity, Nancy Warner, a cheerful development editor who took our words and turned them into a book, and Mark Enochs, without whom nothing is possible!

Special thanks to the following people for their help in providing insight and information along the way, both for this book and more. To the people dedicated to outfitting anyone who's willing with the tools of economic independence through business ownership, a grateful thank you to the Small Business Administration staff, Gere Glover, Mike Stamler, and John Bebrief. Thank you to Paula Aryanpur of the Online Women's Business Center for her enthusiasm over this project to the Palm Beach County Business Incubator directors, Stephen Windhouse and David Fancher.

Thanks as well to the people who supplied the map through the technical maze of the Internet. To William J. Piniarski, owner of Webster Computing Service, www.webcs.com, for his invaluable insight into building on the Web; Dr. Ralph F. Wilson of Wilson Internet Services, www.wilsonweb.com, for sharing his wealth of information on Web hosting, marketing, and more; and Mike Twombly at Zipwell.com, a Web-savvy entrepreneur with lots of spirit. And to the builders and keepers of the Internet, thanks, what a research tool!

It is impossible to hand out thanks without acknowledging one's family. They are, after all, the ones that talk you through the tough times and deserve to share in the victories. So Janet Bigham Bernstel extends a loving thanks to her parents, Harry and Elizabeth, for their steadfast support in all her creative endeavors, and to her siblings, Bill, Harry, Michael, Brian, and Jeanne, for their ballot box full of votes of confidence.

Most of all, she would like to dedicate this book to her husband, Maurice, for his devoted patience through a long summer as lead parent while she researched and wrote. And also to her children, Marissa and Connor, who will come of age in the third millennium and who continuously fill this writer with joy and faith of a bright future.

Part 1
The Internet, Your Money, and You

Seems like everyone has an email address or a Web site these days, no matter if they're a 13-year-old emailing a pen pal in Japan to help with homework or a retiree searching for the highest savings yields on certificates of deposit. In fact, by the year 2002, technology analysts estimate 175 million people will be using the World Wide Web.

Everywhere you turn, the Internet is prevalent and riddled with technobabble. *And while it is important to master the* Net *lingo, it is equally as important to find out how the Internet can help you profit financially.*

From finding the most cost-efficient online bank accounts to paying the lowest commission rates on stock and mutual fund trades, you can use the Internet as a tool to not only help you save time and meet your investment objectives, but also to pave the way to a prosperous future.

Let's begin.

Chapter 1

What Is the Internet and Do You Need It to Make Money?

In This Chapter

➤ How the Internet affects your lifestyle

➤ What you should—and shouldn't—do online

➤ Why your future in personal finance depends on cyberspace

➤ Ways you can profit by logging online

It's seven o'clock in the morning. Your spouse is sitting in your home office paying the mortgage and credit card bills. Nothing unique about that, except she's talking to the computer and telling it what to do. No keystrokes necessary. Within ten minutes the bills are paid, the checkbook is balanced, and you both rejoice over the morning cup of Java.

Off to work. Driving down the highway, you realize you need cash for an important lunch meeting and left your ATM card sitting on your dresser. No problem! Just plug your modem connection from your laptop into your cell phone and request a balance transfer from your checking account to the restaurant's Web site bill pay section for today's dining members. Ah, transactionless cuisine.

Whoops. You also forgot to make your children's hair appointments. Off to the computer where you log on to the Salon-n-Spa Web site, book three haircuts, download a 25 percent off coupon on future services and throw in a facial for your spouse. After all, she did balance that checkbook to the penny.

So, are you ready for the year 2000 and beyond?

We are, and the new millennium is beckoning. More than 100 million people are banking online, trading stocks, and even calculating how much of a house they can afford. This chapter will show you why it is so important to understand how cyberspace works (and what it is), how to plug in and profit, and provide you with a few resources to get started.

The Internet, Cyberspace, and You

What can anyone in the world tap into no matter what time of day or continent? You got it: It's the Internet.

The backbone of the Internet is nothing more than a global communications network connecting computers around the world. According to the Internet Society, Reston, Virginia, there are more than 50,000 of these computers—typically housed at major universities and governmental departments—that make up this *network of networks*.

The *culture* of information available on the Internet is accessed through a system called the *World Wide Web*, also referred to as the *Web*. And boy, is it growing. Hundreds of thousands of businesses have created Web sites to transact business, increase awareness of their products, or offer online services. For some—such as Amazon.com, the first Internet bookstore—an online presence is paying off. Amazon.com increased its book sales to $148 million in 1997, up from $16 million in 1996. Even Pizza Hut made its World Wide Web debut in 1994 as the first restaurant to set up a Web site where consumers could order pizza.

Bet You Didn't Know

In 1996, there were more than 28 million Web users. By the year 2002, technology analysts estimate 175 million people will be using the World Wide Web.

"Okay, Ms. Authors," you say. "I understand all this network mumbo jumbo, but how can the Internet help me manage my money? I'm all for ordering a good pepperoni pizza now and then, even if it's off the Web, but I need to make a few bucks and make the most of what I have."

No problem; it's quite simple. Let's say you're in the market for a new car. Think of the traditional method to auto shopping: get up early on a Saturday morning, go down to the dealer lot, kick a few tires, and hone your haggling skills. This came, of course, after finding out from your bank's loan officer how much you could borrow.

Today, you can log onto the Internet and search and compare local auto loan rates among 15 to 20 financial institutions to find the best deal. Next, you can search for the type of car you'd like to buy simply by visiting the manufacturers' or car dealers' Web sites. Some Web sites, such as Toyota or General Motors, go as far as showing you inside snapshots and different colors on each make and model. Finally, online resources such as Kelly's Blue Book or Edmunds.com, enable you to compare the manufacturer's suggested retail price (MSRP) with the invoice cost. And you did all this without stepping out of your house. Know what the best part is? You save hundreds of dollars in loan interest and MSRP charges in the process.

This car-buying example is just one of the things you can do online to help with your finances. There are others, but first, you're going to need to learn the lingo. We call it *technobabble*.

Learning the Technobabble and Other Important Stuff

You may know how many licks it takes to get to the center of a Tootsie Pop™, but do you know how many Kbps it takes to transfer data from one computer to another via the Internet? Unless Alex Trebek has penciled you in for a round of Jeopardy!™, it's not crucial if you don't know the answer. If you want to profit online, however, understanding the terminology is important.

Get Connected

You know that the Internet is a worldwide communications network connecting about 50,000 computers, and that the World Wide Web is the system on the Net that you use to access information. In order for you to access that information, you need an Internet Service Provider (ISP) or an online service. These both include but are not limited to:

➤ America Online

➤ AT&T WorldNet

➤ CompuServe

➤ MCI

➤ Microsoft Network

➤ Prodigy

➤ Sprint

Money Meaning

You can buy URLs, you know, or at least a portion thereof, called a *domain name*. For example, if you wanted to create a Web site for your shoe manufacturing business called "Shoes-R-Us," most likely you would want your URL to read: www.shoes-r-us.com. You buy the domain name, in this case, shoes-r-us.com, by registering it through an online service called InterNIC.

5

Bet You Didn't Know

As of 1997, there were more than 320 million Web pages. By the year 2000, there may be 800 million.

—NEC Research Institute, March 1998 (NUA Surveys)

Voilà. You're connected to *cyberspace*, which is a slang term for the Internet, and much like we have a home address—you know that infamous 123 Main Street in Anytown, USA—all Web sites have an address called a *URL*, which stands for Uniform Resource Locator. Some folks pronounce it "Earl"; others say "U-R-L." Merriam-Webster offers both pronunciations. Personally, we're divided. You choose. Web site addresses (URLs) typically look like this:

www.buythisbook.com

Knowing Where to Look

What happens if you're looking for information but don't know where to begin to find the right address? Easy. Let's say you need to get up-to-date information on insurance. You can do so through the different types of indexing systems, much like a library uses a card catalogue. These systems on the Web are known as *search engines*, and include but are not limited to:

➤ AltaVista (www.altavista.com)

➤ Excite (www.excite.com)

➤ HotBot (www.hotbot.com)

➤ Lycos (www.lycos.com)

➤ Webcrawler (www.webcrawler.com)

➤ Yahoo! (www.yahoo.com)

Money Meaning

A **hyperlink** is an electronic link providing direct access from one distinctively marked place in a document (Web page) to another in the same or different document, according to Merriam-Webster Dictionary Online at www.m-w.com. Hyperlinks are usually marked in blue and underlined.

You can simply go to a search engine Web site, type the key word(s) in the search field prompt, and press Enter or use your mouse to click on a search button. Your results will be displayed with the headline, a brief description of the Web site, and a *hyperlink*, allowing you to click directly to that particular site on insurance.

When using search engines to retrieve information, it is best to be as specific as possible to help weed out unnecessary links to irrelevant Web pages. If you need information on health care insurance, for example, rather than just typing in "insurance," type in "health care insurance." Be specific; it'll help save time when wading through the results.

Now that you've got the basics, let's find out what you can do online to help you manage your finances.

What You Can Do Online

Flick a switch and tap a few keys, and reams of financial planning information is available on your computer screen. It's easy to get hooked *surfing* on the Net for information, but unless you learn how to use that information properly, you can make costly mistakes.

Whether you're a *newbie* (just getting started) to cyberspace and the investment arena or an online financial pro ready to make a trade, the Web has a wealth of information on personal finance, including buying insurance, preparing taxes, buying a house, and planning for retirement. In fact, many Web sites offer financial transaction capabilities, such as paying bills or buying stock.

And for you shopaholics, electronic commerce is here to stay—and growing. You can buy groceries online and have them delivered to your doorstep, shop for birthday presents at your favorite store, or even trade your old Cadillac for a newer and improved model through online auctions.

The next few sections present Web sites that will help you get started.

Tax Preparation

Where else to begin other than the Internal Revenue Service? Log onto its Web site at www.irs.ustreas.gov, where you won't get advice but you can download hundreds of federal forms and get links to state forms. In fact, you can file right online with the IRS. (Hint: Print out the instructions first.) A color-coded calendar displays important filing dates and summaries of tax law changes. Even IRS regulations are available in easy, idiot-proof, language. Who knew?

Click Here

Want to know what the Internal Revenue Service is up to? Log onto **www.irs.ustreas.gov** to stay on top of tax-related news and how it may affect you and your family.

If you're looking more for advice, stop by H&R Block (www.hrbloc.com/tax), where a tax refund calculator sums up your tax return (if you have one) and a hefty section is devoted to understanding the Tax Relief Act of 1997.

Quicken.com's tax section (www.quicken.com) includes a tax estimator as well as a calendar, tips, and, of course, the option to purchase its software, TurboTax.

Need more of a potpourri of tax advice? Visit TaxWeb at www.taxweb.com, which provides links to dozens of Web sites that offer tax-related discussion groups, federal and state tax sites, and tax software developers.

Buying a Home

With the median home price in the United States at $157,000 as of January 1999, according to the U.S. Census Bureau, it's no wonder we're all singing the same proverbial tune: How much house can I afford? Not to worry. QuickenMortgage (www.quicken.com) has an interactive calculator that will answer that question for you. In addition, QuickenMortgage provides a loan pre-qualification worksheet that produces a comparative analysis of closing and monthly costs.

Several consumer rate organizations—such as Banxquote (www.banxquote.com), Bank Rate Monitor (www.bankrate.com), and Mortgage Market Information Services (www.interest.com/mmis.html)—allow you to search for the lowest 30- or 15-year fixed rate mortgage or 1-year ARM in your area. Basic how-to information on the mortgage process is available as well as weekly rate analysis and commentary.

You don't need to be a realtor to log onto Realtor.com (www.realtor.com) and access its database of 1 million properties. In fact, you can customize your search depending on which city you live in. Once you pinpoint your desired location, plug in the number of bedrooms and baths you want and any matched results will be listed. Your results will also show you a picture of the home you selected complete with information about the house.

Retirement Planning

Do you contribute to a 401(k)? Then you'll probably want to stop by T. Rowe Price's retirement planning section (www.rps.troweprice.com). T. Rowe Price's Retirement Toolset offers an interactive course in retirement planning. It features a powerful Retirement Planning Profiler, which takes information you provide and uses it to tailor the Retirement Toolset presentation to your situation. Plus, there is a free service dubbed "Watch List" that lets you monitor the performance of your personal list of mutual funds.

While mutual funds play an important part in investing over the long haul for your retirement, don't count Social Security out just yet. If you want to know how much you'll receive—if any—from Social Security when you retire, go to Social Security Online (www.ssa.gov). Useful facts from the government agency are available, although most visitors to this Web site will want to request a copy of their own Personal

Earnings and Benefit Estimate Statement (PEBES). Those willing to provide a few details can view some of their PEBES information here, while others can use the site to order a snail mail version of their records. Otherwise, there is plenty to learn about federal retirement benefits, cost of living data, Medicare premiums, and the location of the nearest Social Security office.

Consider Vanguard Retirement Resource Center (majestic1.vanguard.com/RRC/DA/) as a potential online stop when searching for retirement information. Advice on saving and investing for the years when you won't be employed is provided, and a calculator on how much you need to save now to meet your retirement goals is available.

Click Here

Retirement planning is knowing how much it will take to get you from here to there. Find out with American Express' calculator on the World Wide Web at **www.americanexpress.com/401k/cgi-bin/nestEgg.cgi**.

Insurance

Stay on top of insurance news at the Insurance News Network (www.insure.com), where you can find out which pickups flunk the crash test, register a complaint with the State Department, and learn the ABCs of long-term care insurance. Also available is a report on the financial condition and outlooks for more than 70 major insurance companies and groups, including many of the nation's largest insurance companies. These reports include news bulletins that reflect recent developments at these companies plus, for participating insurers, links directly to insurer Web sites.

Quotesmith.com (www.quotesmith.com) allows you to obtain instant quotes from 350 leading insurance companies and to request an application online—without having to speak to any insurance salesmen. Along with each quote, you also get the latest A.M. Best, Duff & Phelps, Moody's, Standard & Poor's, and Weiss Research ratings.

Not sure whether you have enough auto insurance for your car? InsWeb (www.insweb.com), a Web site dedicated to providing information on all types of insurance, offers an interesting tool called the Auto Coverage Analyzer. Learn about auto coverage and tailor your needs to a customized, interactive profile page.

Investing and Online Trading

Many Web sites offer quotes, but most of those quotes are at a 15- to 20-minute delay. Those sites offering real-time quotes often charge, but the best deal going right now for real-time quotes is Reuters MoneyNet.com (www.moneynet.com), which costs $29.95 a month for quotes on stocks, options, mutual funds, and several market indexes.

To research your potential investments and stay on top of your portfolio holdings, visit Zacks Investment Research (www.ultra.zacks.com) for the latest investment analysis and recommendations.

Microsoft Investor, a service available through the Microsoft Network, will track up to ten investments for you (for a $9.95 monthly fee). The bell and whistle? They will email you when an investment hits your target price.

If you're a do-it-yourselfer, online brokerage firms and other online financal service companies let you buy and sell your way to profitability (that's the goal) right through your computer. For example, account holders at Charles Schwab (www.schwab.com) can garner a $29.95 per stock trade order up to 1,000 shares. Another example is Suretrade.com (www.suretrade.com), which charges only $7.95 on stock trades, $25 plus $2 per contract on all option trades, and a $25 fee for all no-load mutual fund online transactions. With Suretrade, though, if a broker assists you, they'll charge you $30 per trade instead.

Online Banking

Atlanta Internet Bank (www.aib.com), which opened its doors in October 1996, is the only bank online that has no branches, no headquarters, no brick or drywall (as of this writing). There are dozens of other banks that have Web sites and offer online banking transaction capabilities, but Atlanta Internet Bank tends to offer higher yields on saving accounts, such as certificate of deposit (CD) and money market accounts. Its *Internet Checking* account typically earns checking account holders a four percent annual percentage yield (APY), almost twice the national average.

Intuit, Inc., the maker of the Quicken home finance software, offers its product called BankNOW on the Web. Through America Online, users can check account balances, transfer funds between accounts, and schedule bills to be paid while the software automatically calculates the impact of transactions that haven't cleared the bank. Some banking customers can even complete loan applications using a personal computer linked by modem to their bank. You can get the BankNOW product from the Quicken Web site at www.quicken.com in its banking section.

For a complete comparative analysis on which banks are offering what types of online banking services across the country, stop by Cyberinvest.com at www.cyberinvest.com. Click on its Banking Guide and view the in-depth chart on which banks offer bill paying services, whether online CD rates are available, and a toll-free number to contact each bank directly.

Buying and Selling Online

The Internet has opened up a vast market for businesses that were unheard of even a few years ago. Whereas last year's Back-to-School shopping trip may have taken you to the local mall, this year's Internet shopping spree can take you as far away as Paris for a Gucci backpack or bargain-hunting at iMall (www.iMall.com), where hundreds of virtual shops wait for customers. This electronic delivery of goods and services is called *e-commerce*—where choice, convenience, and often lower prices rule the marketplace.

Bet You Didn't Know

According to a 1997 CommerceNet/Neilsen study, 10 million people in North America had purchased something online, up from 7.4 million just six months earlier. International Data Corporation predicts that by the year 2000, 46 million consumers in America will be buying online.

Seventy-seven percent of shoppers are going online with a specific purchase in mind. Seventy-nine percent of those are visiting several sites before making a purchase, according to Jupiter Communications. Can you afford not to be there if you've got wares to sell or something to buy?

Forget the Cash

Your money is no good at the virtual store—well, not in the physical sense. Credit cards are still the payment method of choice for Internet buyers, but privacy and security concerns keep some customers as mere shoppers, not buyers. With requests for PIN numbers, much like an ATM, and secret *encryption* codes, however, the heightened concern about online security is diminishing. In addition, forms of electronic cash—such as *digital IDs* and *smart cards*— are gaining popularity, making online purchases quick and easy, without sacrificing privacy.

Money Meaning

Digital IDs, also known as **digital certificates**, are the electronic counterparts to driver licenses and membership cards. With a digital ID, friends, business associates, and online services can be assured that any electronic information they receive from you is authentic, and vice versa. It opens a secure channel for online transactions.

Auctions and Classifieds

You don't have to go to a virtual store to buy something online. Hundreds of thousands of people are seeking bargains at online auctions. At the Home Shopping Network Web site, www.internet.net, you'll find First Auction where people bid in real-time (that means right now) for televisions, stereos, jewelry—just about anything.

At Classifieds 2000 (www.classifieds2000.com) you can even sell your own stuff at auction. All transactions are between you and the bidders; the Web site just gives you a forum to place your ad, set the bidding times, and conduct the actual auction.

Money Meaning

How smart do you have to be to carry a smart card? Listen up, Einstein. Basically, **smart cards** are plastic credit cards imbedded with a computer chip that stores information right on the card. These card-sized computers are used everywhere, from business secure ID cards to paying for highway tolls and buying items on the Internet. An A+ in our book.

Naturally, Classifieds 2000 also has a classified ads section. Place your ad and it automatically appears in the classified sections of their numerous online partner sites. Thousands of daily newspapers also have online classifieds, such as the *Chicago Tribune*, the *Orlando Sentinel*, and the *New York Times*. Most can be found at the paper's name followed by .com, such as www.orlandosentinel.com. Look for instructions to place an ad, and you're on your way. You can check the ads in a North Dakota newspaper for jobs, products, or services when you live in Buck Lick Holler, Kentucky!

eBay.com is one of the largest personal online trading communities on the Net. Using one-to-one trading in an auction format, people buy and sell items in categories such as collectibles, antiques, computers, toys, and jewelry. They offer over a half million new auctions, and 70,000 new items for sale every day.

Pros and Cons of Taking Your Money Online

No one thing has done more to change the look and feel of personal finance than the Net. Here are some reasons why it's so popular:

➤ **Instant access.** Your morning paper is stale news before it hits the sidewalk. If you want really fresh reports, the *New York Times* (www.nytimes.com) updates every ten minutes. Or *webzines*, a term used for electronic magazine, like www.Bloomberg.com or www.businessweek.com, carry up-to-the-minute news on the latest merger or stock split. If you don't want to wade through barrels of pork bellies, customize your own news page on sites such as www.CNNfn.com, www.news.com, or www.pointcast.com. Really, aside from that almost nostalgic feeling of sitting down with a cup of coffee and the paper, who needs the ink-blackened fingers?

➤ **Choice.** There are more than 300 million pages on the World Wide Web. That's a lot of pages, and while not all of them are relevant sites to help you make money, we'll tell you how to find many that are.

➤ **24/7.** That's *cyberspeak* for an around-the-clock operation. The Internet is open and ready for business 24 hours a day, 7 days a week. Not only is this ultra-convenient for nightowls and procrastinators, it puts the entire globe on equal time.

➤ **Lower prices.** Fast and cheap, the way you like your cars, perhaps, is the way the Internet allows you to do business and conduct your online research. Competition and commerce is heating up online, and with little wonder, as the traffic on the Internet has been doubling every 100 days. Most news and information is already free (and you're still paying 35 cents for your local paper—puh-leaze). Instantaneous stock trades can cost as little as $8 with www.Ameritrade.com or $14.95 with www.etrade.com, compared with $40 and up per trade with traditional brokerage houses. Basic online banking functions like performing a balance inquiry or transferring money between accounts costs little or nothing. And, although most banks charge a fee for electronic bill payment, you still save on postage and gain the convenience.

Money Meaning

Cyberspeak is the language of computer savvy Net surfers. You, too, will be fluent in cyberspeak once you've read this book. :)

For every pro, of course, there must be a con, and the Internet has those, too. The Internet is cheap and convenient, but far from perfect. Here are some reasons why people grumble about this modern day electronic wonder. Some of the downsides to the Internet include:

Money Meaning

A **digital footprint** is the information you leave behind when you post messages, stories, or items on the World Wide Web. Do a search sometime for your own name and see what pops up. You may be surprised, or alarmed!

➤ Heavy traffic. Millions of users leads to slow access during peak user times.

➤ Security and privacy. You can leave your *digital footprints* on the Net, a sort of telltale trail of personal postings if anyone cares to search. Also, some employers have ways to monitor which Web sites you're visiting. Dangerous? Sure. You could lose your job if you're consistently doing personal work on company time using company property.

➤ Too much information. With over 300 million pages to sort through, surfing the Net can be a little confusing at times. We call it *information overload* and quite often reach for the Tylenol™.

➤ Scams and shams. It's too easy to believe everything you see. Remember, not all the information on the Net is accurate, so make sure you trust the source.

➤ Y2K bug. A computer glitch caused by a programming error in the 1960's may become the plague of Net. If not fixed in time, this little three-digit nemesis could cause computers worldwide to read the year 2000 as 1900. Yikes! See Appendix A for tips on bug repellant.

Plug In and Profit

You can do it. If you can get yourself past the "I don't even know how to turn on a computer" stage, you are on your way with the best of the Net surfers. We've shown you what you need to plug in (PC, modem, remember?), so now let's journey on to ways to help you profit.

We'll show you how in these chapters, but first, you should decide if making money on the Internet is for you. If you can answer *yes* to any of these questions, then keep reading and be prepared to prosper.

Are You...:

➤ Looking for a job that pays better?

➤ Looking to sell your work?

Do You...:

➤ Have a product or idea that you want to sell or advertise?

➤ Have some cash you'd like to invest but don't want to pay big commission fees?

➤ Want to be competitive and forward thinking?

Let's go make some money!

The Least You Need to Know

➤ The backbone of the Internet is nothing more than a global communications network connecting computers around the world; it's easy to log on.

➤ You can tap into an Internet indexing system to look for information online using a search engine. Some search engines include Yahoo!, Excite, AltaVista, and Lycos.

➤ Web sites of companies and organizations offer you the chance to determine your financial needs through online calculators or read up on the latest news in their editorial stories.

➤ Smart cards are plastic credit cards imbedded with a computer chip that stores information right on the card. These card-sized computers allow you to pay for highway tolls or even buy items on the Internet.

➤ The Internet is a time-saver, and sometimes a life-saver, put it's not perfect. Make sure your source is trustworthy, and don't give out too much personal information.

Chapter 2

The Future of This New Age Tool

Remember the days when you wanted to change the channel on the television set you actually had to get up from the couch? Whew, what a workout. You must admit that the remote control is one of life's sweetest technological advances (especially for the lazy couch potatoes). Today's generation surely balks at the mere exercise, but then again most of them probably haven't even seen a black-and-white television set either.

Of course, the world of technology has grown much more than shuffling through music videos on *MTV* or feverishly searching for *Seinfeld* reruns with your remote control. Consumer appliances and electronic gadgets—such as microwave ovens, cellular phones, fax machines, and voice-recognition computer software—all promise to make your hectic lives easier. Just read one of those buy-in-the-sky shopping catalogues the next time you're on a plane for proof. Devices that can store up to 1,000 names and phone numbers in seven different languages—including Swahili—abound, not to mention a timing device operated by solar power to feed your toy poodle while you're out of town.

What will they think of next?

Our new millennium will reward those people who stay on top of technological trends in their personal and professional lives simply by having the knowledge to make better informed decisions about what to buy and how to invest. This chapter will show you what key trends to look out for in the new millennium, how to benefit by embracing its largest tool—the Internet—and what you can do to profit from it.

You've Come a Long Way, Baby

In order to grasp the future, we must look to the past. Don't worry, we'll keep it brief.

Investments in technology are among the highest-payback investments the United States has ever made. A report issued in the early 90s by the Council of Economic Advisers notes, for example, that over the past 50 years technological innovation has been responsible for half or more of the nation's growth in productivity.

You can see the fruits of this labor every day. Many of the products and services we have come to depend on for our way of life in America—lasers, computers, communications satellites, modems, and even storm windows—are the product of federal science and technology investments made over the past 50 years.

Bet You Didn't Know

Now playing in your living room: the computer. The percentage of U.S. households that have at least one computer was almost 37 percent in 1997, up from 24 percent in 1994. And the more money you make, the more apt you are to subscribe to an online service, according to a July 28, 1998, report issued by U.S. Commerce Department Secretary Daley entitled "Falling Through the Net II: New Data on the Digital Divide."

These innovations also mean more employment opportunities for consumers. There are millions of good new jobs, better health and longer lives, new opportunities for individuals, and enrichment with newfound knowledge that we would not have been able to imagine half a century ago. Francis Bacon was right when he coined the phrase, "Knowledge is power." (And he didn't even have Internet access back then.)

How Far Have You Come?

Our country's wealth is largely based on its activity on various levels, such as what companies manufacture, how much you work, and how much you spend. The more active and productive we are, the greater the national wealth. Technology, especially the Internet, has had a large part in our country's affluence. The U.S. Commerce Department says that electronic commerce, those that do business over the Internet, may surpass $300 billion in revenue by 2002 as more businesses of all sizes take advantage of the Internet to rein in purchasing costs, reduce inventory, close sales, and recruit new customers.

So all this techno-hoopla must mean that Americans are technologically savvy and quite productive to have gathered such great knowledge and are rich beyond belief. Hmmm. Let's think about that for a moment with a pop quiz.

1. True or False. If you're technologically savvy, you are productive, which has a positive effect on the bottom line.

The answer is true *and* false. What makes this statement true is that the advancements in technology are responsible for an increase in productivity, whether you work for a company that produces home heating and cooling systems or own a charming bed and breakfast in western Massachusetts.

Let's say the new machinery with all the bells and whistles you've been lobbying for at work has the capacity to double production output, but you need more information to back up your assumptions. As you learned in Chapter 1, the Internet can be used as a search tool through various search engines, such as Excite, Infoseek, Yahoo, and AltaVista. By digging through search results online, you can select Web sites that provide information to help you determine if this is the best and least expensive product for your company. After thorough investigation, your theories are confirmed. The result? More goods for your company to manufacture and sell. Can you say pay increase?

Take the example of the bed and breakfast owner. A New England inn has the appearance of a quiet place where we busier-than-heck-workaholics can get away from it all—but that's just window dressing. Inside the guts of the operation, the innkeepers are registering their Web site with numerous search engines to make sure potential guests can find them on the Web, checking their email from people who have reservation inquiries, and uploading special discount offers on home products made on the premises. Label them cash-flow positive with a capital C.

Those are two simple examples of how being techno-savvy can work for you. Now, here's how it can work *against* you.

There are more than 4.3 million Web sites on the Internet as of February 1999. Talk about information overload. Everyone has a Web site with a story to tell or a product to sell. All of these millions of pages can make the needle in the haystack of online information you're pouring through overwhelming and—yes—counter-productive. That is, unless you know how to go about implementing the right search techniques to get the information you need.

Search Me, Frisk Me, Whatever It Takes

As of this writing, there are no online police—fortunately, for the Freedom of Information Act fighters—although a crossing guard now and then would really help when sifting through search engine query results. A search engine finds the information you request from its database by accepting listings submitted by authors (people who produce the Web sites) wanting exposure, or by getting the information from their *Web crawlers*, *spiders*, or *robots*.

Bet You Didn't Know

Web crawlers, **spiders**, and **robots** are programs that roam the Internet, searching all the available content. In addition to storing links to these Web sites, they also record information about each page that they visit. The information that comes from these searches is used to match your search query to particular Web pages, and the link is used to give you the Internet address of the page.

So, besides typing in a few relevant—and very specific—words into the search form, what else can you do to condense your troubles...um...we mean, search query? Most search engines allow you to type in a few words, and then search for occurrences of these words in their database. Each of them, including HotBot, Lycos, and Infoseek, has its own way of deciding what to do about the approximate spellings, plural variations, abbreviations, or word abstracts known as *truncation*. If you just type words into the basic search area you get from the search engine's main page, whoa! Be prepared to be inundated as you can get different logical expressions binding different words together.

A key strategy is to search only in titles so that you can eliminate pages with only brief mentions of a concept, and therefore retrieve pages that really focus on the information you're looking for. And, each search engine does have a help file. Use it! After all, time is money.

Excite (www.excite.com), for example, lists an extremely helpful search guideline where they suggest you use more than just one keyword to limit the number of results. Their methodology is based on finding relationships that exist between words and ideas so that the results will be closer to what you're looking for. Excite also suggests that if you find that one of the results better describes what you are looking for, click on the *More like this* link, which will then use that as a basis for a new search to find more sites similar to the result you selected.

Knowledge Is Power and All That Good Stuff

In the Draconian days before the Industrial Revolution in the early 1800s in North America when people used to make their own clothes, and paper and glass were left for the wealthy, the thought of accessing information through a phone line wasn't even a consideration. Okay, you got us—the telephone wasn't even invented yet—that wasn't until the end of the century.

But the seedlings for change were there, as machinery replaced human workers, and inexpensive, mass-produced goods replaced expensive, handmade goods. Many people pushed for the transition into more, faster, better, and cheaper.

Times haven't changed; there's just more to choose from and learn. After all, knowing the basics about technology, especially the Internet and computers, adds tremendous power to your life, whether you're a Math teacher, own a pizza and sub shop, or a college student at the University of Michigan. In today's world, if you don't learn about technology, you will be left at ground zero holding your Atari joystick.

Here are a few motivating facts to show you how technological change is good and how others are getting involved:

➤ Attention female shoppers: Your wallets are talking. Studies indicate that you will spend nearly $3.5 billion by the year 2000, purchasing clothes, housewares, and food online. What does this mean for online storefronts, such as Godiva chocolates (www.godiva.com), clothing from Neiman Marcus (www.neimanmarcus.com) and gifts for the little one at Baby Gap (www.babygap.com)? Revenues.

➤ In 1997, small businesses spent $138 billion on technology, according to Access Media International, up from $118 billion the previous year. As a result, productivity and profits are booming; 74 percent of small U.S. businesses with Web sites received more product and service inquiries; 52 percent expanded their sales to new geographic regions; and 30 percent experienced more timely feedback from customers and suppliers.

➤ With Fortune 500 companies dedicating more resources to their respective Web sites, those employees in the Web-building field are reaping in the bucks. Less than 30 percent of people surveyed in Internet World's 1998 fourth annual survey of corporate webmasters reported earning less than $55,000 per year. About 20 percent reported earning $95,000 a year or more—up 9.6 percent from the previous year.

Money Meaning

In Merriam-Webster's online dictionary, **truncated** means to cut or shorten words, as a search engine would often cut out abbreviations, for example, if you use them in your online search.

Bet You Didn't Know

Faster, better, cheaper: The electronic calculator, introduced in 1971, cost $240. Through advances in technology using semiconductors, chips that act like switches, and continuous mass production, the same but now modern-day calculator now is only about $10.

It's Cocktail Party Fodder

How many times in one day do you think Bill Gates' name is mentioned across America? That is, outside of Janet Reno's office?

All kidding aside, Gates is one of the most influential people in the world regarding technological advances (not to mention one of the richest). He, a spry 21-year-old, along with partner Paul Allen, began the company today known as Microsoft, in 1975. They were with the computer geeks who built the world's first mini-computer to rival all commercial models.

Since then, Microsoft has dominated the software market, and it, along with other technology-related resources—such as America Online, A&T, Yahoo!, IBM, Apple—is penetrating your living rooms (and pocketbooks!), making themselves household brand names just like Betty Crocker.

Here's some proof: In November 1997, the research team Hart and Teeter found that Microsoft was the most admired company in one of the most admired industries in America. When the public was asked to volunteer, without being prompted, the names of one or two companies they admire, 25 percent of those queried said Microsoft. IBM and General Motors came next at 16 percent, respectively, followed by AT&T and Walmart at 15 percent.

Hold On, Batman

The technology industry, especially the Internet, is much quicker to adapt to events than is television or newspapers, where the changes are glacial by comparison. For example, the 400-plus page report issued by Ken Starr, in September 1998, relaying all the information about the events between Monica Lewinsky and President Clinton, was uploaded immediately onto the Net.

What happened next? Well, if you had searched for information on the Internet about Monica Lewinsky or President Clinton your search results would have produced millions of pages for your reading pleasure. In fact, *The Late Show with David Letterman* Web site reveals it is not responsible if your computer crashes if you perform a search through their Top 10 List archive with the phrase "Clinton."

The speed at which information is uploaded on the Web, be it trivial, historical or helpful, is daunting, but like City Hall, you can't fight it. Technology is a reality that's here to stay—just ease up on the Bill Clinton web searches!

But I'm from Camp Clueless

It's easy to fall into one of the two camps: You either spend a fortune by buying all the new gizmos and gadgets just because they look great in the computer magazines, or you don't get involved with any of the stuff because you're not *into technology*. Either way, you're going to lose, since you'll be broke from spending all your money on contraptions or ignorant of an education that could reward you handsomely.

Here are a few concepts to keep in mind to help you embrace the world of technology and not be labeled a total geek in the process:

➤ **Think Ol' MacDonald.** He had a farm with plants, chickens, pigs, goats, and cows, right? They all need to be nurtured to grow. And so do you, your brain that is; with all this new information, it just needs to be done *slowly* so you can absorb every single detail. Farmer MacDonald wouldn't take a firehose to a delicate patch of carrots just because it needed water. He would sprinkle the plants with water daintily, allowing enough droplets to moisten the soil. The same concept applies to your studying, accepting, and practicing new information. Slow and steady is the approach. E-I-E-I-O.

Click Here

Subscribing to several email newsletters that discuss all the technological changes going on in the world is a good way to introduce yourself to the Internet and all it offers. The newsletter library (**pub.savvy.com/subject.htm**) has a database of more than 11,000 free newsletters that can be sent to your email address. All you do is fill out a free questionnaire and select your interests (investing, health and fitness, or art and lifestyles, for example) and your email address will be sent to all newsletter publishers.

➤ **Once you've absorbed this information, be prepared to think and react quickly.** The Internet industry operates at an exponential growth rate, and the people and businesses who are on (or at least follow) the Net every day react just as fast. For example, if you work for a travel agency, it pays to watch what the competition is doing with its Web sites, especially if they're accepting online reservations and credit card payments. Or, for instance, maybe you despise trekking down to the bank lobby so you opt for online banking. Will you know how it works once its loaded onto your computer?

➤ **Can you spell D-E-M-O?** Test out new gadgets *before* you buy them. You want proof that whatever latest and coolest stuff you have your eyes on is just as easy to work with at home. That's right, whether it's a new VCR, a software application that helps you manage your finances, or a souped-up computer that works as a laptop and a workstation, you need to play with it first. Any store you are considering purchasing new toys from should give you a hands-on demonstration.

➤ **Get connected the right way.** We don't necessarily advocate getting a cellular phone or subscribing to more than one Internet Service Provider, but if you cannot stay in touch with other people, especially for business, you could lose out on potential money-making opportunities. With the rate at which software is developing and gobbling up space on your computer's hard drive, as well as the increased time it takes to download a Web site, you should consider adding more memory to your computer and opting for a faster modem. Adding additional memory, such as upgrading to 16MB from 8MB on a PC, will run you typically **$79 to $99.** A 56K modem is also a worthy buy as a 28.8 modem is as out of date now as a black phone with a rotary dial and costs roughly $100.

➤ **Try, try again.** The key to success in this new age is to try new techniques frequently. If something doesn't work, learn from it, re-tool, and try it again. And then call customer service for help. Getting someone to assist you will help you learn quickly and efficiently.

Bet You Didn't Know

Men and women accept technology differently. (What else is new?) Men tend to display more positive attitudes toward computers regardless of their level of familiarity, whereas women's attitudes become more positive as their level of familiarity increases, according to a 1993 study by Sacks, Bellisimo and Mergendoller. Can they say the same thing about gender differences with sex?

Just Jot It Down

As multitasking people of the new millennium, we both can attest to needing a place where we can jot down all our assignments, meetings, children's doctor visits, dates with husbands, and pet vaccination appointments. You get the picture.

We live in a society where technology has implemented and improved the notion of *faster, better, cheaper*, but the end result is also *more*. There are more appointments, more assignments, and more meetings, leaving little time for extracurricular activities (although those get sporadically thrown in, too). Someone, or rather, something, has to juggle all of these things if we plan on staying on top of and profiting from online trends.

Good examples of products that can manage your life are organizers such as a Daytimer (www.daytimer.com) or a Franklin-Covey Planner (www.franklincovey.com)—dubbed "the time management workshop for the entire business of living." Both companies offer useful time management systems that you can order online and keep you up to date with any new products or services each offers.

Franklin-Covey Planner's Web site offers a quote of the day, a customer service center to help you with purchases, and even coupons that can you save 20 percent off the next purchase at a local Franklin-Covey Planner store.

Click Here

For those of you looking for self improvement, a free weekly newsletter is available via email with suggestions on improving your life. Motivational quotes, products, and book reviews are included. Log on to **www.selfgrowth.com/form-newsletter.html** and fill out the form.

Stay Wired, Get Hired

Whether you're choosing a career, changing your job, or trying to balance work with the rest of your life, the following information will help you take control of your career course.

Technology jobs, for one, pay higher than average wages due to the basic laws of supply and demand: There are more computer jobs than there are professionals to fill them. Salary expectations can vary widely depending on which region of the country you live in. According to the 11th annual salary survey done by *Computer World*, a trade publication, top industries such as business services and rubber and metal manufacturing pay technology professionals who manage their Web sites more than $60,000 per year.

No need to be a tech guru to gain ground in the technology industry. You can improve your chances for a raise, promotion, or even a new job at a new company by improving your computer skills.

Several national computer stores, such as CompUSA (www.compusa.com), Best Buy (www.bestbuy.com) and Circuit City (www.circuitcity.com), either offer or have affiliations with local schools that give one-, two-, or three-day software or Internet training workshops. These classes include but are not limited to:

Microsoft Windows 95 and Windows 98

Microsoft Office 97

Microsoft Office 98

Microsoft FrontPage (for Web site publishing)

Microsoft Word

Microsoft Excel

Microsoft Powerpoint

Netscape Communicator

If your schedule is about as hectic as ours, you can also pick up one of the latest *Complete Idiot's Guide* books on any of the preceding subjects. Check your local bookstore or log on to Barnes and Noble online (www.barnesandnoble.com) or Amazon.com (www.amazon.com)—and save at least 10 percent off the cover price!

By learning more about computers, technology, and the Internet—whether it is to gain more skills for your career, find a career in that field, create your businesses' Web site, or even research investments and manage your money online—*you* have the power to profit in more ways than you'll ever know.

The Least You Need to Know

➤ Over the past fifty years, technological innovations have been responsible for half or more of the nation's growth in productivity.

➤ When you need to find information on the Web, a search engine will find that information for you from its database by accepting listings sent in by authors (people who produce the Web sites) wanting exposure.

➤ Whenever you test out a new product or piece of equipment, such as a computer or software package, see if you can get a demo. Technology, although rampant, is expensive, and a free demonstration of how your potential purchases work could save you money if you don't understand the application—or worse, if it's broken.

➤ Get on the technology bandwagon and perhaps get a raise or even a new (and better) job! Contact local and national computer stores to learn about inexpensive computer and software training packages they may offer.

Chapter 3

Using Technology to Help You Budget Your Money

In This Chapter

➤ Kick those old spending habits out the door

➤ Pick a plan to suit your style

➤ Worldwide help for your budget

➤ Budgeting for your life stages

It's pointless to talk about how to make money if you are unsure about how to keep it or manage it. In other words, we really can't take you any further unless we say the "B" word...budget. Yours. Don't turn away or turn the page, please. This doesn't have to hurt.

A budget should be many things, but it should not be painful. It's a tool to help you find out where your hard-won cash goes, and to help you free some of it up to spend on real money-making goodies, such as the fast-track investments we'll tell you about in Chapter 7, "Finding the Hot Stocks for the New Millennium."

So, all you non-CPAs out there, listen up. We're going to fine tune the cash flow in your life, and we're going to do it with some cyber-help. Free budget calculators, interactive worksheets, and reasonably priced software are constantly being upgraded to attract you, the math-dodging procrastinator! Check out some of today's tools by plugging in your own numbers, and test future scenarios of wealth building. Playing *what if* can be fun, and guess what, you're really working on your budget. See, and it didn't hurt a bit.

Before we log on and play with all these technology tools, however, let's look at budget basics that apply whether you're using pen and ledger or pull-down, pop-up super cyber-budgets.

It's Habit Forming

What is a budget anyway? An excellent tool for laying out your expenses, something concrete that you can pull out and analyze, discuss with your mate if you have one, and act on. It's a look at past spending and a road map for future wealth.

Do you have one now? Yes, and you may not even know it if you're not keeping track, because then you're not in charge. Every month you pay bills. You write checks and hope you have enough to cover all your expenses. All your time is focused on making the money to cover these costs, and it could be that not enough energy is spent on tracking the outflow.

Well, it's time to stop holding your breath at the end of every month and let out a deep sigh of satisfaction instead. The first step towards creating a healthy budget is to get organized. Just the process of gathering information alone is liberating. Once you know where it goes, you can control the flow of your money.

Stop the Panic

This may take a little time; getting organized always does. You are really training yourself in a new habit—that of budgeting your money—so expect some setbacks. Old spending habits die hard, but in the end a budget will save you hours of stress and anxiety.

If you're waiting for a good time to start, you've found it. Right now. Maybe you're getting married or starting a new job. A raise or promotion are also good budget triggering events because they involve financial decisions. So get going and start working smart.

A budget needs a few essential elements:

➤ **Flexible**. The idea is not to constrict you but to free up cash for other things like saving and investing.

➤ **Easy to maintain**. If you share a household, everyone involved in financial decisions should know how to work the budget.

➤ **A source of information**. You should be able to pull up your budget at any time and know where you stand financially.

➤ **Painless**. You may be doing better than you even knew but were afraid to look.

Now is the time to dig through those shoeboxes and old coat pockets. Gather up the paperwork and put it in the right place and we're on the way. Here are the organizing basics, the absolute minimum must-do's to succeed.

Click Here

For a comprehensive listing of financial freeware and software, go to **www.e-analytics.com/soft2.htm**. You can quickly download the software right off the Equity Analytics Quality Information on Investing site. You may not need the math software to create Pi to a million decimal places, but the calculators, home budget and retirement planning applications could help you compute.

Dedicate the Office Space

One of the biggest headaches at bill paying time is finding everything. It's frustrating and counter-productive. Even if it's one shelf in the kitchen, it's imperative to have a space strictly for budgeting materials. Put all the office supplies you need to handle bills—such as stamps, envelopes, and file folders—in that space. Let others know these supplies are off limits for schoolwork or personal use.

Get a Hard Drive (or Clean Up the One You Have)

If you don't already have a computer, financial management software is a compelling reason to buy one. With powerful PCs coming out under $1,000, you owe it to yourself. With the right personal finance software you can achieve almost instant control of your financial records. Sure it takes a few hours to enter your various accounts and their numbers, but it saves so much time month after month.

If you're already wired, make sure you have the right hardware. You need at least 8 MBs of RAM, and Windows 95 or higher. The software makes it easy to keep a budget in line and to predict your financial future. You can forecast long-term goals and veer around the pitfalls of bad budgeting. Here are the top two most popular software packages:

➤ **Quicken** (www.quicken99.com/new/newa.html). This very popular software comes in many forms, from basic to deluxe. It has a checkbook-based register and supports online banking and bill paying. And forget all that data entry drudgery; now there's Quicken Quick Entry.

➤ **Microsoft Money** (www.microsoft.com/products/prodref/698_ov.htm). This newly designed package is fairly easy for the average person to use. It includes the Money Basic Lifetime Planner for long-term financial decisions, as well as the Decision Center for worksheets, calculators, and specific budget items like insurance or home buying.

Money Meaning

Envelope accounting or budgeting is also referred to as "Bag" accounting, and is very simple. A certain amount of money is set aside on a regular basis in an envelope marked for a specific purpose or category. If you want to buy something in that category, you check to see if the funds are available. If yes, go ahead. If not, you don't buy.

The following are some less-expensive packages that may offer just the help you need:

➤ **Smart Home Manager 2.0** (www.surado.com/shm.html). Extensive information management features, calendars, reports, and an address book.

➤ **Make$.Cent3** (www.empowers.com). A powerful and flexible budgeting program based on the envelope accounting system. Now has Scheduled Transactions. Download a copy for free 30 day trial.

➤ **Monthly Bill Manager** (www.mjksw.com/shareware/mbm99s.exe). Has a higher learning curve but is good once you know the system; based on the envelope budgeting system. Download a free sample.

Once you've mastered your software program, you'll feel it's worth the money spent, and that's good budgeting! But you can't even get started if you don't know where you put the paperwork.

File the Paperwork

Contrary to popular hope, computers have not yet reduced paperwork in our lives. Those old printed bills are still coming in, receipts and warranties are still handed over with new purchases. And they have to go somewhere or they're useless. So what's really important and what can you throw out? We'll help you get started:

➤ **What goes.** Three-year-old credit card statements; pay stubs; bank deposit and ATM receipts; old loan payment books, and even certain mutual fund statements (keep the annual report and current statement); expired guaranties, warranties and manuals.

➤ **What stays.** Current credit card statements, any tax-related expense, canceled checks. The IRS recommends that you keep tax returns for at least three years after you've filed. Accountants advise you keep any scrap of paper that may help you defend yourself in an audit. Don't laugh at the old shoebox idea, it actually works and is semi-respectable. As long as they hold separate account headings like the following, a shoebox works just fine:

  ➤ Credit card statements

  ➤ Medical receipts

  ➤ Income statements, from sources such as salary and dividends.

➤ Utility bills

➤ Home improvements receipts

Make sure to clearly mark the Inbox separately from the receipts and bills already noted and filed. We like the accordion files that have separate areas you can mark clearly for filing receipts and bills. Also make sure to switch to new boxes or files every year to keep accounts straight for tax purposes. Changing colors each year provides a good visual distinction.

Schedule Your Tasks

This is a habit, remember? So try to sit down and enter data into your budget at the same time every week, or month, or whatever works best for you. Most of the money management software mentioned earlier has a scheduling program to make it easy for you. Here are a few things to remember when scheduling the work:

➤ Pay your bills on time to avoid late fees or interest charges. Subscribe to an online banking service to ensure automatic monthly payments. In Chapter 4 we explain how to find the best online bank for you, and how to find the Internet deals.

➤ Balance your checkbook and charge statements every month. Don't forget to check your ATM deposit and withdrawal receipts. Guess what is the single largest reason people overdraw their checking accounts, according to the American Banker's Association. Math errors! Use your personal finance software to tally up your totals. Or go to www.powersource.com/cccs/ and use the Consumer Credit Counseling Services's online Account Balancer.

➤ Pay off your highest interest credit cards first, and then pay down the rest.

All right, you have space and a filing system; now you need a plan. To figure out where the money should go, you need to know where it's been going.

Where the Money Goes

Budgeting is a little like playing hide-and-seek. If you want to find out where the money goes, you have to know where to look. This is what puts the "personal" in personal finance. Ready? You're it...start looking:

➤ **Credit history**. Look at your debt patterns, both old and new, paid and unpaid. This includes such things as car loans, mortgages, school loans, and installment plans for equipment.

➤ **Spending habits**. Are you an impulse buyer or do you shop with a list?

➤ **Philosophy**. Do you carry credit cards everywhere you go or stick to cash. Spend freely or only when you absolutely have to?

You're facing up to the spender in you and your household. There are no wrong answers here, by the way. There is only the way you have done things and the way you would like to do them. Getting in touch with your inner spender is kind of Zen like, but it will help you to form better habits.

When you're ready to add up some numbers, why not log on and compute? Answering the pre-set questions online should trigger your memory, and even suggest some categories you didn't know about. Check these out:

1. Financenter.com has over 100 calculators in 12 areas of personal finance, including budgeting, savings, credit cards and investing. These online interactive tools not only offer explanations so you understand what the results mean, they also generate graphs and charts for illustration.

   ➤ How Much Am I Spending? (www.smartcalc.com/cgi-bin/smartcalcpro/ bud3.cgi/FinanCenter). Plug your numbers into both the current and desired spending columns. Then click on the tab marked Results. A handy tool to see the dramatic impact a slight spending cutback can have on your bottom line.

   ➤ What's It Worth To Reduce My Spending? Again at Financenter.com (www.financenter.com/budget.htm). Helps you to create a "what if" chart related to spending so you can see how fast your savings accumulate if you don't spend.

2. Money.com Instant Budget Maker (cgi.pathfinder.com/cgi-bin/Money/ instant.cgi). Analyze your spending habits and see how your spending measures up to the average American household.

3. Idea Café's Instant All-In-One 1st Year Budget Worksheet (www.ideacafe.com/ getmoney/fgr budget.html). An online calculator that includes both personal and business expenses. Great for someone also considering starting up a business.

4. MoneyMinded Budget Worksheet (www.moneyminded.com/incomego/start/ a7budw15.htm). Simple and quick, fill in the blanks for a personalized budget analysis.

Maybe you don't even know where your money slips away to, so let's keep track:

1. Ask for and save every receipt for one month.

2. Keep a notebook and write down the little things you may not have receipts for, such as vending machine purchases. What you spend on soft drinks and snacks in a month could astound you!

3. Add it all up.

4. Subtract these expenses from your income.

Congratulations! You have created an expense sheet that tracks where all your money goes.

It's Your Budget, You Can Cry If You Want To

Before you decide to break out the tissues because you realize you've been gobbling up your cash in munchies and magazines, let's zoom in for a closer look at this budget. A budget has two basic parts: income and expenses. Income can come from many sources but still amounts to money in.

Although income is usually fixed, expenses are more flexible. There are two types of expenses: fixed and variable. We're most concerned with variable expenses because when those are adjusted, it has a big effect on our bottom line.

It's time to break both expenses and income into categories to help you keep track. We'll explain what the categories should generally consist of. Old-fashioned hand-written budget worksheets will probably never go out of style, but these days it's a little like using a screwdriver when the power tools are nearby. But even with online number crunching, you need to know what the entries mean.

> ➤ **Income.** Include salary, bonuses, dividends or interest, child support, unemployment, pension or Social Security and income from any rental properties. Estimate on the low side.

> ➤ **Gross monthly average.** Insert a line for every income earner in the household.

> ➤ **Payroll deductions.** All taxes taken from your pay, such as Social Security, Medicare, and federal and state income taxes.

> ➤ **Expenses.** Estimate on the low side.

> **Housing.** Rent or mortgage, Insurance, Housing, medical, dental, etc.

> **Utilities.** Electric, gas, water, and sewer. Cable doesn't count here; it's entertainment.

> **Telephone.** Include cell phones and pagers.

> **Transportation.** Vehicle payments, public transportation, and any related expenses such as gas, oil, licenses, insurance, and inspection fees.

> **Savings.** No matter how modest your income, you have to put something aside for yourself and your future. Ten percent is the *minimum* you should pay yourself.

> **Entertainment.** Movies, dining out, vacations, music, books, and online services (unless that is a business expense for you).

> **Home maintenance.** Cost of repairs and upkeep.

> **Loans.** Any outstanding debt not covered under another title, such as school loans, etc.

> **Food.** Groceries, not dining out which is considered entertainment.

    Personal care. Body maintenance and toiletries.

    Clothing. Uniforms may be tax deductible, keep separate.

    Medical/dental. Any expenses not covered in or under your insurance.

When you've reached that infamous bottom line—the income minus the expense—you have a clear idea of the kind of adjustments you need to make in your habits and lifestyle, if any. If there's a lot left over, lucky you! If not, here are some tips on shifting the balance.

Cut Expenses, Not Living Standards

We don't want you to give up the life you lead, only to make some changes. Budgeting doesn't have to be looked at as cutting expenses, but more like conserving cash. After all, the goal is to have some money left over for investing, which means it's making more wealth for you, not taking it away. Here are some tips:

➤ **Make solid goals in setting money aside.** If you are emotionally ready to save, you'll be able to do it. Don't allow yourself to get sidetracked from your end goal…wealth! Go to LabPuppy (www.labpuppy.com/tools.htm) for an assortment of the top online financial planning calculators available to help you set some goals. The National Center for Financial Education (www.ncfe.org/index.htm) has good tips on how to avoid getting into debt.

➤ **Shop with a list.** Advertisers are very good at bringing out our impulsive nature. Fight it. Buy what you need and get out. Save the rest. If you want to learn to squeeze pennies out of rocks, go to Frugal Corner's Tip of the Week at (www.brightok.net/~neilmayo/index.html). That should help shorten your shopping list!

➤ **Buy smart, not cheap.** Quality purchases save you money in the long run because they don't need frequent replacement. Use periodicals and online resources, such as *Consumer Reports* at www.consumerreports.com, to steer you to quality at the right price.

➤ **Treat yourself.** Don't deny yourself the little pleasures, but reward yourself when you've reached a budgeting goal. No Web site needed, just make sure you budget for it!

Here is a reminder of why you're busy budgeting. You'll have extra money on hand to:

➤ Take advantage of opportunities

➤ React calmly to emergencies

➤ Have the money it takes to make money—invest

Computerize Your Lifetime Plan

The nice part about planning for your future is that you can enjoy life's special events instead of being controlled by them. Here is a guide of online resources to help you do that:

➤ **Buying a home:** Join the wave of homeowners as they search for the best mortgage rates online. Read Chapter 14 for a comprehensive look at Real Estate in the Millennium, but here are some additional Web sites for fast loan rates and prequalifications.

Eloan.com   Search the top lenders to find a loan, whether it's for a first time buy, a refinance or a home equity loan.

GetSmart Mortgage   www.getsmartinc.com/mgotokwbuyingahome

The American Relocation Center (www.buyingrealestate.com)   All about Buyer's Agents, or real estate professionals who work for home buyers, not the sellers.

➤ **Buying a car:** There's nothing like that new car smell to life your spirits on the drive to work. But what will all that ease of handling and aromatherapy cost?

www.autoweb.com. Buy, sell or finance an automobile.

www.carfinance.com. Instant rate payments and analysis for auto loans.

www.edmunds.com. Extensive consumer information about new and used automobile purchasing including tips, strategies, and update pricing information.

Money.com (pathfinder.com/money/smartcalc/pages/sav3.html). Use this calculator and find out what it will take to save for a new car.

Microsoft Carpoint (carpoint.msn.com). A complete automobile site with links to everything from Kelly's Blue Book to Virtual Auto shows to financing deals.

➤ **Getting married:**

Modern Bride (www.modernbride.com/weddingplanning/whopays.cfm). Ever wonder who should pay for what? It's all here, plus an interactive budget chart and tips on keeping true to your budget.

WedNet (www.wednet.com/wedsense/wedsense.asp). The Dollars and Sense column is loaded with practical advice.

MetLife (www.metlife.com/Lifeadvice/Family/Docs/getmarriedintro.html). There's a wedding worksheet here guaranteed to clue you in on costs. You just might decide to ditch the big reception and elope!

Womens Wire MoneyMode (womenswire.com/money/quiz). Before you walk the aisle, test your financial compatibility with Your Mate's Money Quiz.

➤ **Starting a family**: Find out how much it will cost to raise a child from diapers to dorm room with these helpful tools.

Quicken's Life Events (www.quicken.com/life_events/parenting). Advice and calculators on budgeting for baby and saving for school. Find out if one spouse can afford to stop working when the little one arrives with an online calculator.

Kiplinger (www.kiplinger.com/kids). A financial planning center, college calculators and a kids and money forum to help the young ones learn along with you.

Money.com (pathfinder.com/money/smartcalc/pages/bud7.html). A calculator designed to help you create a budget for child-related expenses until he or she reaches the age of 20.

➤ **Planning for Retirement**: Company pensions plans are quickly being replaced with self-directed investments, like the 401(k)and IRAs. But are you ready to be your own investment manager? Online information can keep you up-to-date.

Quicken (quicken.com/retirement/qanda). Answers to questions like "How much should I contribute to my 401(k)?" and "What do I need to retire early" are custom-tailored with online calculators.

The Mining Company (retireplan.miningco.com). Timely articles and links to help you wade through the complexities of retirement planning.

Administration on Aging (www.aoa.dhhs.gov/aoa/pages/finplan.html). Provides booklets, brochures, calculators, links and resources for retirement planning.

The Least You Need to Know

➤ Budgeting doesn't mean cutting back; it means taking control of your financial management.

➤ A simple, easily understood and updated budget plan ensures success.

➤ Online calculators take out the guesswork in budgeting "what–if" scenarios.

➤ Many software programs can help you track spending, pay bills, and more.

➤ Online interactive tools can help you plan for all the stages in your life, including college, marriage, having children, retiring and more.

Chapter 4

Sending Your Money into Cyberspace

In This Chapter

➤ Why online banking is the ticket to the future

➤ How to get your feet wet and find the right online bank for you

➤ Knowing the right questions to ask about cyberbanking

➤ Where to get special Internet banking deals

➤ How to find out if your institution offers online banking

Did you know that most consumers these days opt to purchase a new computer rather than a new microwave? That's right; the PC is gaining ground on a major kitchen staple. According to the Digital Living Room Consumer Index, almost 90 percent of people surveyed in 1998 will buy a new computer within the next year. Although you can't nuke a TV dinner with a PC, there are many other everyday tasks you can do, such as pay bills, transfer funds between bank accounts, apply for a mortgage, or earn higher savings yields.

If you're still banking and paying bills the old-fashioned way, forget it. Those sheaves of envelopes and books of stamps may soon become collector's items as more banks and businesses become wired to help you balance your checkbook, pay bills, and even directly deposit your Social Security checks. If you have a computer, a modem, and a phone line, you're all set with the latest tools to take you out of the bank lobby and directly into your living room. Bank when *you* want.

This chapter explains the basics of booting up and banking online, online security issues, and key questions to ask your banker about banking in cyberspace.

Makes You Feel Like Rip Van Winkle

In an age when some of us still fret at programming the VCR to stop flashing 12:00, along comes the notion of using a computer to pay bills. None of us has been asleep at the cyberwheel for 20 years, but where did all this come from and how the heck do you do it anyway?

Home banking has been discussed for dozens of years, yet ironically it has been slow to take off. Chalk it up to customers concerned with the security of sending their money into cyberspace or even the lack of knowledge on just how to perform the darn transactions.

That's why it took nearly a decade and a half for online banking to make it into at least one percent of the households in this country—and that wasn't until 1996. By mid 1996, 38 percent of the top 150 banks in the United States offered PC-based home banking services, and most of the remainder plan to offer services by the new millennium. And virtually all have some sort of telephone-based banking service.

Bet You Didn't Know

As of fall 1998, approximately four-and-a-half percent of all households in the United States are performing some type of online banking or bill payment transactions. Look for that figure to grow.

Online Banking Report, an industry newsletter, projects that over the next three years online banking and bill payment usage should increase by four to five million households per year, hitting 22 million in the next 48 months.

The pros are as follows:

➤ Your checkbook is always balanced. By calling up your bank's Web page and typing in a password, all you have to do is click on a button that says "account history." No having to wait for your statement in the mail.

➤ Your bank is a 24/7 shop. Online banking enables you to transact your banking business whenever you want. You are not at the mercy of lobby hours.

➤ Some online savings accounts pay more interest than regular savings accounts. Atlanta Internet Bank, for example, offers higher yields on money market accounts if you open an online bank account. And, depending on your balance, you can earn almost *double the yield*!

➤ You save time paying bills. Rather than writing out checks and using stamps and envelopes, you can pay all your bills in less time with the click of a few keyboard strokes.

And the cons are as follows:

➤ Adios, techno-phobes. With most banks offering the basics—such as being able to check account balances, transfer money, and pay bills electronically—you must be comfortable using your computer.

➤ Wasted time and effort. If you switch banks, all the time and effort you spent keying in all your financial data must be redone…usually.

We make it sound so simple….

Just when you thought all the kids had gone to sleep, you hear cries of "I've got it!" and "That was so easy!" coming from the den. Your 10-year-old is still up, playing on the family computer. You know, the 300 MHz-Pentium with the 3.2 GB hard drive and 32 MB of RAM the children begged and squealed for during the 10 weeks before Christmas.

You're hip; you know that "edu-tainment" is in. You ask your child if he's having fun with the Megablaster Tri-color-rama battlefield game on the CD-ROM. Your child gives you one of those "get real" stares, turns to you, and says, "Nope. I just balanced your checkbook, paid off your credit line at the bank, and reconciled your Visa account. Wanna update your stock portfolio? I got the 56K modem all set up on COM port 2."

"Geez," you muster under your breath, as all the pride of learning the difference between the floppy drive and hard drive flushed right out of your toes. Welcome to managing your money in the 21st century. So, just like Oprah Winfrey told everyone when she ran the Marine Corps Marathon in 1994, if she can do it, anyone can—and that includes you and your computer.

Okay, I'm Hooked…Now What?

You've got the itch. Now let's make the switch to paperless banking.

First, you need to find out if your bank offers online banking simply by contacting an account representative or calling customer service at the institution's toll-free number. According to the *Online Banking Report*, as of November 1998, the United States has almost 250 "true" Internet banks—institutions that provide account balances and transaction details to retail customers over the Web.

If you currently do not have a bank account but are looking to boot up with a bank anywhere in the country, consider checking out the Internet Banker Scorecard published by Gomez Advisors. Their Web site (www.scorecard.bom/finance/) lists more than 54 banks and bank holding companies in one place that allow their customers to bank online. Each bank is ranked by ease of use, customer confidence, onsite resources, relationship services, and overall cost.

Another resource to help you find an online bank is Bankrate.com (www.bankrate.com), which not only lists Web site reviews on a weekly basis but also compares the fees of more than 75 financial institutions (banks, thrifts, and credit unions).

Click Here

Compare fees for online banking at institutions across the country by logging on to
Bankrate.com (**www.bankrate.com**). You'll be surprised to see how many banks do not
offer a free trial period. (Some offer as many as 90 days.) And, with PC banking fees as high
as a $10 set-up fee, a $5 access fee, or even a $7.50 bill-payment fee, it will help you and
your wallet to do the research first.

Keep in mind that banks offer two distinct ways they provide their online services:
dial-in networking services and Internet-based services (some banks offer both.) While
most financial institutions require you to have the bank's proprietary software stored
on your computer's hard drive, many Internet-based systems allow you to dial in and
use the bank's software or software provided by an Internet Service provider, such as
America Online. An Internet-based service simply means you're using your browser to
bank over the Web. Once you determine which method of delivery you will use, it's
time to start asking some questions of ol' Mr. Banker.

Bet You Didn't Know

By the mid to late '90s, virtually all banks have some sort of telephone-based banking
service, and more than a third of the top 150 banks in the United States offer PC-based
home banking services.

I'm on a Need-to-Know Basis

Some banks offer both Internet-based and dial-up access. The fees for account transactions and investments vary among banks as much as the services they offer. Most
banks with an online Web site, for example, let you view account balances and
transfer funds among accounts for free. Paying bills, on the other hand, can generate
another monthly charge.

If you are considering banking online, here is a list of questions you should ask the customer service representative at your bank:

➤ Does the bank offer or plan to offer its own online banking service, either through its own Web site or a software application with online access to its central computers? You will want to find out all the charges and fees involved and what types of transactions you can and cannot do online.

➤ What are the system requirements to process online banking and bill payment transactions? Typically, an IBM-compatible 386 or higher PC running Windows 3.1 or later with eight MB of RAM is required. Note that if you have a 386 machine anytime you use the latest browser your "user experience" will take a long time because of your slower machine.

➤ How long does it take for each transaction to become executed? Does a funds transfer take place immediately? If you pay your mortgage on a Monday, when will the payment be debited from your account and credited to the recipient?

Here's why. Let's say you pay your electric bill via cyberspace on Tuesday. Once many financial institutions' processing departments receive your "electronic request," however, they may still have to print out a check and mail the payment to the electric company. The result? Your electric bill payment might not get paid until five business days later. Find out the details from your financial institution. Some banks debit your account the day the check clears.

➤ What type of security does your bank offer with its online banking services? Typically, the types of encryption used in online banking allow only you and the bank to see your account information. Ask your banker to explain the details in laymen's terms.

➤ What happens if an error occurs? Sure, online banking may have been around a decade or so, but mistakes can happen. What can you do if there is a technical glitch that results in a duplicated transaction? Ask your banker what steps you need to take to rectify any situation—be it your error or not. If you inadvertently duplicate a transaction or send money to the wrong creditor, you need to know how to correct the error and not pay substantial bank fees in the process.

➤ What is the process to close an online bank account, and what types of charges are involved? It may be easy to open an online banking account, but how difficult is it to close it? Your banker should tell you what is involved from a financial as well as a technical perspective.

➤ How are monthly fees charged? Typically, monthly fees are automatically deducted from the primary checking account (designated by you on the enrollment form) on the date of your statement. If you sign up with a financial institution on an online service or the Internet, make sure you understand all of the features and whether or not additional charges are assessed.

➤ How do you deposit money into your account? Most financial institutions recommend that you have your paycheck directly deposited into your online bank account. If not, you can ask the bank to give you postage-paid, pre-addressed envelopes for mailing in your deposits.

Is My Financial Data Secure?

Computer hackers are everywhere, which is probably why online security is the number one concern for consumers. Banks take online security very seriously, especially since even the slightest flaw could severely damage customer confidence. Bank of America, for example, explains to its customers all the security problems that occur on the Internet and, thereafter, the countermeasures that are taken.

Even so, security, of course, is always a major concern of customers. When you're sending credit card numbers, passwords, electronic cash, and personal information over the Internet, it makes you wonder if this information can be intercepted by others.

Click Here

One online bank is putting their mouth where their money is. Security First Network Bank at www.sfnb.com guarantees security of customer deposits and in the event you ever have funds removed from your account without your authorization they will pay you back in full.

Banks and solution providers are stacking up *firewalls*, encryptions, pin codes, and passwords against hackers like sandbags against the flood. Tip: Change your password often as a measure of protection. (Just don't forget it!)

Money Meaning

A **firewall** is a computer mechanism that is installed on computer servers to protect unauthorized/insecure transactions taking place, for example, "hacking."

Typical online banking services are protected with a PIN number—a personal identification number that you choose—that verifies and confirms each banking transaction that you perform.

You should look for a bank that features key encryption measures—security "codes" implemented so that only you and your bank see your account information. Through encryption, your data—everything from account numbers to account balances—is converted into a series of unrecognizable numbers before being exchanged over the Internet. This series of numbers creates a mathematical lock—a lock that only your financial institution and browser have the key to. Furthermore, every time you perform a new transaction, a new lock and key combination is randomly created.

Click Here

If you work in a bank, or want to work in a bank, you can find a job in the banking industry right online. Careers, Inc. works with the country's largest banks to publicize available positions through its weekly newspaper, *Jobs for Bankers*, which is online at **www.bankjobs.com**.

America Online's Banking Center, for example, features a product called BankNOW that is used along with several of AOL's banking partners to transfer funds between accounts, get balances, and pay bills. The BankNOW software, created by Intuit, the makers of Quicken, uses a 128-bit encryption method and states that it is virtually impossible for anyone using current technology to steal information. Simply put, it is like sending your money inside a steel safe. Restrictions do apply; the 128-bit standard is so powerful that the United States government has made its sale overseas illegal. Federal regulations allow only American and Canadian customers to download the 128-bit encrypted software.

Bet You Didn't Know

Another reason for diving into cyberspace? The average time spent setting up new accounts at a traditional bank branch is more than five hours, whereas online accounts can be set up in a little over an hour. With customers demanding flexibility and responsive services, it's no wonder that millions of consumers are choosing to save time by banking online.

Have We Got a Deal for You

Special deals are available, even to online banking customers. The trend is for banks on the Internet to offer higher yields on money market accounts and checking accounts, especially if you carry a high account balance, as we've seen the past several years on online banks. To give you an idea of what has been available as of fall 1998, the following institutions offered special deals to Internet shoppers. Of course, these are just examples and as rates and yields change, so do special offers from online banks. These offers in no way represent any future possibilities of these institutions offering the same types of products or deals to online customers.

➤ **Salem Five Cents Bank** (www.salemfive.com). Offers an annual percentage yield of 4.61 percent on its money market account.

➤ **Net.Bank** (www.netbank.com). Offers Internet banking shoppers the chance to open a checking account with only $100, no minimum balance, no monthly fee, *and* an annual percentage yield of 3.05 percent.

➤ **Commerce Bank** in Philadelphia, South Jersey, and Jersey Shore (www2.yesbank.com). Allows customers to stay connected by offering a free cellular phone and a $10 checking or savings account credit when you open an account on the Internet.

On the Sneak

There are a few unscrupulous people out there. Sad, but true; and unfortunately, they're in the Internet banking industry. That's why the Federal Deposit Insurance Corporation (FDIC) has created a searchable database on its Web site that will help you determine if an institution has a legitimate charter and is a member of the FDIC. You can search by institution, holding company, or branch office to see if they are legitimate. Any bank that is not FDIC insured we would recommend avoiding—both online and off!

The Least You Need to Know

➤ With online banking, you can balance your checkbook and pay bills when convenient for you, not at the mercy of lobby hours.

➤ One of the most important questions to ask your bank about online banking is how long it takes for transactions to become executed. You should find out if fund transfers and bill payments take place immediately.

➤ Look for a bank that offers the 128-bit encryption method if you are doing your online banking using a Web browser. With this type of "security code," it is virtually impossible for anyone using current technology to steal your information.

➤ Just because you don't need to go into a bank branch doesn't mean there aren't charges associated with online banking. Find out from your banker how much it costs, as well as if there are fees associated with closing the account.

➤ If you are unsure about the legitimacy of a bank, contact the FDIC (www.fdic.gov/suspicious) to report your findings.

Chapter 5

Making Money in Cyberspace

Ever have one of those days where after drinking your morning cup of Joe, you read a newspaper headline that just stumps the heck out of you?

Such as when NASA successfully field-tested an oil-spill-catcher made of 1.4 million pounds of hair in mesh pillows. C'mon, hair? Or that dreadful day when NBC announced *Seinfeld* was leaving its Thursday night line-up and would live on only in syndication. No more Jerry, Kramer, George, or Elaine.

Or even that the number of people trading online has expanded so far—up 14 percent in the third quarter of 1998 versus the second quarter—that broker cyberwars are flourishing. Consumers can actually *save* money on commissions by opening up a brokerage account through their personal computers.

They're all true folks; a hairdresser, the cast of *Frasier*, and millions of online brokerage account holders all can confirm these facts.

No need to shorn your locks or live without your *Seinfeld*, but you should sit up and take notice of the online trading activity happening all around you. This chapter will show you which online brokers are leading the way with reduced fees, better customer service, and easy-to-use online applications. In addition, we will provide you with the basics you need to invest on the Web, how to find the best research tools, and the right questions to ask before you place a trade.

Traditional or Non-Traditional Online Brokers?

There are two types of online brokers: traditional and non-traditional. Traditional brokers online include companies such as Charles Schwab & Company, Fidelity, and Quick & Reilly. They have the ol' brick-and-mortar offices where you can call or visit with account representatives in addition to placing trades online. Non-traditional online brokers, such as Datek, E*Trade, Suretrade, and DLJdirect, were born on the Internet and are typically discount- or deep-discount brokers—meaning no reduced commissions.

Is one better than the other? Well, just like in the banking industry, it's up to you to decide whether trekking down to an office to meet with a live person is a necessary preference. But know this: Most online trading customers are choosing traditional brokers, according to a report issued by Piper Jaffray, a full-service investment firm as the report indicates customers want to go with a name they are familiar with. Online operations for traditional discount brokers, including Schwab, Fidelity, and Ameritrade, averaged 20 percent gains in average daily trades in the third quarter of 1998 compared with the second quarter. During the same period, those pioneering firms founded on the Web grew slower than the rest of the online market—increasing only six percent—as their relatively inexperienced customers sat on the sidelines.

What's driving this market? If you're new, then it's you. New customer accounts are exploding, with the top 10 online brokers alone reporting a 15 percent increase to 5.8 million accounts in mid-1998.

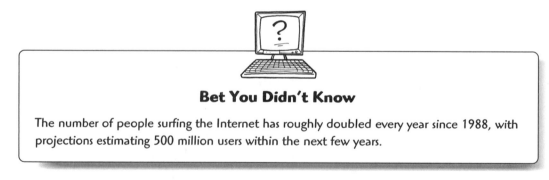

Bet You Didn't Know

The number of people surfing the Internet has roughly doubled every year since 1988, with projections estimating 500 million users within the next few years.

Whom to Trade With?

Choosing an online broker is probably the hardest part as each firm offers different features, services, and commissions. Each broker has strengths and weaknesses, and not everyone sees a broker in the same way. What works for your great uncle Milton may not work for you.

Click Here

If you're in the market to open up an online trading account, check out Gomez Advisors' Web site that rates online brokerage firms. Log onto www.scorecard.com/finance for details.

Here's what you need to have in mind when you compare and contrast each online broker:

➤ **What services are offered?** Find out if you can buy and sell the investments of your choice online. Do they offer services besides straight buying and selling of stock? Can you invest in other products, such as mutual funds or options?

➤ **Do they have research available?** No good deed goes undone when thorough research is available to help you make your investment choices.

➤ **How much does it cost?**

   ➤ **To place a trade.** While no brokers offer free online trading, the online wars of who can offer it cheapest certainly benefits investors. For example, many online brokers offer reduced commissions the more shares you buy.

   ➤ **To research companies.** Free research can sometimes make or break a decision on which online broker you choose, as there are dozens of companies on the Web that offer free investment research.

   ➤ **To get real-time quotes.** Quite often, Web sites offer 15-minute delayed quotes; to get real-time quotes you will typically incur a fee.

Bet You Didn't Know

While paying low commissions to execute trades online may seem appealing, some online brokerage firms require you to pony up several thousand dollars to open up an online account. Check the account requirements information typically found in the "Frequently Asked Questions" section on the Web sites.

Bet You Didn't Know

Even though you can save money in commissions by trading online, online brokers do charge for other things that you need to watch out for. For one, there are transaction, postage and handling fees that apply to all trades. In fact, it can cost as much as $25.00 to have a stock certificate issued and delivered into your hands. Make sure you understand all fees involved with online trading.

➤ **Are there handling fees tacked onto each trade?** Yep, there is a charge for processing your trade confirmations, especially if they're the paper kind sent to you via the United States Post Office.

➤ **How are confirmations sent?**

  ➤ **By email.** Make sure if this is the option that you print out your confirmed email and save it in a folder. Tip: Have your email confirmations sent to a personal email account rather than a work email account to ensure privacy.

  ➤ **By snail mail.** Your hard copy trade confirmation should also be filed to maintain an organized system—plus it's easier come tax time.

  ➤ **By phone.** In addition to a phone confirmation, you should have a hard copy or email confirmation sent to you for recording purposes.

Click Here

Looking for a broker but unsure of its financial health? Consider Weiss Ratings (www.weissratings.com), which issues financial safety ratings on nearly 250 brokerage firms in the United States each year. Their ratings are based on our analysts' review of publicly available information collected by the SEC. You can get a verbal rating over the phone by calling 800-289-9222.

➤ **Does it cost extra to talk with a broker if you need help with your account?** Some banks do this to speak with live tellers; are online brokers following suit? In the day and age of faceless financial transactions, find out how many dollars it costs if live help is needed.

➤ **What hours are brokers available?** Not everyone works 24/7, so find out if the online brokers you're interested in are available at the hours *you* need them.

➤ **Are accounts in real-time, any time?** This is an awesome feature and can help troubleshoot any potential problems or errors.

➤ **What is the financial strength of the firm?** Although the Securities Investors Protection Corporation (SIPC) offers up to $500,000 of insurance on accounts, it pays for you to find out the asset size and safety of the firm.

What the Cyberboys of Wall Street Offer

The Internet has helped democratize the investment process by providing widespread access to even the most specialized information and types of things you can do with that information: Namely, invest your money without leaving your living room.

There are more than 67 online brokerage firms, each touting its own bells and whistles. With this many choices it can often be confusing which firm has the brightest bell or shiniest whistle for the cheapest price.

Several brokerage firms, both traditional and non-traditional, are listed below to help you begin your search. Happy hunting!

Table 5.1 contains contact information of 15 well-known and often-utilized online brokers.

Bet You Didn't Know

There is a lot of online broker competition to capture the current $300 billion in assets that is trading in cyberspace. As a result, the big cyberboys of Wall Street are reducing the fees they charge you to buy and sell investment securities online—some even as low as $7.95 per trade!

Table 5.1 Online Broker Contact Information

Name	Address & Phone	URL	Min. Opening Balance	Commission Rates		
				Online	Touch Tone	BrokerAssisted
ACCUTRADE	4211 S. 102 Street Omaha, NE 68103 (800) 228-3011	www.accutrade.com	$5,000	$29.95		
Ameritrade	PO Box 2209 Omaha, NE 68103 (800) 454-9272	www.ameritrade.com		$8	$12	$18
Brown & Co.	One Beacon Street Boston, MA 02108	www.brownco.com	$15,000			
Charles Schwab & Co.	(800) 435-4000	www.eschwab.com	$2,500	20% off broker	20% off broker	$29.95
DATEK Online	100 Wood Ave., South Iselin, NJ 08830 (888) GO-DATEK	www.datek.com	$2,000	$9.99 up to 5,000 shares	N/A	$25
DLJ Direct	PO Box 2062 Jersey City, NY 07399 (800) 825-5723	www.dljdirect.com		$20 up to 1,000 shares	$20 up to 1,000 shares	$20 up to 1,000 shares
E*TRADE	2400 Geng Road Palo Alto, CA 94303 (800) 786-2575	www.etrade.com	$0	$14.95 market, $19.95 other	$14.95 market, $19.95 other	add $15, add $15
Fidelity	PO Box 770001 Cincinnati, OH 45277	personal12.fidelity.com	$5,000	$48.95–$98.95		
National Discount Brokers	7 Hanover Street 4th floor New York, NY 10004	www.ndb.com	$2,000	$14.75	$19.95	$24.95
The Net Investor	(800) NET-4250	www.netinvestor.com	$5,000, $2,000 IRA	$20.95	$20.95	
Quick & Reilly	(800) 833-5838	www.quick-reilly.com				
Suretrade.com	PO Box 862 Lincoln, RI 02865 (212) 566-2031	www.suretrade.com		$7.95	$7.95	$30.00
Waterhouse Securities	7242 SW 42 Terrace Miami, FL 33155 (888) 925-5783	www.waterhouse.com	$1,500	$12.00	$35.00	$45.00
Web Street Securities	1200 Shermer Road Northbrook, IL 60062 (800) WEB-TRADE	www.webstreet-securities.com	$0	$14.95		
Jack White	(800) 216-2333	www.jackwhiteco.com		$25.00		

And the Winners Are...

Buying and selling stocks with the touch of a key. Check your portfolio at two o'clock in the morning. Know what all this means? Your account is available whenever *you* want. Of course, these very features that make online trading more and more appealing to investors come with a price tag: commissions.

According to a 1998 *Smart Money* survey, Ameritrade and Suretrade were the winners. At $7.95 per trade, Suretrade's commissions are half as expensive as the average commission of other online brokers, with Ameritrade following suit at $8 per trade.

Who brought up the rear? Accutrade and Charles Schwab, where investors pay rates three times that of Ameritrade and Suretrade, according to the survey.

Not all cyberinvestors should look at commissions alone, of course, although they're a top contender when selecting an online broker. Easy access and tech support rank right up there. Imagine being unable to log on to your account or complete your trade instantaneously, as many of the brokerages promise. And when there's heavy market activity, as we've seen throughout 1998 in terms of shares changing hands on the Big Board—volume as high as 600,000,000 to 800,000,000 shares—you want ease of use.

Bet You Didn't Know

If you trade frequently and are concerned about tech support, consider an online broker that provides multiple trading services, such as the Internet, proprietary software, telephone availability, and in person. This way, if the Internet service goes down, you'll have an alternative.

Technical support is key. Does your online broker offer around-the-clock availability seven days a week and *not* make you wait on hold for 15 minutes or longer after placing your call? If so, that firm is something to consider. Price is important; it's difficult to turn down the cheapest trading rates. Not being able to trade on busy days or get help when you need it, however, can spell M-I-S-S-E-D O-P-P-O-R-T-U-N-I-T-I-E-S.

And You Can Quote Me on That

Many online brokerage firms offer you the ability to get real-time quotes or up to a 15-minute delay quote on stocks and mutual funds. Some charge a fee and some offer a specified number of free real-time quotes and charge thereafter. Others provide unlimited quotes. There are even online brokers that charge up to $30 for unlimited quotes.

Here's our suggestion: If, in your quest for the perfect online broker, you find that the broker you've selected assesses a fee for real-time quotes but offers lower fees on commissions, consider the following online data resources as supplements to your real-time quote needs:

➤ **BigCharts** (www.bigcharts.com) This is one of the world's most comprehensive and easy-to-use online charting and investment research Web sites, providing access to interactive charts, quotes, reports, and indicators on more than 50,000 stocks, mutual funds, and market indexes.

➤ **Quote.com** (www.quote.com) In addition to a wide array of stock quotes available for the online investor, this Web site includes access to quotes for after-hours trading with a live quote feature.

➤ **FREErealtime.com** (www.freerealtime.com) Savvy investors, this one's for you. Get free access to real-time stock quotes, financial news, corporate profiles, economic calendars, and more.

➤ **PC Quote** (www.pcquote.com) Looking for streaming real-time quotes that update before your eyes as trades and quotes occur? This Web site offers intraday charts, alerts, and tickers.

➤ **CBS MarketWatch** (http://cbs.marketwatch.com) In addition to up-to-the-minute market commentary, this Web site offers as many quotes as you want from all the major exchanges on demand. Data about futures and equity options are also available.

Online Boot Camp

You've done your research on what online brokers offer, where you can save money on trades, and which resources provide you with the data and financial and economic news you need. Now it's time to...wait!

Huh?

You heard us. Before starting to throw your money into cyberspace, you must know how to trade online. That's right, it's time to brush up on the ol' jargon.

It's Either One or the Other

Let's assume you're thinking about investing in stocks. Well, the first, most basic question on the menu is whether you want to *buy* or *sell*. That's straightforward enough. If you're buying, you enter a *buy order* on the online application. (All online brokers have this.)

Next, you must specify the *quantity of shares*. You'll select how many shares you'd like to buy (or sell). This can be any number, from one share to 100,000 shares. Enter the full number of shares. Don't abbreviate or spell it out; just enter the number. And don't worry about entering less or more than the traditional 100-shares of stock order, known as a *round lot*. There used to be a real problem with less than round lot orders (called *odd lots*), but that's no longer the case. You'll get the same price for a round lot or an odd lot in most cases.

Money Meaning

When you buy 100 shares, you are buying a **round lot**. In the past, round lot stock trades tend to receive quicker execution than, say, if you were to only buy or sell five shares.

What Else Is on the Menu?

You have the following five different types of orders to choose from:

➤ **Market orders**. This means you're willing to buy or sell a stock at whatever the market maker (the person in the trading pits) is willing to sell or buy the stock to or from you. This is the quickest way to buy and sell stocks.

Bet You Didn't Know

There are two terms to remember in your investment transactions: bid and ask. When you sell stocks, you will do so on the *bid* side of the market (the sales price); when you buy stocks, the quote you'll get is on the *ask* side of the market. The difference between these two prices is called the *spread*.

➤ **Limit orders**. Limit orders mean that you want to limit your transaction to a certain price. If you're looking to buy a stock and it's trading at $25 a share, and that's as much as you want to pay for it, then enter a Buy Limit order with a price of $25. Use limit orders if you have plenty of patience and are willing to take the risk of not buying or selling your stock.

➤ **Fill or kill orders**. Sometimes confused with "all or none orders," this means you either want to sell all your stock at once or forget it.

➤ **All or none orders**. If you have a large order and want to be sure you'll sell all your shares and not just pieces of it, consider this type of order. Know, however, that your trade might not get executed.

Bet You Didn't Know

When filling out an order to buy or sell stocks—and depending on the type of order you want executed—don't forget to fill in the price. Most online brokers have a price box you can fill in or leave blank. If you don't fill in the price box, the online broker automatically executes it as a market order.

➤ **Stop orders**. Stop orders are when you own a stock and want to be sure that you limit your loss on the stock. You do not automatically sell the stock at the stop order price, however. It's just a red flag that says "I want out."

➤ **Stop limit order.** A stop limit order combines both a stop and a limit order. This type of order specifies both a stop price where the trade is activated and a limit price. Once the stop is elected, the order becomes a limit order. This type of order is useful when the trader wants to control the price paid or received.

Bet You Didn't Know

When you look at a quote and enter an order with a limit price, also look at the size of the market. Why? It determines how many shares of stock are being bid for on the bid side of the market and how many shares are being offered on the ask side.

If Not Today, Then Maybe Forever

Another thing you should keep in mind is how long you want the order to live. A *day order* means you're putting in your order for the day only—the day you enter your order. If you haven't bought or sold your stock by the end of the trading day, the order is automatically canceled, and you have no trade pending.

If, however, you use the GTC, or Good 'Til Canceled, order, you have a live bid or offer for the next 90 days or until you call and cancel the order. The re reason we don't recommend this order is that a lot can happen to a stock after the market closes: earnings announcements, mergers, executive hirings or firings.

With a GTC order, one of two things could happen within the next 90 days: Either your order will get filled or it won't because it will expire. Don't use GTC orders unless you can monitor your stock continuously.

Three Different Account Types

There are three different types of accounts you can trade online with: cash, margin, and short. Until you really get your feet wet understanding all the online and Wall Street jargon, we suggest using a cash account.

Cash Is King

Cash is cash. That is, every trade you make, whether it's buying stock, selling shares in a mutual fund, whatever, you will settle in cash. When you buy or sell stocks, you have three business days in which to settle a trade. This is known as *T plus 3* or *trade day plus three business days*.

With a cash account, you must pay for your stock within three days with a check or have enough cash in the account to pay for it. If you have sold a stock, you will receive the proceeds of the sale on the third business day after the stock was sold in the form of a check sent to you or money deposited in your account (by far the most common way).

Be Careful to Stay Within the Margins

Using a *margin* account can either help you or cause you a big financial pain in the tush. Here's why: Trading on margin allows you either to borrow money from the brokerage firm to buy stocks or to take money out of your account. You must have stocks or money in the account, of course, but this account allows you to leverage your investing or spending. We do not recommend this type of account to people who love to gamble or have pushed their credit cards to their limits. You will only dig your hole deeper by having one of these accounts.

With a margin account, the stocks or bonds you buy can be used as collateral to borrow money; up to 50 percent of the value of the stocks can be borrowed. Let's say you have $5,000 worth of stock, fully paid for, in your margin account. You can either take out $2,500 or buy more stock—up to $5,000 worth provided all the stock you own and are about to buy is allowed to be bought on margin. A lot of zip and power for a little account, huh? With margin trading, you can buy double the amount of a stock, and if that stock goes up, you can make much more money.

It sounds as sweet as lemonade on a hot summer afternoon, but read what happens if the trading gods don't work in your favor. When the stock goes down, you get wiped out twice as fast and receive what's known as a *margin call*. This is when your account goes down in value so much you only have 25 percent equity left in the account. You then need to meet a margin call to bring the equity back up to 50 percent.

Using the previous example of buying $5,000 worth of stock with only $2,500, if the stock value goes down by 25 percent, then your equity shrinks by that amount, too.

Money Meaning

When you trade on **margin**, you are borrowing monies from a brokerage firm to buy additional securities. You are charged an interest rate, known as the **margin rate**, for borrowing this money. Typically, low margin rates run less than seven percent.

It's Not Tall, It's Short

Okay investing veterans, this one's for you. Shorting stocks requires a complete understanding of having a trading account without having stock in it, and actually "betting against" positions that you don't outright own—a concept most people have a great deal of trouble comprehending. If you understand shorting stocks, you know enough about this account to open one. If you don't understand shorting stocks, don't bother with this type of account.

Here's how it works. First, you must set up a margin account in order to sell the stock that you don't own but rather borrowed from the brokerage firm. Why would you do this? Because you are hedging your bets that the stock price will fall. And, when you sell a stock that you don't own and the price drops, you would then buy the stock back at the lower price and keep the difference as your profit. Think sell high, buy low—in that order, please.

There are risks, however. The market value of the security could go up. Then you would be selling short and buying the stock back at even a higher price. This investment strategy is extremely risky because your maximum loss is unlimited.

I'm Scared!

You've got the goods (your cash); you've asked the right questions; you know the trading lingo and are comfortable with the online broker you've selected. You're still as nervous, however, as a cat in a room full of rocking chairs when you fill out the online application. Let's walk through the process using a typical online account application provided by one of the online brokers in Table 5.1.

First, tell us about yourself. No, not *us*, the application form. (Of course, we always want to know how you're doing.) You'll need to fill out the following information:

➤ Name (first, last, and middle initial)

➤ Street address, city, state, and zip code

➤ Country (non-U.S. citizens have special instructions to follow regarding tax laws)

➤ Home telephone number

➤ Email address

Next, you'll most likely have to fill out a personalized user name and password for when you log on. Most online brokers prefer that your user name is eight to ten characters long, and quite often you'll have to enter your password twice.

Now it's time to create a secret code. You'll enter a word or a phrase that only you know, such as your mother's maiden name. This secret code will be used to retrieve your password should you ever lose it.

To continue, they'll ask you questions such as:

➤ What type of account are you opening?

  ➤ Individual, Joint, Other

  ➤ Brokerage or IRA

  ➤ Cash/Margin/Option Trading

➤ How will you initially fund this account?

  ➤ Check

  ➤ Wire

  ➤ Account transfer

  ➤ Security certificate

Click Here

Many brokers, such as E*trade (**www.Etrade.com**) and Web Street Securities (**www.webstreet.com**), offer you the chance to put your money where your mouth is without even ponying up the dough. Fictitious accounts with $25,000 to $100,000 investment portfolio are given to players. Typically, the highest return for the month is deemed the winner, and quite often cash prizes are awarded.

Thereafter, for all accountholders, employer and salary information will be required.

If you're still apprehensive, brokers such as E*Trade allow you to request an account kit to be sent to you in the mail.

Click Here

Hello, cyberinvestor. The CyberStocks Investor Report offers free market commentary in its weekly stock newsletter. All you have to do is enter your email address to subscribe. Log on to **www.thewebinvestor.com**.

Online, Offline—It Doesn't Matter

When the Securities and Exchange Commission, fondly known as the SEC, was formed in 1934 as the federal arm that protects the investing public against malpractice in the securities markets, little did it know back then that it would be lassoing in scam artists through a computer.

Online trading, for all its benefits, does warrant some warnings to investors. Here's why: The proliferation of investment-related Web sites produced by reputable companies has grown tremendously—but so have personal Web pages, message boards, newsgroups, and chat rooms by unqualified people promising quick profits. Offers to share inside information or investment recommendations are rampant on the Web.

Pseudonyms are common online, and some salespeople will try to hide their true identity. What can you do about it? Avoid Web pages and the like that use words such as "guarantee," "high return," "limited offer," or "as safe as a CD (certificate of deposit)." No financial investment is risk free, and a high rate of return usually means greater risk.

The SEC aims to promote full public disclosure of all types of investments and investment practices. With any investment you consider for your portfolio—whether it's promoted on the Internet or even through regular mail, the phone or in person—the SEC advocates that you *slow down*. Ask questions and get written information.

Here are the top ten questions you should ask about any investment opportunity, according to the SEC:

1. Is the investment registered with the SEC and the state securities agency in your state, or is it subject to an exemption?

2. Is the person recommending the investment registered with your state securities agency? Is there a record of any complaints about this person?

3. How does the investment match your investment objectives?

4. Where is the company incorporated? Will it send you the latest reports that have been filed on this company?

5. What are the costs to buy, hold, and sell the investment? How easily can you sell it?

6. Who is managing the investment? What experience do they have?

7. What is the risk of losing the money you invest?

8. What return can you expect on your money? When can you expect it?

9. How long has the company been in business? Is it making money, and if so, how? What is its product or service? What other companies are in this business?

10. How can you get more information about this investment, such as audited financial statements?

You are only as safe as you are smart, and while most individuals have honest intentions and use the Internet as a legitimate investment tool, there are still some shady characters out there. Any information you find on the Internet should be double-checked and verified.

Bet You Didn't Know

The Internet is vast and resources to monitor all the message boards that discuss stocks are limited. Regulators, such as the NASD and SEC, just can't keep up with the millions of message posts, so be careful. You don't know the motives of the person who has posted the message. *En guarde!*

Like any technology still in its infancy, the Internet has its own set of growing pains; many dangers are only beginning to surface. An informal study of half a dozen stocks conducted by NASD Regulation, Inc., showed a close correlation between Internet postings and changes in both trading volume and price. It's impossible for agencies such as the NASD or SEC to police every Internet post or monitor every investment chat, so it's up to you to be your own watchdog.

On its Web site, the NASD suggests the following guidelines for making investments:

➤ **Question all advice.** If you don't know the source of the information or the motives behind the source, challenge the validity of the information.

➤ **Consult other resources.** Never make investment decisions solely based upon what you read on the Internet.

➤ **Do your homework.** Although the Internet opens up access to a variety of new information sources, there is no substitute for your own detailed research.

➤ **Use good judgment.** After all, every investment has its risks. As the saying goes: If something seems too good to be true, it probably is.

➤ **Call on the experts.** If you suspect something is shady, trust your instincts and notify the regulators before you act.

You can contact the NASD at:

NASD Regulation, Inc.
1735 K Street, NW
Washington, DC 20006–1500
(301) 590-6500

The Least You Need to Know

➤ Consumers can actually save money on commissions by opening brokerage accounts on their personal computers. Commissions have been reported as low as $7.95 per trade at brokerage firms such as Suretrade.com.

➤ If the online broker you've selected to do business with does not offer free quotes, consider online alternatives such as CBSMarketWatch, PCQuote.com, and BigCharts.

➤ Before you start trading online, know the five different types of orders you can execute: market, fill or kill, all or none, stop, and limit.

➤ Make sure you remember your password and security code—such as your mother's maiden name—when filling out your online application.

➤ If you suspect online investment fraud, call the NASD at (301) 590-6500, or write them at 1735 K Street, NW, Washington, DC 20006–1500.

Part 2
Making Money in the Millennium Marketplace

Making money takes more than just sheer motivation and a few dollars in your pocket. The process requires consistent dedication to a plan—your investment plan made up of all your investment goals—that you create simply by determining why *you're investing in the first place. Do you want a new home? Pay your children's college tuition bill in one fell swoop? No matter what your financial goals are, they are a required variable in the formula in building wealth.*

Without a plan, you cannot profit from any hot stocks, be they in the Internet, pharmaceutical, or industrial sectors. Even yesterday's mutual fund winners won't ring any millennium bells if you haven't created your plan first.

Of course, knowing how economics work and which financial Web sites to use as resources are integral parts to your personal plan. Understanding how foreign countries count on each other for financial aid and how that affects our American economy will enable you to make better investment decisions. Plus, you get to see who the biggest component is in our economy—you!

Let's create your investment plan for your future.

Chapter 6

Simple Wealth-Building Strategies

In This Chapter

➤ Why wealth doesn't buy happiness—but it does pay the bills

➤ What lessons to learn from 1998 for the future

➤ Simple investment strategies even the rich use

There's an amazing tale of how the satisfaction in life changes with the more money you make while working and living in the United States. It begins with the theory of happiness of someone who has $10,000 in income. If this person's income increases to $20,000, a dollar buys only one-third as much happiness. By the time you jump from $40,000 to $60,000, the same dollar buys only 12 percent as much happiness.

Granted, this is based on a simple mathematical calculation, but there is a point here: When you're rich, a dollar simply doesn't do as much for you as when you're poor. So, the idea is to not get rich. Nope, that's a terrible investment philosophy. The idea is to build wealth—s-l-o-w-l-y.

The tried-and-true principles practiced by the wealthy are simple and based on one foundation: You must have a success strategy.

This chapter will show you how to profit from not just creating an investment portfolio but also create simple investment strategies to build success for you and your family.

A Year in Review

Life is change, no doubt. Nothing can ever be the same a minute from now as it was a minute ago. Everything you own is changing in price and value. You can find the last price of an active security on the stock ticker, but you cannot find the *next* price anywhere. Even the value of your money—and your house—is changing, though no one walks in front of it with a sandwich board posting the changes.

Across the Big Blue

The year 1998 was riddled not only with change but also with opportunities and challenges, especially worldwide. The crisis of investor confidence that unfolded in the summer of 1997 in South Asia and spread to Japan and then on to Latin America (although not as in-depth as in fall of 1993) spilled over into 1998, showing that the global business environment does not always run smoothly.

The main worldwide event for 1998 was the final preparation for the Economic and Monetary Union (EMU), in which member-states (Germany, France, and ten other countries) positioned their economies to run congruently and have one singular denomination of currency that began in early 1999. This currency is known as the *Euro*. There has been some resistance to participating in the EMU—usually due to the fear of losing old-world historical value—which is why several countries, including Britain and Sweden, sat on the sidelines for the first several months of 1999 to see the outcome.

Bet You Didn't Know

Croatia is not participating in the new currency market. Is it fear of losing thousands of years of history? No, in fact, *contradictory religious* beliefs prevent the country from participating in this new economy.

Okay, you say. All those events take place *over there*. What do they have to do with me? A lot. You see, if you own stock in companies like Coca-Cola, Microsoft and McDonald's, then you are already participating in the global economy by owning multinational companies that do much of their business overseas. International business provides valuable diversification within these companies. A large portion of stock mutual funds with growth as their investment objective often invest a fragment of their portfolios in worldwide issues—including European-based companies. (Check the prospectus for confirmation.) If you want to know what's happening to your money, pay attention to what's happening overseas. The wealthy do.

America, America

Back here at home, the United States—along with Japan and Germany—still shapes much of the global economic landscape. Fifty-one percent of global gross domestic product (all the goods and services bought and sold in the world) originates in these three countries with low inflation.

Give credit to the Federal Reserve, which has kept its watchful eye on inflation and will seize upon any sign of wage or price pressures and step on the brakes with higher interest rates.

Hot Stuff Online

With more than 100 million documents on the information superhighway, cyberspace not only exploded in 1998 but mushroomed into the cracks and crevices of every American living room that garners a computer.

In fact:

Money Meaning

The **gross domestic product** is the sum of all the goods and services bought and sold in the United States. This differs from real GDP which not only measures the sum of all the goods and services bought and sold in the U.S. but also takes into account inflation.

➤ Christmas 1998 was the launching pad when online retail shopping really took off. Analysts at Ernst & Young, Forrester Research, and Jupiter Communications tally the Internet sales anywhere from $220 million to $1.1 billion.

➤ Nua, one of Europe's leading online consultants and developers, estimates the number of Internet users worldwide to be 100.5 million. By the end of the year 2000, analysts predict that number to jump to 200 million.

➤ Keep counting…FIND/SVP's Emerging Technology Research Group expects 800 million web documents to arrive by the year 2000.

And wow! Those financial markets. During 1998, we experienced a tumultuous yet on-the-double-digit-plus-side annual return of the DJIA and, in particular, the S&P 500, a benchmark that many portfolio managers try to outperform. It seemed as though the sky was going to fall, however, on March 8, when the Dow nose-dived 171 points (three percent) in a single day, only to rebound in two weeks. If you're a small investor in for the long haul, treat the Dow like your scale; don't get on it every day.

You Got the Goods. Next?

What is the biggest reason you bought this book? Information. Wherever you turn today, information plagues our society. From the moment you turn on a radio, boot up your computer, buy a newspaper at the drugstore, or read a magazine in your dentist's waiting room, how much more can you absorb?

Rather than launch into esoteric prose on the brain's capacity to store insurmountable amounts of data, we'd rather you know this: While information is important to digest, the *types* of information and how you *choose* this information enable you to stay on course with your wealth-building plan.

Not all information is relevant to your investment success "campaign." Here's an example: If you were to log on to the Internet and go to your favorite search engine and type in the word "investing," do you know how many entries will be returned? Try more than six million. Your time is precious, leaving little to wade through all those entries. Plus, not all of those entries are relevant to *your* specific needs. And while a specific search string would be more helpful (see Chapter 2 for a hint on how to do this), there are other methods of retrieving specific information to help foster your plan. Please consider the following:

➤ **Read a major daily newspaper everyday.** By staying on top of local, national, and international news, not only are you staying on top of current events, but after a time you will begin to see trends develop that hit your wallet. When a number of companies are laying off workers (do you own their stock?) and weather in the Southeast is below normal (what happens to orange juice prices?), are small examples of how current events affect the consumer pocketbook.

➤ **Subscribe to at least one financial newsletter.** This is not a green light to put your money where the editor's mouth is, but many reputable financial newsletters do summarize recent market events. Where to begin? Subscribe to *The Hulbert Financial Digest*, written by editor Mark Hulbert, which tracks the performance numbers of the recommendations given by dozens of financial newsletters available to investors. For subscription information, go to his Web site at www.hulbertdigest.com.

➤ **Go to the library.** Visit *your* books on library shelves; after all, the library illustrates your tax dollars hard at work. Most libraries across the country have computers that give you suggested titles for whatever subjects you are looking for. If your library doesn't have a computer, you can ask for help from the librarian at the business reference desk.

Click Here

Stay on top of information by reading *The New York Times*, available online at **www.nytimes.com**, or on all major newsstands and available for home delivery.

Look in Your Own Backyard First

Before you can improve your investment picture, you must make sure your overall finances are sound. Being organized is key. At one point or another, many of you have probably had the motivation to sort out your financial affairs; now before the millennium hits is the time to do it!

Here's a snapshot of what you need to do before embarking on your wealth-building efforts:

➤ **Figure out your goals.** Buy a house? A new car? Vacation home?

➤ **Determine your time horizon.** When do you expect all these things to take place?

➤ **Assess the cost.** What is the price tag on each of the items you are trying to reach or accomplish?

➤ **Look at your budget.** When was the last time you balanced your checkbook?

➤ **Reduce your debt.** Are you paying down debt from Christmas—of 1996?

Click Here

New to using computers? Opt for Quicken Basic, budget-planning software by Intuit, as part of your financial organization strategy this year. Intuit offers demos and information about this product on their Web site at **www.quicken.com**.

How the Wealthy Folks Do It

What defines wealth? For some, it's a portfolio that consistently wreaks of double-digit gains and living off the interest because all the bills are paid for. For others, wealth means flying in Lear jets and downing bottles of Cristal with your partner. For others, the phrase "being wealthy" connotes a meaning unto itself.

There is no true answer to what signifies wealth, no matter how large your bank account or expensive your sports car. While the *Merriam-Webster* dictionary defines wealth as "riches, fortune, and opulence," that's not necessarily what we're shooting for here.

So, forget buying the Rolls Royce or spending $100,000 for New Year's Eve at the Ritz Carlton for their "Millennium Experience™." (Of course, the Rolex™ watch of your choice it offers in the package sounds tempting.) The goal is to *not* do this overnight; building wealth takes time, motivation, attention to detail, and a lot of patience. Sounds like a plan, doesn't it?

Click Here

Looking for investment analysis at the click of a button? Log onto **Briefing.com** for expert market commentary of what's happening on Wall Street, from sector (industry) ratings, individual stock analysis and any news from the Federal Reserve.

Unless they were born into it, married into it, or inherited it, all wealthy individuals know it is nearly impossible to reach investment goals without a plan.

Let's get started with yours:

➤ **Define your investment objectives.** Do you want growth, income, or a combination of both? Do you need tax-free income? Discerning your answer will help you determine an integral part to building wealth.

➤ **Know your risk tolerance.** Generally, the greater the risk, the greater the reward potential. Like they say at the gym: No pain, no gain. The longer your investment horizon, the more risk you can usually tolerate.

➤ **Build a portfolio that fits your objectives and risk tolerance.** Too much risk and you'll be too nervous to sleep nights. Too much safety and you may find the returns too low. Remember: Building wealth is long-term planning, so design an investment program that you can modify as you get older and your objectives change.

That's only the beginning. Adopt these fundamental principles to get started creating a simple wealth-building plan, and you are on your way.

Wait, There's More!

Suppose you "fell" into some cash, about $100,000. That doesn't qualify you as wealthy, at least by today's standards, but it's a nice chunk of change that would help build your portfolio on the road to wealth.

One of the initial steps in creating a successful portfolio is deciding what you should invest in. You make this decision by determining what each investment product is, how it works, and how risky it is. Once you figure that out, the next step is to decide which stocks, bonds, mutual funds you should consider. That decision is based upon investment research.

The three-step process to investment research includes:

➤ Learning about the company

➤ Learning about the industry

➤ Monitoring the company and the industry

Use your eyes in all three phrases. These "personal observation tools" are quite often the foundation for all investment research. You're reading a major daily newspaper everyday and watching for trends in consumer behavior, right? What are you noticing? When you drop off the kids at school, what cars are other parents driving? What are the kids wearing?

It's as simple as that.

Let's say you notice that many parents are driving Chevrolet vans, or, as one of us refers to it, "The Mommy Mobile." Vans, vans, everywhere! Then, on your way to work, you notice that the school grounds aren't the only place you see these vans; they're tooting along the highway, not necessarily at breakneck speed, but definitely in droves.

Click Here

First Call, an investment research firm, provides earning estimates, buy/hold/sell recommendations on stocks, earnings announcement dates and other important data to investors on its Web site at **www.firstcall.com**.

As you flip radio stations, you hear an Associated Press wire report that the Big 3 Automakers in Detroit are reporting stepped up production requirements to handle consumer demand for all these vans. Thinking back to the basic laws of economics, higher demand means higher prices; and for the Big 3 that spells higher cash flow.

You can learn about the Chevrolet company by contacting its headquarters in Michigan and speaking with a shareholder services or investor relations person. Most often, when you have a question regarding a company's business or practices, you can contact either of these departments (although the Web can be used now as a supplemental research tool).

Click Here

Touted as the ultimate source for company information, Hoover's Online provides more than 13,500 company descriptions and financials – all for free. Also available are company histories and their market strategies, but you must subscribe online to that information. Sign up at **www.hoovers.com**.

You'll need documentation, such as financial reports, and any brochures you can get your hands on. Ask to be put on their mailing list. And definitely find out the following:

➤ How long has the company been in business?

➤ How profitable is it?

➤ How much bad debt versus good debt does it have?

➤ Who is running the company?

➤ Who is the competition?

➤ Are there any new products or services coming out on the market?

➤ Which analysts at the brokerage firms follow this company, and what do they have to say?

Once you have done your research and have answers to all your questions, check out the entire industry on the Internet, keep an eye out for news stories in your daily paper, or do a little digging at the library.

The KISS Principle

One of our favorite examples of what a little effort can do over a long time is based on the KISS principle: Keep It Simple, Silly.

Suppose, at the age of 25, you invested $100 a month in an equity mutual fund that earns an average return of 12 percent, and kept investing it until you retired. At retirement, you would have close to $1 million—not counting the money from reinvested dividends or capital gains. Imagine that! One million dollars by the time you retire just because you socked away a $100 every month. It's possible, especially if you're younger, because you have time on your side. It's also a strategy the wealthy implement; how do you think they got that way? It's called *dollar cost averaging*. While it does not guarantee against loss, it is a system you should commit to for several years.

Dollar cost averaging allows you to take advantage of the markets when share prices are low, and helps you avoid paying inflated prices when markets are high. Yet even the most experienced investors find it almost impossible to time the markets. By investing at regular intervals, you can take advantage of market downturns *and* benefit from stock and bond market rallies. Plus, you don't have to think about timing the markets just right.

With dollar cost averaging, you invest a fixed dollar amount on a scheduled basis, regardless of market directions. Using this strategy, you can reduce your average cost per share. This disciplined approach to investing can help long-term investors improve their chances for strong returns and build significant assets over time.

Bet You Didn't Know

Don't have enough money to buy 100 shares of stock? No problem. Charles Carlson, CFA, and author of *The Individual Investor Revolution*, notes that companies that offer dividend reinvestment programs, known as DRIPs, enable you to buy fractional shares directly from the company. Bypass the brokers and their commissions. Log onto **www.dripinvestor.com** to find out more information.

By investing a fixed dollar amount at regular intervals, you automatically buy more shares when prices are low and fewer shares when prices are high. As a result, your average share *cost* could be less than the average share *price*.

Let's say, for example, that you invest $500 every month for six months during a period of fluctuating prices. As the table below illustrates, your average share cost is *less* than the average share price. Using dollar cost averaging, you take advantage of market rallies while getting more shares for your money when the market turned down.

When?	How much?	Price?	Shares?
January 15	$100.00	$15.00	6.67
February 15	$100.00	$16.00	6.25
March 15	$100.00	$14.00	7.14
April 15	$100.00	$12.00	8.33
May 15	$100.00	$14.00	7.14
June 15	$100.00	$15.00	6.67
July 15	$100.00	$16.00	6.25

continues

continued

When?	How much?	Price?	Shares?
August 15	$100.00	$15.00	6.67
September 15	$100.00	$17.00	5.88
October 15	$100.00	$18.00	5.56
November 15	$100.00	$20.00	5.00
December 15	$100.00	$22.00	4.55
TOTALS:	$1,200.00	$16.17 avg price/share	

Own 76.11 shares

Total amount invested: $1,200

Value of portfolio now: $1674.42

Net profit (loss): $474.42 (does not include dividends being reinvested)

The Least You Need to Know

➤ The tried-and-true principles practiced by the wealthy are simple and based on one foundation: You must have a success strategy.

➤ Planning for the long-term does not necessarily mean you should react to the DJIA every day. Use it, along with other financial benchmarks, such as the S&P 500, in your daily monitoring of the financial markets.

➤ Stay informed. A subscription to a major newspaper and financial newsletter, as well as a frequent visit to the library, will keep you on your toes with current events and ready to be proactive should any investment opportunities come your way.

➤ Before investing in a stock, bond, or mutual fund, you should learn more about the company, the marketplace, and the industry. Start today simply by contacting the shareholder or investor relations departments at each organization.

➤ Dollar cost averaging is an investment strategy that does not guarantee a profit but does provide a way to build wealth over a long period of time.

Chapter 7

Finding the Hot Stocks for the New Millennium

In This Chapter

➤ Why making money in stocks requires more than just patience

➤ How to interpret performance information easily

➤ Which industries will make the grade in the next century

➤ When you should use a few tricks of the trade in dealing with bear markets

---

You may not recall the Dutch tulip craze of the 17th century in which ordinary citizens speculated on tulip bulbs as a surefire way to get rich only to end up bankrupt. We're sure, however, that you've read the headlines of the thousands of at-home investors who are acquiring shares of Internet stocks hoping to double and triple their money.

It's easy to say you've never seen anything like the Internet stock phenomenon that occurred during the last half of the 90s; but in fact, market crazes have happened time and time again.

Stop and smell the tulips, for one. In 1634, thousands of people in the Netherlands ponied up their life savings hoping to fetch that one precious and rare tulip bulb to sell for a profit on their investment. Three years later, however, the market collapsed and their wallets dried up quicker than the bulbs.

Of course, not all historical speculations ended up as financial losses. Personal computers were introduced in the early 1970s and widely used when Steve Jobs and Apple Computer, Inc. brought powerful and affordable computers to individual users. Good thinking. According to the Electronic Industries Association, more than 60 million PCs were sold in the United States in 1996. Personal computer sales now exceed those of televisions. And publicly traded companies like Compaq, IBM, and Hewlett-Packard are ringing in the new millennium with incredible balance sheets—and happy shareholders.

Still, trying to get your arms around the value of any publicly traded companies in the year 2000 and beyond—especially Internet-driven companies—is like trying to hug the air. This chapter will help you determine how to choose the right stock, which industries are poised for growth and profit potential, as well as offer stock trading strategies that even some of the investment pros use.

It's More Than Patience, My Dear

It's a brand new world out there. Any investor who wants to make money in the next few years better get used to it, because the opportunities are likely to be no less exciting. They will be quite different, however, from what we've witnessed during this past century.

A market cycle, as you know, always brings new stocks to the fore, and that takes some adjustment. (See a trend here? Think "change.") We are now dealing with a completely different sort of financial animal—a dangerous one if you don't understand it.

The stocks that were market darlings in the beginning of 1998, for example, got slaughtered in early fall. Not slaughtered but definitely hit were companies like Coca-Cola and Gillette, which warned of disappointing earnings results and saw their stocks tumble. Yet the losses were symptoms of underlying global financial problems, not necessarily the main cause of market decline.

Whether you believe we are in good market times or the Wall Street bubble is about to burst, you should know that finding the hottest companies in which to invest—and hopefully profit from—in the new millennium requires you to learn everything you can about the company.

Many investment research Web sites offer "Company Overview" information, such as where they're headquartered, how many employees they maintain, top competitors, key officers, and brief-but-current commentary. Follow this information; it's a prerequisite to your stock research. Also be sure to:

> ➤ **Find out who is running the company.** If there has been poor management in the past, it will be indicated on the company's financial statements, such as balance sheets and earnings estimates. Note if and when there is a change in management so that you can check into the background of the new manager.

> ➤ **Check how long the company has been profitable or, at least, how close they are to a profit.** Try to get a five-year financial history. Make sure the company didn't consistently post losses for all five years; even the IRS wonders about small businesses that post losses after five years and labels them as "hobbies."

> ➤ **Determine how much and what types of debt the company is carrying on its books.** Like consumers, companies have good debt and bad debt. An example of

good debt is when companies issue bonds, such as an IOU, to investors who loaned them money for capital infusion with a promise to pay the money back with interest. Bad debt, however, includes loans companies made to other businesses that have gone unpaid for several quarters.

➤ **Assess the competition.** Think of McDonalds and Burger King. How financially strong and how much market share does each competitor have? If the company is new, like many of the Internet stocks in the late 90s, and is entering an already saturated market, what type of competition—and future—does it face?

➤ **If any new products are coming out, find out why.** In an established company, new products or services can be either good or bad. Check the company's history to see whether it's ventured into that territory before and what type of competition it faces with the new products.

Bet You Didn't Know

It took the Dow Jones Industrial 25 years to recapture all its losses prior to the stock market crash of 1929.

Realize that your research will be an ongoing process. Learning about the company and the industry is the first part. You must consistently monitor the company after you have invested by following its performance information.

The Basics of Performance Information

The most available source of performance information is in the financial section of your local newspaper where you'll find the most widely read performance indicator: the closing price of an investment. The *New York Times*, *Los Angeles Times*, and *Chicago Tribune* all list the *closing prices* for thousands of stocks, market indexes, and mutual fund and commodities information that traded the previous trading day. Such investments are listed either by their ticker symbol or an abbreviation.

Money Meaning

The **closing price** represents the last price at which a listed investment security was either bought or sold. That price is what investors usually look for.

In addition to the closing prices, other performance information is given. This includes, but is not limited to, the following:

➤ **High and low.** The numbers in these columns represent the highest and lowest price of an investment during the previous trading day (yesterday).

➤ **52-week high and 52-week low.** This represents the highest and lowest price of an investment during the last 52-week period.

➤ **Close.** This is the price at which the security closed on the previous trading day.

➤ **Volume.** Sometimes shown as "VOL" in the table, the volume indicates how many shares, issues, or contracts of an investment traded and exchanged hands for the entire previous trading day.

➤ **Net change.** The net change is the difference in price from the previous day's close to that particular day's close. For example, if you are reading the financial tables on Thursday morning, the net change listed represents the difference in price from Tuesday to Wednesday.

These are the elements of ticker talk you should be aware of when monitoring your stocks. Make sure, however, you don't base your investment decisions on yesterday's closing price. You need to complete some other steps.

Interpreting Performance Information

Our lives are filled with numbers. Just pick up a *Barrons* and read how Internet giant Yahoo! traded at 320 times the projected 1999 earnings. Or turn on CNBC-TV's *Power Lunch Hour* and listen to Bill Griffith's remarks on how stocks like Cisco, Lucent, and Northern Telecom are down five, six, and even seven points—*in a day*—and suddenly selling at half the price they were two or three months ago. Even basic numbers cross your daily path when you shop at the grocery store and find you paid more than three dollars for a gallon of milk!

All the performance information is given when you become a *shareholder*, but how do you figure which end is up? Here is a basic primer to understanding what performance information tells you:

➤ **Total return.** Total return gives the sum of the price appreciation and income derived from an investment. For example, if you invest in a stock that reports a total return of 16 percent, the 16 percent is what you earn from the appreciation in price of the stock (the stock price moving up) and the income derived from the stock (in the form of dividends you receive).

➤ What happens, however, if you invest in a company that doesn't pay dividends? The majority of the performance (the total return) comes from the price appreciation. High-paying dividend stocks focus on income rather than price appreciation.

➤ **Annual return.** Annual return is the total return measured over a 12-month period. An annual return of 23 percent means the investment earned 23 percent—either in price appreciation, income, or a combination of both—over a period of 12 months.

➤ **Cumulative return.** The cumulative return is usually expressed in a period of three, five, or ten years as the *sum* of the annual return for each of those years. So, for example, if your stock earned 19 percent in 1995, 16 percent in 1996, but only 3 percent in 1997, your cumulative return would be 38 percent. Keep in mind when interpreting performance information on a company not to look solely at a cumulative return; those triple digit numbers can be misleading when you start picking about annual returns year by year.

➤ **Average annual return.** This return number represents the cumulative return number expressed as what you would earn for each year given. For example, if the cumulative return of a mutual fund was 126 percent for three years, the average annual return would be 42 percent—the cumulative return divided by the number of years.

Money Meaning

A **shareholder** is a person who has bought ownership, or shares, in a company that maintains a value of at least one dollar per share.

Analyze This!

When researching stocks, you need to analyze company financial statements. Now put down the Mylanta and hold on for one moment. If you think that a business runs its operations just like you do, meaning there are:

➤ Expenses to pay, such as utility bills and telephone bills to pay

➤ Income to earn to meet those expenses, like from sales of products or services—to you, it's your paycheck

Then you can easily learn the basics of how to decipher balance sheets and income statements to assist you in your stock selection. A *balance sheet* is a company's statement of assets, liabilities, and net worth at a particular point in time. It is a static report of the company's financial condition as of a particular date. The fundamental equation of the balance sheet is as follows:

Assets = Liabilities + Net Worth

In the case of a corporation, however, the net worth could be defined as stockholder's equity. Therefore, the formula changes to the following:

Assets = Liabilities + Stockholder's Equity

Assets, as you know, are anything that you own. Your house is an asset, unless, of course, you're renting. Assets are divided into the following three major classifications:

➤ **Current assets.** Current assets are items such as cash, marketable securities, accounts receivables, prepaid expenses, and inventories that can be turned into cash within one year. Coins, short-term investments like Treasury bills, and negotiable CDs are considered assets. So are trade receivables that are expected to be received within one year. Inventories, such as raw materials, goods-in-process, or finished goods, are usually current assets because they generally can be converted into cash within a year.

➤ **Fixed assets.** Assets that are not easily converted into cash (illiquid) are fixed assets. These are tangible properties—such as land, plant buildings, and equipment—used in the production of income. Ordinary plant buildings and equipment are listed at cost, less any amount that has depreciated in value due to wear and tear. Remember: Fixed assets on a balance sheet are shown as *cost less depreciation*.

Bet You Didn't Know

The primary purpose of accounting for depreciation is to enable a company to recover its cost, not replace the asset or reflect its declining usefulness. To determine the value at which asset is carried on a balance sheet you will look at its book value. If a piece of manufacturing equipment is put on the books at cost when purchased, its value is reduced each year as depreciation is charged to income. The book value is its cost minus accumulated depreciation.

➤ **Intangible assets.** This third typical asset classification consists of assets that are not physical in nature. Ordinarily, intangible assets represent a small portion of the corporation's total assets. Examples of intangible assets include goodwill, leases, patents, copyrights, and franchises.

Switch to the next part of the equation: liabilities. You have liabilities, just look at your credit card bills. A liability represents a financial claim by a creditor against a corporation's assets, and is categorized as either current or long-term.

➤ **Current liabilities are the amounts owed by the corporation that will come due within one year.** These include accounts payable, notes payable, and other payables, such as taxes and dividends that need to be paid.

➤ **Long-term liabilities are debts that will come due after one year.** Examples are bonds, mortgages on real property, and long-term promissory notes.

Net worth and stockholder's equity mean the same thing. Net worth, in a corporation, is the owner's equity or claim against the assets.

Next on the balance sheet are capital accounts. These include:

Money Meaning

Book value is the value at which an asset is carried on a balance sheet.

➤ **Common stock.** The number of shares issued and outstanding is listed at the par value, which is an arbitrary dollar amount assigned to a share of stock by the corporation when the stock is issued. Common stock is an *equity security* because it represents ownership in a corporation.

➤ **Capital surplus.** This represents the amount of common stock sold above par value at the initial offering—if it was sold above par. This is part of the net worth of the common stockholder.

➤ **Retained earnings.** Also called earned surplus, retained earnings represent a company's total profits minus the paid dividends.

➤ **Preferred stock.** The usual par value of preferred stock is $100 and is listed on the balance sheet in the stockholder's equity section but is not part of the common equity.

Total capitalization is another item you will find on a balance sheet. This is the invested capital made up of five components:

➤ Long-term liabilities

➤ Common stocks

➤ Capital surpluses

➤ Retained earnings

➤ Preferred stocks

The income statement is another important financial statement to review. Also known as a profit and loss (P & L) statement, the income statement summarizes a company's revenues and expenses for a given period. This fiscal period can be any 12-month period designated by the company. It is the history of the company's operations for the year and shows whether there was a profit or a loss as a result of the company's activities for that time period. The fundamental equation of the income statement is as follows:

Total Revenues – Total Expenses = Total Profit

Beginning to sound a bit familiar to *your* personal finances? Of course, corporations usually have more intense operations on their books, especially publicly traded companies. All you need to remember is to review these financial statements before you invest, not only to make sure the company's goals and objectives meet with your own, but that they're not three steps away from going out of business.

Creating a Customized Search

As of December 1998, there were more than 10,000 publicly traded stocks. Of course, reading all the financial data on every single one is impossible. The thought alone offers nightmares cured only with hefty doses of herbal tea and a few deep breathing exercises.

That's why several companies, such as America Online, Morningstar, and Hoovers, have created (free!) interactive technology to help you sort through stocks and find the ones that you think would make the best investments. This all depends on your investing priorities, such as:

➤ You only want stocks valued less than $20.

➤ You prefer companies that pay dividends.

➤ You don't want stocks that have a high *beta*, which is a measurement of risk.

It's your call! For example, here's how AOL's Investment Research Stock Screening resource works once you log on to AOL's Personal Finance Channel (keyword: personal finance):

➤ **Choose which order you want your results to appear.** This feature can appear as "ascending or descending," meaning, you get to pick whether you want your best choice to appear first or last.

➤ **Rank your stocks by the variables you select.** Depending whether you want information on a *price-to-earnings ratio*, book value, or some other sort of financial variable, you set the groundwork on which variable ranks the highest in terms of priority. If *price-to-book ratio* is the most important factor, you would select that as your top priority. You can even select which stock exchange you prefer, if that is a factor.

➤ **Get picky with your variables.** If you want to choose a specific price-to-earnings ratio, for example, you can choose a range of numbers with the click of your mouse.

Money Meaning

Beta is a measurement of the sensitivity (volatility) of a stock relative to current market activity.

Money Meaning

A **price-to-earnings ratio**, also known as p/e ratio, measures how much an investor is willing to pay per share given the stock's current level of earnings. You take the stock's market price and divide it by its current or estimated future earnings.

A **price-to-book ratio** is the price per share divided by the book value per share.

➤ **Select an industry.** All stocks belong in at least one industry. AOL's stock screening capabilities allow you to choose among the 12 business sectors listed, such as transportation, retail, and automotive.

➤ **Screen your stocks.** After filling in all the variables, click on the Screen Stocks button to sort through its database for the information you need.

Click Here

E*Trade, the online brokerage firm, offers stock screening tools that allow you to sort through thousands of publicly-traded companies based on a variety of financial variables, including key ratios, income statements, and earnings estimates. Log onto **www.etrade.com** for details.

Beyond the Numbers: The Ideal Company

What types of 21st-century businesses will be ideal to invest in? Well, you need to understand that we live in a global economy. Doing so will enable you to embrace the first component of your research: looking for companies that sell to the world rather than to a single neighborhood or even a single city or state. In other words, companies with an unlimited global market.

Click Here

The United States is no longer a self-sufficient country, and neither is any other industrialized or emerging country. Countries depend on each other for capital, customers, and commodities. Stay on top of stocks at the exchanges in 40 different countries by logging on to the global stock exchanges at **www.wiso.gwdg.de/ifbg/stock1.htm**.

This is more important today than ever, since world markets have now opened to an extent unparalleled in either of our lifetimes. Wall Street is quite optimistic about investing in global economies. For example, Mark Holowesko, CFA and president of

Templeton Global Advisors Limited, likens many of the emerging markets' crises in recent years to overcorrections, with the fallout based on emotions and not reason. As a result, during the last two years of the 20th century, foreign currencies were under-valued, and an intriguing competitiveness in the export business existed in countries such as Hong Kong and Singapore—some of the world's busiest seaports.

You don't have to go to the Far East, however, to witness competition. How many times have you seen a retail store that has been doing well for years only to have a bigger and better store move nearby and put it out of business? That's why it's crucial to find companies that market a product or a line of products that cannot be easily copied. This means that the product is an original or at least something that can be copyrighted or patented.

You also should look for companies that operate with low overhead or minimal labor requirements. Companies that do not need an expensive location to do business, such as large amounts of electricity, advertising, legal advice, high-priced employees, and large inventories, may fare better during both good and bad economic times. Profit-ability doesn't hurt, either.

Not all the popular publicly-traded companies of the late 90s maintained these charac-teristics, however. That's okay; we are providing the basic guidelines for developing your stock research skills.

For example, those cherished—yet volatile—Internet stocks were so overvalued toward the beginning of 1999 that small investors bought stocks like eBay, an online auction house, at $125 a share. Amazon.com, the Internet's no-brick-and-mortar bookstore, predicted a target price of $150 a share by the year 2000 but hit it in three weeks.

Ironically, many Internet stocks have been riding on millions of dollars in losses. How can this be? Are these the types of companies you should be investing in for the future?

Like a Flying Trapeze

Henry Ford said, "Life is a series of experiences, each one of which make us bigger, even though sometimes it is hard to realize this." If you can chalk up investing in stocks as an "experience," you can definitely say buying shares in Internet companies at the turn of the 21st century has been an adventure!

For one thing, people have adopted the Internet faster than nearly any other information-age invention. Although automobiles were first mass produced in the early 1900s, it took 55 years for even 25 percent of all U.S. households to buy a car. The television and PC fared better; it took a little over 15 years for 25 percent of all Americans to own a PC. The information superhighway, however, has been so entic-ing that it took only ten years to reach 25 percent of the population.

The Internet has changed not only the way people get their information but also how they spend their money and time. It's an intangible lifestyle product that you cannot get your hands around. According to Jupiter Communications, nearly 10 million American households will have high-speed Internet connections by the year 2001 and, coupled with advances in payments and securities technologies, will probably put online commerce into hyperdrive.

Bet You Didn't Know

The value of electronic commerce is expected to reach a staggering $223 billion by the year 2002, up from just over $11 billion in 1997.

Does this Internet interest smell of mania rather than steadfastness? Many technology fund managers hope not, but one cannot help comparing Internet stocks to the radio stocks of 1929. Back then, the stock market rocketed to new highs before crashing. Radio, however, the newest craze, and broadcast industry-related stocks, started a slow decline that ended with the death of empires such as RCA.

There is no doubt that Internet stocks are volatile. theStreet.com, a popular investment Web site, reported that its Internet Sector index lost 6.6 percent in just *one day* during the first week of January 1999.

So, if you're anything like the small investors that made 100- and 200-share trades in Internet stocks during the last half of 1998—thereby the most active traders in Net stocks—you're the one who is driving the market, as you can see from the following table.

Table 7.1 Small Investors Drive Internet Stocks in the Late 1990s

Stock	Number of Trades (Million)	Number of Shares Traded (Million)	Average Trade Size (Million)
eBay	183,691	57	310
Yahoo!	424,016	185	438
Amazon	239,550	108	453
Lycos	178,843	104	580
AOL	59,621	241	4,051

Birinyi Associates, Inc., November 1998

According to Birinyi Associates, Inc., a firm that tracks program trading (the purchase or sale of 15 or more stocks tallying $1 million), except for America Online, the small size of the average trade suggests retail investors rather than big institutions dominate Net investing.

Even though these small investors take advantage of cheap online commissions and loads of information on the Internet about Internet stocks (good practices, we must say), those strategies do not complete all that you should do in the investment process. While you might make money chasing the latest Internet stocks, you should understand that the frenzy surrounding them is as volatile as the stock prices themselves. Buy stocks where you can make a case for strong fundamentals in the company.

Although some of this information might seem basic, you cannot make money on Wall Street without doing your homework.

Industries Poised for Growth

As you look at the stock market today, your view of it depends upon your own situation and your investment objectives. For some of you who do not mind taking on more risk in exchange for potentially higher returns, the current volatile market should look very good, especially with some stocks experiencing double-digit price swings in just one day.

At the same time, however, those of you who need to pull money out at this time will look unfavorably at today's market. We are never happy when we sell low or at a price other than our target price. If this is your situation, make sure you use the proper perspective. In today's volatile market, your investment may be worth less than it was several months ago. You should not focus on that, however. Instead, focus on whether your investment is worth more or less than it was when you invested several *years* ago.

When Two Becomes One

A joke floating around the financial services industry depicts one of the most lucrative types of business transactions on Wall Street: mergers and acquisitions. If Sondra Locke, the movie actress who has appeared in several *Dirty Harry* movies, married Elliot Ness and then divorced him to marry Herman Munster, she'd be known as Sondra Locke Ness Munster.

This witticism is an excellent example of what has been taking place during the last decade on Wall Street when two or more companies combine assets. Merger activity can be extremely lucrative to shareholders, especially the transactions that took place in 1998 in the financial services industry, as shown in the following table.

Table 7.2 Global Financial Service's Merger and Acquisition Activity—Top 10 Transactions

Target Name/Country/Sector	Acquirer Name/Country/Sector	($ billions) Deal Value
Citicorp/US/Bank	Travelers/US/Insurance	72.6
BankAmerica/US/Bank	NationsBank/US/Bank	61.6
Wells Fargo/US/Bank	Norwest/US/Bank	34.4
First Chicago NBD/ US/Bank	BancOne/US/Bank	29.6
General RE/US/Insurance	BerkshHathwy/US/ Insurance	22.3
SunAmerica/US/Insurance Insurance	Amer Intl Gp/US/	18.1
Tor Dom Bank/ Canada/Bank	CIBC/Canada/Bank	15.4
Bank of Montreal/ Canada/Bank	Royal Bank/Canada/Bank	12.5
Generale/Belgium/Bank	Fortis/Belgium/Insurance	12.3
Genl Accident/UK/ Insurance	Comml Union/UK/Insurance	11.2

The reasons for all the mergers and acquisitions? In the financial services industry, for example, you can chalk it up to the following main factors:

➤ **Deregulation.** In the mid-1980s banks challenged the *Glass-Stegall Act of 1933* by offering money market funds, discount brokerage services, commercial paper and other investment services.

➤ **Lifting of restrictions on insurance activities.** Many financial institutions are becoming involved in distributing insurance products to its customers.

➤ **Increased sales of financial products.** Yesteryear's allure of certificates of deposit has given way to investment products such as stocks, bonds and mutual funds.

Money Meaning

The **Glass Stegall Act of 1933** was legislation passed by Congress authorizing deposit insurance and prohibiting commercial banks from owning brokerage firms. Under Glass-Stegall, these banks may not engage in investment banking activities, such as underwriting corporate securities.

➤ Continued consolidation. The financial services industry will continue to see heavy mergers and acquisitions activity not just in the United States but virtually in all countries, leading to increased concentration.

It's not only the financial services mergers from which you can profit. High-tech deals have been on the upswing, with global mergers and takeovers in the information technology, communications, and media industries hitting record levels in the first half of 1998. Expanded products, services, and distribution—not to mention healthy balance sheets—are ingredients to success.

Between January and June 1998, mergers and acquisitions rose 15 percent from the same period in 1997, according to a study from Broadview investment bank in London. The value of these deals skyrocketed 148 percent, from $117.7 billion in the first half of 1997 to $292 billion in the first half of 1998.

Mega-deals, such as SBC Communications' deal to take over Ameritech Corp., and AT&T Corp's deal to acquire Tele-Communications for $48 billion, have left shareholders in all corporations with dividends in their pockets and smiles on their faces. And with little wonder: In the first six months of 1998, telecommunications-sector deals rose 589 percent, from $24 billion to $165.4 billion worldwide.

Paul Deninger, Chairman and CEO of Broadview and author of a report that follows merger activity, credits the furious pace of merger activity in the information technologies and communications industries to urgent strategic needs. Call it consumer demand.

The perfect example of another industry to watch is the software industry—again, with you the consumer playing a major role—with deals rising 33 percent in the first half of 1998. A *Complete Idiot Guide* forecast? The software sector will probably see continued concentration for the next year or two as software companies continue using mergers and acquisitions to address product and technology needs.

Bank on It

If your images of the banking industry include passbook savings accounts and free toasters and lollipops, guess again. Banking is a global industry that has grown immensely. In fact, there were 68,814 total bank and branch offices in the United States in 1997, up from 35,350 in 1970. Even small investors are noticing the difference and putting their money where, well, where their money is.

And panicking; remember late summer 1998 when bank stocks such as Citicorp fell $47, Banc One Corp. fell 30 percent, and Bank America skidded from $100 to just under $78? This massacre took place in *one month* in August 1998. It certainly gave bank stockholders the jitters.

If you own stocks in technology or Internet-related companies, volatility is nothing new to you. However, it has been odd to see volatility in the banking sector, as reported by the Standard & Poor's financials index.

It was hard to believe when Standard & Poor's financials index rose 51 percent in 1995 and 42 percent in 1996 and 1997, respectively. And then on the heels of the financials index rising we saw a slump in this sector in 1998. Think of what could be considered 1998's short-term slump this way. Remember when we said that we live in a global economy? In 1998, Asia, Russia, and Latin America experienced their own financial crises, which tumbled over onto Wall Street. Couple these foreign financial crises with the incredible merger activity in the financial industry and you can see why there has been so much volatility in the financial sector.

The question investors have is whether to consider these banking stock price drops as a signal to buy or as a warning to wait. You have to decide for yourself, of course, based on your investment objectives and time horizon. Many bargains we saw toward the end of 1998, however, certainly appeared enticing for long-term investors willing to ride out the storms at the time.

Who Gets the Crown?

Big stocks, such as Yahoo!, Lucent Technologies, and Merck, did well in 1998, and, according to the most recent study of *Dow Theory Forecasts*, an industry newsletter, the S&P 500 outperformed 47 of the 60 industry groups.

Even though the rule in the investment industry is that past performance is no indication of future performance, use the following table as a guide to those industries and groups that performed well in 1998 and are possible contenders for the next century.

Table 7.3 Stock Performance by Industry for 1998

	0%	10%	20%	30%	40%	50%	60%	70%	80%	90%	100%
Technology											
Computers/ information	xxxxxxxxxxxxxxxxxxxxxxxxxxxxxxxxxxxxxxxxxxxxxxxxx										
Computer services/ software	xxxxxxxxxxxxxxxxxxxxxxxxxxxxxxxxxxx										
Semiconductors	xxxxxxxxxxxxxxxx										
Non-Cyclical Consumer											
Biotechnology	xxxxxxxxxxxxxxxxxxxxxxxxxxxxxxxxxxxxxxxxxxxxxxxxxxx										
Telephone— long distance	xxxxxxxxxxxxxxxxxxxxxxxxxxxxxxxxxxx										
Drugs	xxxxxxxxxxxxxxxxxxxxxxxxxxxxxxxxxxx										
Food retailers	xxxxxxxxxxxxxxxxxxxxxxx										

continues

Table 7.3   Stock Performance by Industry for 1998

	0%	10%	20%	30%	40%	50%	60%	70%	80%	90%	100%
Domestic Consumer Cyclical											
Retail—specialty	xxxxxxxxxxxxxxxxxxxxxxxxxxxxxxxxxxxxxxxxxxxx										
Media— entertainment	xxxxxxxxxxxxxxxxxxxxxxxx										
Retail—discount	xxxxxxxxxxxxxxxxx										

SOURCE: Dow Theory Forecasts (www.dowtheory.com)

Bet You Didn't Know

January is the best time of year to invest in small company stocks, according to Ibbotson Associates. This has been true with such regularity over the past century that since 1926, small cap stocks have returned five percentage points more in January, on average, than large cap stocks.

Click Here

If you want to know something about technical analysis or technical indicators and software, log on to Market Technicians Association at **www.mta–usa.org**. It provides links to more than 300 sites that offer investment information, such as a list of 800 money managers, an index to initial public offerings (IPOs), a patent search system, and commodity and foreign stock exchanges.

A Quick Word About Bear Markets

Although the S&P 500 posted an annual return of 28.3 percent in 1998, not every year is going to be on the plus side. The Forum for Investor Advice, a non-profit organization based in Bethesda, Maryland, offers the following story about what to do when a bear market approaches.

Two campers are far from civilization when they hear an ominous growl behind them. They turn and see an angry bear headed right for them and moving fast. One camper reaches into his backpack for a pair of sneakers and calmly begins to lace them up. "You must be crazy," says the other camper. "You can't run faster than a hungry bear!" "I don't need to," the first camper points out. "I only need to run faster than you!"

The moral of the story is that bear markets happen. While the stock market, historically, has lost 20 percent every three years or so, the purpose of investing is to reach a goal—not to outrun a bear market.

With that in mind, remember the following should you hear a nasty growl approaching your investment portfolio:

➤ **The bear may not affect you.** The only share prices that matter to you are those of the shares you own. If the market is down, it doesn't mean your holdings are. Even during the October 1987 crash when the DJIA dropped 508 points, some stocks gained ground.

➤ **Review how your investment's track record relates to your goals and your time horizon.** Have you gained more than enough since the last bear market to put you well ahead of inflation? Look at how your investments have performed during previous market downturns.

➤ **Don't panic.** If you do, you're bound to make ill-considered moves that could cost you, not just in profit or loss of capital, but also in taxes. Whenever you sell shares, you're on the hook for taxes on any capital gains.

➤ **Remember what follows a market decline: a market gain.** If you are not invested in the market when it rebounds, you cannot enjoy the rewards.

Three-Step Battle Plan for Investment Survival

As you know, life is change; nothing can ever be the same a minute from now as it was a minute ago. But exactly how do you profit from that change? Well, as long as you're adjusting your investment goals accordingly, keep the following in mind:

➤ **Write things down.** You will score more investment success and avoid more investment failures if you write things down. Very few investors have the drive and inclination to do this.

➤ **Keep a checklist.** If you aim to improve your investment results, get in the habit of keeping a checklist on every issue you consider buying. Before making a commitment, write down the answers to the following basic questions: How much am I investing in this company? How much do I think I can make? How much do I have to risk? How long do I expect to take to reach my goal?

➤ **Have at least one explanation.** Writing things down is the best way to find out the "ruling reason." When all is said and done, there is usually a single reason that stands out above all others why a particular stock transaction can be expected to show a profit. All too often many relatively unimportant statistics are allowed to obscure this single important point.

Any one of a dozen factors may be the point of a particular purchase or sale. It could be a technical reason—expected earnings increases by Wall Street, for example, a change in management, or the promise of a new product. However, in any given situation, one of these factors will almost certainly be more important than all the rest put together.

Bet You Didn't Know

The year 1995 had the largest gain in the Dow Jones Industrial Average since 1928, up almost 34 percent. The years 1989, 1991, 1993, and 1986 round out the top five, with annual returns of 27 percent, 20.3 percent, 22.6 percent and 13.7 percent, respectively.

The Least You Need to Know

➤ Before buying a stock, you should look at the company financials. One of the most commonly reviewed financial statements is the balance sheet, which shows the company's assets, liabilities, and net worth at a particular point in time.

➤ Some of the industries you should keep your eye on as potential stock investments include banking, technology, software, transportation, and retail. Internet stocks can be considered as long as the company has strong fundamentals.

➤ One of the most important things to remember in a bear market is not to panic. You could end up making poor investment decisions and incur taxes on any capital gains from selling your stock.

➤ Your investment survival plan should include writing things down, keeping a checklist of your current investments, and making sure you have a reason not just for buying a stock but also for keeping or selling it.

Chapter 8

Picking the Best Mutual Funds

In This Chapter

➤ Why now is the time to invest in mutual funds

➤ How easy it is to join in the fun and pave the way for your financial future

➤ Why the Securities and Exchange Commission is worried about the mutual fund industry

Remember your first kiss? Your heart was pounding, your palms were a bit sweaty, and, of course, your knees were knocking. And then? Right when you go in for the smooch of a lifetime, you sneeze everything but your brain right through your nose on your new love.

It's okay; nothing is perfect when you're doing it for the first time. That rings especially true for the world of mutual fund investing.

First, you have more than 10,000 funds from which to choose. (It's no wonder getting started is the hardest part.) We understand that sometimes it's difficult to choose between egg salad and tuna salad at lunch, and that to now wade through thousands of funds seems as challenging as running 26.2 miles with your shoelaces tied together.

Second, information overload abounds. How do you know what to look at when comparing and choosing mutual funds? The wealth of available information—from helpful resources such as the Mutual Fund Education Alliance, the Investment Company Institute, and Morningstar—can more often confuse than clarify. Even discount brokerage firms, such as T. Rowe Price, Muriel Siebert & Co., and Charles Schwab & Co., offer investors basic how-to guides and comparison tables on mutual funds.

This chapter will explain not only how to help you pare down the mutual fund universe to find a fund or two that meets your investment objectives, but also why now is the best time to jump on board. Plus, we'll look forward to the future and see how Y2K can either help or hurt your mutual fund portfolio.

Dip Your Toe In and Then Jump

$5.719 trillion dollars.

That's how much money people have socked away in mutual funds as of January 1999, according to the Investment Company Institute, a Washington-based non-profit institution that surveys mutual fund data. And that's just the combined assets of mutual funds in the United States; it does not include monies invested overseas. Yowza!

Unless you've been sleeping under a rock the past ten years, you've noticed just how much cash small-time investors like us have been infusing into mutual funds. And with a profitable glee, we might add. Look at the following table for proof.

Net Assets of Mutual Funds, Billions of Dollars

	Jan 99	Dec 98	% chg	Jan 98
Stock Funds	3,083.8	2,978.2R	3.5	2,392.6
Hybrid Funds	369.9	364.7R	1.4	322.2
Taxable Bond Funds	544.2	532.0R	2.3	465.6
Municipal Bond Funds	303.2	298.6R	1.5	276.0
Taxable Money Market Funds	1,218.7	1,163.2R	4.8	928.6
Tax-Free Money Market Funds	198.8	188.5R	5.5	169.9
Total	5,718.6	5,525.2R	3.5	4,554.9

Source: Investment Company Institute (www.ici.org).

Bet You Didn't Know

More than 40 million people, or one out of every three households in America, invest in mutual funds, according to the Mutual Fund Education Alliance.

Okay, you're hooked. Now, mutual fund investing basically is a three-step process:

1. Understand what a mutual fund is.
2. Determine why you want to invest in a mutual fund.
3. Pick your fund.

Let's go.

Tell Me More

Mutual funds have been around since the 1920s, yet their popularity has really only increased the past 15 years. The reasons? Mutual funds make it easier and less costly for investors like you to invest for the long haul, and offer diversification and professional money management.

It's really a simple concept. A mutual fund is a company that pools the money of many investors, known as shareholders, to invest in a variety of different securities, such as stocks and bonds. These securities are professionally managed on behalf of the shareholders; each investor holds a percentage of the portfolio and is entitled to any profits when the securities are sold, but is subject to any losses as well.

That's it!

I'm High Maintenance, Darling

If you live in a frazzled world like we do, you know how precious time is. The thought of calculating investment records to the penny, although necessary, is, well, just plain anal. Fortunately, it's one of the luxuries mutual fund investing offers its shareholders.

For the individual investor, mutual funds not only provide the benefit of having someone else manage your investments but also take care of the recordkeeping for your account. And, you can diversify your dollars by having your money invested over many different securities that may not be available or even affordable to you otherwise.

A mutual fund, by its very nature, is diversified. Its assets are invested in many different securities. There are many different types of mutual funds with different objectives and levels of growth potential, furthering your chances to diversify your monies.

Money Meaning

The **Net Asset Value** (NAV) is the value of one share in a fund. When you buy shares, you pay the current NAV per share, plus any sales charges (called a sales load). When you sell shares, the fund pays you the NAV minus any other sales load (where applicable). A fund's NAV goes up and down daily as its holdings change in value.

Other benefits of mutual funds include the following:

➤ Because your mutual fund buys and sells large amounts of securities at a time, its costs are often lower than what you would pay on your own.

➤ Buying shares in a mutual fund instead of individual stocks or bonds directly allows you to spread the investment risk.

➤ Initial investments are typically quite low, often $1,000–$2,500.

There are many sources of information you should consult before you invest your money in mutual funds. Begin with the most important source: the prospectus. (A mutual fund company is legally required to mail you a fund's prospectus.) A prospectus is the fund's selling document and contains information about costs, risks, past performance, and investment goals.

Bet You Didn't Know

You should know that mutual funds are not risk-free investments. Even mutual funds whose portfolios consist only of guaranteed U.S. government bonds contain an element of risk. Before you pick a fund and invest your money, be sure you completely understand the risk. When you invest in a fund, the risk of total loss is lessened due to the diversity in the portfolio. Anyone who tells you there is no risk involved, however, is lying.

Matchmaker, Matchmaker

It's time to assess your goals and risk tolerance and help you match your investment profile with the right mutual fund. If you begin with a clear investment purpose in mind, as well as an understanding of how you might react if your fund loses money, you'll be less likely to purchase a fund that doesn't fit your needs.

Why are you investing your money anyway? Is it to buy a home within the next five years or maybe save for your daughter's college education? Consider the basis for your mutual fund selection based on:

➤ **Your goals.** Are you saving for a house, college education, or vacation home?

➤ **Your time horizon.** Do you plan on being in the market for 0–3 years (short term); 3–5 years (medium term); or 5 years or longer (long term)?

➤ **Your risk tolerance.** Can you afford to lose any of this money at any time?

Answering these questions will help you begin choosing the right fund for you. Your next step is to determine the fund's investment objective. A fund's investment objective tells you the goals the fund seeks to achieve and how it intends to achieve them.

Funds seeking growth, for example, typically hold stocks. Funds seeking income with little or no concern for growth generally hold bonds. Can you guess what balanced funds do? That's right; balanced funds hold stocks and bonds. The objective of a fund is so fundamental that it generally determines the category into which a fund will be assigned. This information is found in the prospectus.

Immediately following the investment objective is a discussion of what investments are allowed, and in what percentages. Stock funds, for example, must conform to legal limits for maximum holdings in any one stock or industry. On the other end of the spectrum are sector funds, which may hold stocks from a single industry only. Risks of the various allowed investments are explained in enormous detail in the prospectus, so don't feel too bad if you get bogged down in the legal verbiage and technical detail.

Finally, Picking a Fund

Let's say you don't know which fund company to research first for a prospectus. No problem; a myriad of resources are in print and online to help you. Some of the most popular and easy-to-understand resources include:

➤ **Morningstar**. Considered the most informative and user-friendly survey of mutual fund performance, its twice-monthly newsletter, *Morningstar Mutual Funds*, compiles information into full-page reports along with commentary on each fund by mutual fund analysts. It costs $365 per year, but much of their information is also available in cyberspace at morningstar.net www.morningstar.net for free. The latest data on the top 25 performing funds by asset class (growth, international, corporate bond, and so on) is available. Online all you have to do is:

1. Determine whether you want to search your funds by star rating (on a scale of 1–5, with 5 being the highest) or investment objective (growth, income, growth and income). If you are looking for an equity-income fund, for example, you'll find a screen that offers the top contenders based on total return in the past year. Also included are fee information and annualized three- and five-year returns.

2. Get more information by clicking on the fund of your choice and pulling up a performance sheet listing the fund's ticker symbol, along with the investment objective and fund performance.

➤ **Lipper Mutual Fund Profiles**. Get an evaluation of past performance of thousands of the largest load and no-load mutual funds from Lipper Analytical Services. Each profile tells how a fund has performed during a certain market cycle. This information is available in print for $132 per year by calling 212-208-8000. You can also log on to the Internet and get Lipper data from its partnership with CNNfn at cnnfn.com/yourmoney/lipper. In addition to updated NAVs on funds, profiles are available.

➤ **Value Line**. Get a full-page analysis on thousands of mutual funds from *The Value Line Mutual Fund Investment Survey*. A three-month trial subscription costs $49. A six-month and annual subscription are also available for $155 and $295, respectively. Call 800-284-7607 for more information.

➤ **CDA/Weisenberger**. Known as the country's first mutual fund tracking service, its three publications, *Mutual Funds Update*, *Mutual Fund Report*, and the *Investment Companies Yearbook* are available. The *Mutual Fund Update* includes expert analysis on industry trends and events, and is the only publication in the industry that reports on fund mergers, name changes, liquidations, and splits. The *Mutual Fund Report* offers a quick reference when you just want the numbers. The *Investment Companies Yearbook*, Wiesenberger's flagship publication, is 1,700 pages chock full of information found in *Update*, and includes full-page profiles on almost 1,000 of the most widely held funds each year. Call 800-232-2285 for subscription information.

Consider using the library as a reference tool in your mutual fund research. Quite often, companies like Value Line and Morningstar distribute their print newsletters to the Business Reference Desks at your local library for you to review for free.

You're Halfway There

Now that you know where to look, what should you be looking *at*? In today's Information Age, when confronted with massive amounts of mutual fund data, it's not uncommon to feel a bit threatened by information overload.

Bet You Didn't Know

If you're considering investing in an index fund that mirrors the S&P 500, check out the average annual returns: In 1995, up 37.6 percent; 1996, up 23.0 percent; 1997, up 33.4 percent; 1998, up 28.6 percent. Compounded annually in an S&P 500 Index fund, $100 invested in January 1995 would have nearly tripled, to $290 by the end of last year.

While a review of the performance history of the fund is important, it's not as conse-quential as you might think. Advertisements, rankings, and ratings tell you how well a fund has performed in the past. Studies show, however, that the future is often differ-ent. This year's number one fund can easily become next year's below average fund.

When comparing performance, check the fund's total return, which is located in the Financial Highlights, near the front of the prospectus. The total return measures increases and decreases in the value of your investment over time, after subtracting costs.

Also watch out for:

➤ Three-, five-, and ten-year compound average annual returns provide a quick summary of a fund's performance. However, one high-return year may mask a couple of subpar or even loss years. Solution? Look at year-by-year returns, noting any extreme performance years and remembering the market conditions that prevailed during those years.

➤ What is the ideal time period to examine? Clearly, one year is too short. In some cases, however, ten-year figures may be misleading if the character of the fund has greatly changed. At a minimum, look at the three-year figure and spend some time with the five-year figure. Funds with less than three full years of data are a blind bet unless the portfolio manager has prior fund management experience that you can evaluate.

➤ Bull market and bear market performance numbers are most useful when exam-ined as a team. That is, when compared to each other they add to an intuitive feel for performance and risk. It is an unusual fund that leads in a bull market and avoids a bear market. Usually, a fund does well in one but not the other.

Is ten years of performance data better than five years, five years better than three years, and so on? You need enough years of data to observe how a fund has performed in different market environments. If you go too far back, however, you may be looking at a fund that differs greatly from the one you are considering now.

Bet You Didn't Know

If you save $1 a day, or $365 a year, and invest it for long–term growth that averages 10 percent, from the day you're born until you are 65, you will wind up with a retirement nest egg of more than $2 million on your 65th birthday. Get a compound rate of return of 11 percent, and you have $3.2 million; 12 percent gives you $5.4 million.

Is Your Manager in Style?

Next on your list is to observe the portfolio manager's style. This is the investment approach used by the fund's portfolio manager. In general, there are two camps: those seeking growth, and those seeking value, although not all managers are either one or the other.

Value managers are often characterized as seeking "undervalued" stocks. Yet, what investor would not seek stocks that are, at least in their opinion, undervalued? The key is knowing how a fund manager approaches the search for undervalued stocks and among what types of stocks he searches.

When a stock is priced low relative to the earnings it generates, the dividends it pays, its cash flow (monies coming in), or even the total value of its assets, you can bet a mutual fund portfolio manager wants to know about it. Portfolio managers who seek this type of information are known as *"value" managers*. What defines low? Well, "low" can be measured relative to the overall market, relative to the industry, or relative to a specific financial variable, such as earnings. Stocks that are neglected or have had setbacks are part of a value manager's repertoire.

Money Meaning

Mutual fund portfolio managers who look for companies whose stocks are priced low relative to the earnings it generates, the dividends it pays and its cash flow are known as **value managers**.

The growth-oriented style of management is opposite from the value-oriented style. Usually, growth stocks have not only demonstrated rapid earnings growth but also are anticipated to have much better than average long-term growth. Sales growth figures are also equally likely to be high. And in both cases, earnings and sales growth rates are accelerating.

Because growth stocks are companies that need money to expand their businesses, they often pay lower dividends than value stocks. Furthermore, growth stocks trade at prices that are high relative to earnings, dividends, and cash flow. And finally, growth stocks are volatile. Why? Because growth-style managers have shorter time horizons— keep that in mind when selecting your fund!—and may trade more frequently. The result is that they "turn over" their portfolios more rapidly.

Is one management style better than the other? Not at all. It just depends on whether the portfolio manager's style and the fund's objective meet with *your* objectives.

You should add one more item to your checklist: fees. The following section discusses what to look for when comparing the fees that different companies charge.

Comparing Costs

Costs are important because they lower your returns if they are too high. A fund with a sales load and high expenses has to perform better than a low-cost fund just to stay even with the low-cost fund.

A November 1998 study by the Investment Company Institute found that the overall *total* cost of owning mutual funds dropped by 33 percent from 1980 to 1997. In fact, the average cost of investing in equity funds decreased from 2.25 percent in 1980 to 1.49 percent in 1997. Investors must be sensitive to costs, because more than 75 percent of mutual fund shareholders invest in funds that charge annual fees below the industry's simple average.

So take note, fund shareholder, and compare fund costs in the fee tables near the front of the prospectus. The fee table breaks costs into two main categories:

➤ Sales load and transaction fees (paid when you buy, sell, or exchange your shares)

➤ Ongoing expenses (paid while you remain invested in the fund)

Bet You Didn't Know

The actual and maximum front–end sales load (fees charged when you first invest in a fund) has dropped more than three times its original fee, according to Investment Company Institute. In 1960, the average actual load on a mutual fund was 7 percent. In 1997, it was 2.3 percent.

No-load funds do not charge sales loads. When you buy no-load funds, you make your own choices, without the assistance of a financial professional. However, even no-load funds have ongoing expenses (not the same as sales loads), such as management fees.

Typically, the sales load a mutual fund charges pays the salesperson's commissions and marketing costs. Sales loads buy a broker's services and advice; they do not ensure superior performance. In fact, funds that charge sales loads have not performed better on average than those that do not charge sales loads.

Different Types of Loads

The following are two types of load funds:

➤ **Front-end load.** A front-end load is a sales charge you pay when you buy shares. This type of load, which by law cannot be higher than 8.5 percent of your investment, reduces the initial amount of your investment in the fund.

For example, if you invest $1,000 in a mutual fund with a five percent front-end load, $50 goes to pay the sales charge, and $950 is invested in the fund.

➤ **Back-end load**. A back-end load (also called a *deferred load*) is a sales charge you pay when you sell your shares. It usually starts at five or six percent the first year and gets smaller each year thereafter until it reaches zero—typically in the sixth or seventh year of your investment.

For example, if you invest $1,000 in a mutual fund with a six percent back-end load, the load decreases to zero in the seventh year. Let's assume that the value of your investment remains constant at $1,000 for seven years. If you sell your shares during the first year, you receive only $940, because $60 goes to pay the sales charge. If you sell back your shares in the seventh year, however, you get back all your initial investment.

Expenses to Be Aware Of

Even if you choose a mutual fund that does not carry a sales load, you will incur other expenses while invested in the fund. The fee table in the prospectus shows the expenses—such as the management fee—as a percentage of the fund's assets generally for the most recent fiscal year.

Let's see how expenses can eat away at your portfolio. Let's say you invest $1,000 in a fund and (hypothetically) earn a flat rate of return of five percent before expenses. If the fund has expenses of 1.5 percent, after 20 years you would end up with roughly $1,990. If the fund has expenses of 0.5 percent, you would end up with more than $2,410—a 22 percent difference!

Another type of charge is a Rule 12b-1 fee, which is most often used to pay commissions to brokers and other salespeople, and occasionally to pay for advertising and other costs of promoting the fund. It is usually between 0.25 percent and 1.00 percent of assets annually.

Bet You Didn't Know

Funds with back-end loads usually have higher Rule 12b-1 fees. If you are considering whether to pay a front-end or back-end load, think about how long you plan to stay in the fund. If you plan to stay in for six years or longer, a front-end load may cost less than a back-end load. Even if your back-end load has fallen to zero, over time you could pay more in Rule 12b-1 fees than if you paid a front-end load.

Keep in mind that high expenses do not mean superior fund performance. There may be circumstances, however, in which you decide it is appropriate for you to pay higher expenses, such as when the fund provides special services such as toll-free numbers (although most already do) and check-writing and automatic investment programs.

Also remember the following:

➤ Check the fee table to see if any part of a fund's fees or expenses has been waived. If so, the fees and expenses may increase suddenly when the waiver ends. (The part of the prospectus after the fee table should tell you by how much.)

➤ Many funds allow you to exchange your shares for shares of another fund managed by the same portfolio manager or at least within the fund company (often referred to as the *fund family*). The first part of the fee table should tell you whether there is any exchange fee.

➤ Beware of a salesperson who says, "This is just like a no-load fund." Even if there is no front-end load, check the fee table in the prospectus to see which other loads or fees you may have to pay.

Jump Start It with a Few Bucks

Another item on your fund checklist is to ask whether the mutual fund company offers an automatic investment plan. An automatic investment plan enables you to, well, automatically invest a fixed amount per month. Check your fund's prospectus or the shareholder services department for more details. Some of the following might apply if a fund offers an automatic investment plan:

➤ You have the option of investing in the fund for as little as $50 a month.

➤ Many fund families waive the $1,000, $500, or even $250 minimums, thereby allowing you to begin investing with a small amount of money.

➤ All monies are electronically transferred, typically between your bank checking account and your mutual fund account.

Click Here

FundAlarm (**www.fundalarm.com**) is a Web site that keeps track of all portfolio management changes. It is only updated once a month but does list every fund in which a portfolio manager leaves or is fired. And it's free!

It's easy and a highly advisable investment strategy. By completing the application in the section marked "automatic investments," you are giving the mutual fund company the authority to electronically transfer a fixed amount of money each month—without having to lift a finger or remember to place a phone call. With your completed application, you will need to provide your bank's ABA number, which is the nine- or ten-digit routing number, along with a voided check.

The biggest benefit to participating in a fund's automatic investment plan is that you take the guesswork out of when to buy low and sell high. When you invest automatically on a monthly basis, you get to take advantage of any dips in the NAV of the fund. Therefore, if the price drops from $15 a share to $12, your monthly contribution, assuming $100, will buy more shares. When the share price rises after you purchase these shares, the value of your mutual fund portfolio rises as well. How can you figure this out? Simply multiply the number of shares you own by the current share price to calculate the value of your portfolio.

Bet You Didn't Know

Call it the Santa Claus rally. Since 1950, December ranks as the best month for performance of the S&P 500 with an average monthly gain of 1.7 percent. Guess ol' Kris Kringle won't be receiving any coal in the new millennium.

A Feel Good Mutual Fund Strategy

If you are looking to further develop your "environmental consciousness", you have an option: socially-responsible investing or ethical investing, as it's also known. These are mutual funds that do not invest in companies that, for example, produce environmentally hazardous materials, manufacture cigarettes or work in the nuclear-testing industry.

You may have read articles knocking ethically screened mutual funds for underperforming the market. Some funds deserve the criticism for weak performance and for not being well diversified. Managers may assume their customers will excuse weak performance as long as they are "green". Some ethical funds are small and new, which tends to make expenses eat into the returns. Many are "load funds" with sales fees which will hurt your returns.

From 1991 to 1994, one of the top performing funds in any category was the Parnassus Fund. Then, beginning in 1995 (a great year for the market as a whole), Parnassus stumbled badly. It eked out a gain of only 0.6 percent while the S&P 500 was up 38 percent.

Another socially responsible fund is the Domini Social Equity Fund, which boasts the best record among all ethical funds. The Domini fund is actually an index—it tracks the Domini Social Index, an ethically screened list of about 400 companies. The Domini fund tends to have more small and mid-size stocks than the large-company S&P 500.

How to find out more about socially responsible funds? Check out Morningstar's Web site for more information at www.morningstar.net.

Now What's All This Y2K Business?

The Securities and Exchange Commission (SEC) is in a tizzy. As of November 1998, whereas most large mutual fund companies and banks in the United States have been adequately preparing for Y2K (some since 1995), fund companies that invest in developing countries haven't adequately reprogrammed their computers. This glitch could make it difficult for funds to determine their net asset value, or share price, according to the SEC.

Bet You Didn't Know

Even the Federal Reserve acknowledges that the Y2K problem will affect the U.S. financial system, if only temporarily. In fact, the Fed announced it will print $50 billion *extra dollars* by the end of 1999, in case people rush to move their investments into cold, hard cash.

The Y2K computer glitch is when computer systems worldwide will mistake January 1, 2000 as January 1, 1900, and fail. Although many U.S. corporations are spending billions of dollars treating this problem, not all worldwide, publicly traded companies found in emerging market fund portfolios are up-to-date. Couple that with the wild ride emerging market investors had in early 1998, and the phrase "Tequila Effect" makes the 1998 "Asian Flu" seem like a sniffle.

If you're invested in an emerging markets fund and are concerned about the Y2K problem, contact the shareholder services department at the fund company and ask them how they are dealing with the global Y2K problem and what is the portfolio manager's position on this important issue. The answers you receive may help you decide whether or not to liquidate your accounts and bring your money back to the States and into funds that are Y2K compliant.

The amount of money that fund companies are spending on Y2K ranges from $14.4 million by PIMCo Funds to $35 million by Putnam Investments. In fact, many fund companies are beefing up their Y2K workforce. For example, Fidelity announced it has dedicated 500 workers to its Y2K project.

A fall 1998 Morningstar unscientific survey queried 15 mutual fund companies about the status of dealing with the Y2K problem. The majority of the firms tally December 1998 as the completion dates; this way, they have 1999 to work out any technical kinks. These firms include AIM Group, American Century, Charles Schwab Corp., Dreyfus, Fidelity, Franklin Templeton, Janus, MFS Investment Management, Prudential, Putnam, and Robertson Stephens Funds. The fund companies in Morningstar's survey that are already Y2K-compliant are American Express Financial and Nicholas-Applegate. Oppenheimer and PIMCo Funds are slated for compliance in spring '99.

It is up to you to contact your fund company to monitor the ongoing Y2K progress. Ask for its full Y2K plan disclosure.

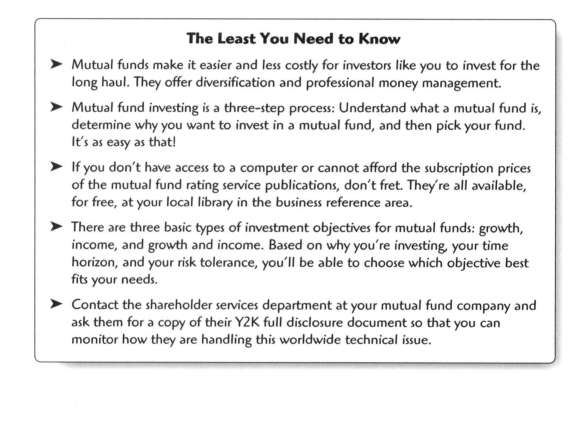

The Least You Need to Know

➤ Mutual funds make it easier and less costly for investors like you to invest for the long haul. They offer diversification and professional money management.

➤ Mutual fund investing is a three-step process: Understand what a mutual fund is, determine why you want to invest in a mutual fund, and then pick your fund. It's as easy as that!

➤ If you don't have access to a computer or cannot afford the subscription prices of the mutual fund rating service publications, don't fret. They're all available, for free, at your local library in the business reference area.

➤ There are three basic types of investment objectives for mutual funds: growth, income, and growth and income. Based on why you're investing, your time horizon, and your risk tolerance, you'll be able to choose which objective best fits your needs.

➤ Contact the shareholder services department at your mutual fund company and ask them for a copy of their Y2K full disclosure document so that you can monitor how they are handling this worldwide technical issue.

Chapter 9

Our Economy in the New Millennium

In This Chapter

➤ Why the United States prospers economically but isn't the leader

➤ Why understanding economics will help you succeed in the new millennium

➤ How the debacle of getting your financial information could affect our economy

We are a lucky nation, and you're the one who's holding the dice.

The United States remains one of the world's most industrialized countries. We are the largest exporter and importer of goods, have the largest economy, and enjoy the highest standard of living. Of all the countries in the world, we are the sixth freest economy.

Great trivia, but what does this have to do with you? A lot.

You are the largest component to the future of economics, because you are a *consumer*. The amount of money you spend on purchases—from large appliances such as washers and dryers to clothing and even cars and homes—is tabulated monthly in U.S. government reports. When you lose your job, you and your previous watercooler buddies aren't the only ones who know about what really happened; so does Uncle Sam.

Your data—along with everyone else's—is then released to economists, Wall Street movers and shakers, and the business media. It is from those reports that small investors make decisions on how to allocate their investment portfolios, or moms across America choose how much to spend on groceries this week. Without even knowing it, so are *you*, too, making the same decisions.

The decisions you make on a day-to-day basis influence the economy. For example, when you purchase a Toyota rather than a Chevrolet, your money is being spent on an imported car. If not enough American cars are sold in the United States or overseas, our trade deficit (the difference between the amount of money we spend buying foreign goods versus the amount of revenue we collect from other countries buying our goods) increases. Not a good thing.

Knowing how economics plays a role in making money in the new millennium will keep you well informed and prepared for your future. By understanding how interest rates work and which indicators to pay attention to, and how the Year 2000 bug may affect the ability to get economic and financial information, you will be able to take a proactive rather than a reactive role with your finances.

U.ncle S.am Is A.uspicious

Ever wonder why the United States has become such a prosperous nation? Observers of the world economy, from academics to investors to ordinary workers, have long questioned why some countries prosper while others do not.

Click Here

Follow key economic rates, such as the prime rate, Fed funds rate, discount rate and even Treasury yields at Snap.com's Finance channel. Log onto **www.snap.com**, click on Snap Finance and then select "Today's Economy."

The Heritage Foundation, an economic think-tank in Washington, D.C., has identified trends that point to only one thing: Countries that have the most economic freedom also tend to have higher rates of long-term economic growth and are more prosperous than those that have less economic freedom.

Credit the Reagan Administration's two office terms for yielding progress toward our high economic rank. Its move toward deregulating specific industries—such as railroads, trucking, airlines, and banking—was the catalyst. But deregulation—a decision that results in a freer economy with no "caps" on profitability or productivity—didn't stop there. In 1996, President Clinton signed a major telecommunications deregulation law and enacted new tax reforms. The Clinton Administration also worked out a balanced budget for the first time in more than 30 years.

As successful as America has been, however, we still aren't the head economic honcho. As of 1998, Bahrain, New Zealand, and Switzerland all surpass the United States as freer economies. What do they have that we don't? Low inflation rates for one, averaging two-and-a-half percent annually, with Switzerland boasting only a half percent annual inflation rate. Or maybe it's all those bank accounts and Swiss cheese!

Understand that following how prosperous or poor other countries are is an integral part of the overall health of our economy; foreign countries are players in our economics equation. We depend on foreign countries, not just those with freer economies than ours, to buy the products that we make. And, these countries invest in the United States by purchasing U.S. Treasury bills, notes, and bonds—basically, our government's debts and IOUs. The amount of Treasury securities foreign countries purchase makes up less than 20 percent of the total amount of existing Treasuries. The interest rates offered on these debt instruments have to be attractive enough to entice foreign buyers. If they aren't, and foreigners don't buy them, the rates have to rise in order to attract other buyers.

Speaking of Interest Rates...

Our country's central bank, the Federal Reserve, watches all the activities of all banks nationwide. It also minimally regulates the banking system, in that Congress, although not part of the Fed but an icon that works congruently with the Fed, passed legislation in 1996 to permit domestically owned banks to open branches across state lines—something foreign banks already were allowed to do.

The biggest influence the Fed has is controlling the supply of money and the direction of interest rates. When the Fed decides too much money is in the system, it dilutes the supply by selling government bonds that it owns. The Fed has to be cautious, however, because when there's not enough money in the system, a recession can result. Just the opposite occurs when there is too much money in the system. This scenario can lead to inflation because it tends to raise the prices of goods and services; there are more dollars chasing the same number of products.

What about the interest rates you hear about every day? Well, the big cheese in Washington who raises or lowers the rate at which smaller banks borrow from the Fed (the bellwether for all interest rate activity) is Federal Reserve chairman Alan Greenspan. The rate that he and his 12 board of governors discuss—among other important economic issues—is known as the *discount rate*.

To understand why it's important for you to know this information, let's use this example. If you owned a bank and needed to borrow money to add to your reserves, you would go to the Federal Reserve's discount window—similar to a bank teller window. When you borrow this money, you pay interest, which is based on the discount rate. As of the first week of March 1999, the discount rate was 4.50 percent. Now, as a consumer, the key is knowing that when the Fed changes the discount rate, other rates usually follow—which affects *you!*

Money Meaning

The **discount rate** is the rate at which the Federal Reserve charges banks for borrowing money from the Fed.

Here's another example. The law requires a bank to keep 20 percent of customers' deposits in its vaults overnight. When a bank falls short, it borrows money from another bank, typically overnight or for a few days. Ah, but as you know, there is no such thing as a free lunch; there is an interest rate tied to this loan. It's called the *federal funds rate*, or *fed funds rate*, for short. While the Fed doesn't set the rate, it can affect it by either adding or subtracting the reserves to or from the banking system (our nation's money supply).

Bet You Didn't Know

Due to the uncertainty whether consumers will want to hold onto their cash come the year 2000, the Federal Reserve has printed an extra $50 billion to have on hand. This money, however, is *not* being circulated throughout the economy; it's just on the sidelines in case of the emergency of bank runs.

Another key rate to watch is the prime rate. This is the interest rate that banks charge to their largest customers—such as huge corporations—when the customers want to borrow money. If you, however, want to borrow money, either to get a mortgage on a new home or a car loan on a used car, the loan is based on the prime rate, with a few extra percentage points added in.

Bet You Didn't Know

The prime rate is *not* a leading economic indicator. The prime rate normally follows movements in the general economy and is a lagging indicator. Now do you see why it's important to know what the discount and fed funds rates are and how they affect our economy?

Although you never get a loan exactly at the prime rate, other loan rates are based on the prime rate. That's what it means when a loan is tied to the prime. When the prime rate is 7.75 percent, corporations get loans at 7.75 percent; consumers get loans at 7.75 percent, plus a few percentage points.

Click Here

Go to **www.bankrate.com/mortgages** to watch for weekly mortgage analysis reports that follow the latest Treasury rate fluctuations and how they affect mortgage rates.

Y2K Bump to an Economic Slump?

As you know by now, the Y2K problem has been such a high-profile issue it's been debated more often than whether to keep *The Jerry Springer Show* on the airwaves. This computer glitch, which began 30 years ago, has been the focus of many media reports once the clock turned January 1, 1999 as many broadcasters reported daily "Countdown to Millennium" stories, thereby increasing the awareness of this computer problem.

How did all this begin anyway? Well, chalk it up to trying to save a few bucks on computer memory. Back then, computer memory was very expensive. Companies spent at least $1 million for a mainframe with little memory. No big deal until you realize that the limited memory was shared by the entire company, not just for one personal computer. As a result, computer programmers created a solution by shaving off a few numeric digits so that dates would be represented by two-digits—nothing more. They were able to save valuable storage space. What they didn't realize was that they were also creating technological issues that affect our economy and financial markets.

The Y2K problem has had financial ramifications for sure, with companies such as Disney spending more than $200 million to get their computers fixed. (Ah, but think of all the jobs that opened up.) With respect to our national and global economy, one thing has been certain: The securities industry has been spending millions of dollars to combat the Y2K problem. As a result, the industry is one of the most Y2K compliant.

In fact, the Bank Administration Institute reports that the financial services industry is the number one industry in terms of being Y2K prepared. In addition, early 1998 tests involving simulated trading among a select number of brokerage firms and exchanges found several small glitches, but left the industry optimistic that the physical trading system would remain intact. Still, that didn't stop SEC Chairman Arthur Leavitt from mailing 9,000 letters to financial institutions telling them to get their Y2K act together.

Why talk about Y2K in a chapter on economics? Because many elements affect the United State's economy: consumer demand, industrial supplies of goods, and foreign demand, for example. And yes, even the Y2K issue.

The $64 million question is, over the long haul, *how* will this Y2K bug affect the industries that permeate our pocketbooks, namely, the banking and financial services sectors? Are we going into a full-blown recession with lower interest rates and higher unemployment? Well, the inability of most computer programs to tell the difference between the year 1900 and 2000 does pose risks to all things financial, especially financial institutions, be they banks or brokerage firms. While it is important to be concerned and prepared for any Y2K problems, it is not necessarily the case that Armageddon is approaching at the turn of the century.

Click Here

Log onto **www.dismal.com** to read *The Dismal Scientist,* one of the most entertaining Web sites about every day economics. Easy-to-understand information, analyses and statistics that make learning about economics actually fun!

Which Way, Chicken Little?

Many people believe the sky will fall during the early stages of the 21st century, while others think technological problems will occur but not of the magnitude that the economic free world will go down the toilet. Who's right? No one. You can count on the local and national media, however, to promote the Y2K problem and its affect on global financial markets and economies throughout the entire year of 1999, and beyond.

So, can millions of computers and mainframes misinterpreting the date January 1, 2000 as January 1, 1900, causing miscalculations or system failures, lead us into a recession? You must understand what a recession is before you can say one will occur. By definition, a recession is a reduced period of economic activity. However, as one of us likes to say, a recession is when your neighbor is unemployed and a depression is when *you're* unemployed.

A recession is also a period of time in our economy that makes up the business cycle. (Egads! Here comes Economics 101.) A business cycle is a roller-coaster motion that shows whether the economy is moving up or down. Economic indicators, such as the prime rate, consumer confidence survey and durable goods orders, are the variables used to find out where we are in the business cycle. In the business cycle, if the indicators report that businesses are slowing down, production and sales of many goods and services drop, and the market may be heading for a drop and, possibly, a recession.

Dr. Edward Yardeni, national Y2K gadfly, purports that there is a 70 percent chance of a worldwide recession, which could last for one year, beginning in January 2000, equating the level of severity to the 1973–1974 global recession due to the OPEC oil crisis. Dr. Yardeni likens Y2K "information shortage" to the oil shortage because information will be disrupted, thus impairing economic activity.

Will economic information be more difficult to obtain because of computer problems? Not necessarily, but if so, it won't be for long. Most likely consumers will be paying for the millions of dollars spent on fixing and upgrading computer systems to become Y2K compliant, either through companies raising prices on their goods and services or the government raising taxes.

While the financial services industry ranked first in year 2000 preparedness, according to a study by the Gartner Group, a Connecticut-based technology consulting firm, it doesn't necessarily have to be a direct Y2K event to spark an economic downturn. It can also be because of lack of investor confidence—confidence that stocks will be delivered on time, trades will or won't be executed, and that stock portfolios will continue to grow as they did in the last few years of the 90s.

So, will Y2K trigger a recession—directly or indirectly? No one knows for sure. In the year 2000 and beyond it's important to be aware of all the facts and be prepared for any eventuality.

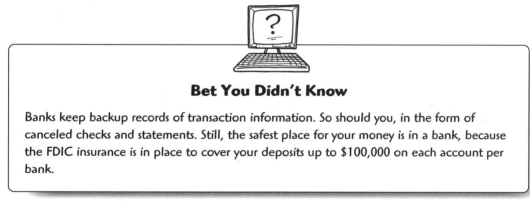

Bet You Didn't Know

Banks keep backup records of transaction information. So should you, in the form of canceled checks and statements. Still, the safest place for your money is in a bank, because the FDIC insurance is in place to cover your deposits up to $100,000 on each account per bank.

Because, as a consumer, you play a major role in our economy, you can help make an economic difference. How? Be like the Boy Scouts.

Getting a Y2K "I'm Prepared" Badge

The next time you visit your bank, thrift or credit union, speak to a bank officer (as long as they don't charge a fee) and ask the following questions:

➤ What are you doing to ensure your company is year 2000 compliant?

➤ How can you satisfy me that your firm will be ready on time, and how could I be affected if you are not ready?

109

➤ Are you participating in industry-wide tests?

➤ If you are ready, what are you doing to make sure that clearinghouses, exchanges, and other market participants are also ready?

➤ How can I be assured that my interest and dividend payments will not be affected by the Year 2000 problem?

Always take safety measures for any potential problems, be they Y2K or something else. Contact your stockbroker, 401(k) plan administrator, and your financial planner. Ask them to send you notarized copies of your current portfolio holdings. The idea is to create a paper trail.

Scouts honor.

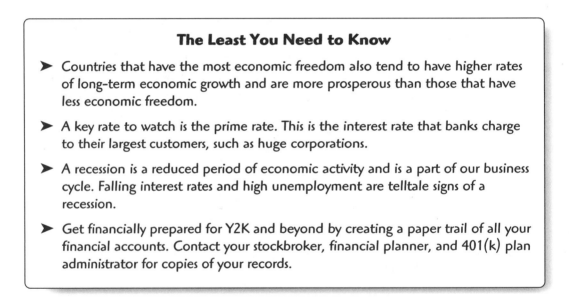

The Least You Need to Know

➤ Countries that have the most economic freedom also tend to have higher rates of long-term economic growth and are more prosperous than those that have less economic freedom.

➤ A key rate to watch is the prime rate. This is the interest rate that banks charge to their largest customers, such as huge corporations.

➤ A recession is a reduced period of economic activity and is a part of our business cycle. Falling interest rates and high unemployment are telltale signs of a recession.

➤ Get financially prepared for Y2K and beyond by creating a paper trail of all your financial accounts. Contact your stockbroker, financial planner, and 401(k) plan administrator for copies of your records.

Chapter 10

Selecting the Right Investment Advisor

> ## In This Chapter
>
> ➤ Find out if you really need an investment pro
>
> ➤ Know what questions you should and shouldn't ask
>
> ➤ Tips for selecting the right advisor

Boy, has the stock market been good to us these past several years. In 1998, the S&P 500 boasted more than a 28 percent annual return. Couple that with a skyrocketing Dow Jones Industrial Average in early 1999 and you've got a formula for investment profits.

When most people think of investing in the market, such as buying stocks, they think they need a stockbroker. Most trades are still conducted using a stockbroker. The stockbroker and even other investment advisors of today bear little resemblance to those of a few decades ago.

How do you know if your stockbroker, financial planner or overall investment advisor is doing all he or she can be doing—or at least should be doing—with your investment portfolio? You don't, really. With the dawn of online trading and brokerage firms on the Internet, the process has been made incredibly easy for you to get the same research and execute the same trades as a stockbroker. These days, there's no middleman anymore. You can easily sign up for an online trading account and click, you're off.

Within the next two years, stock markets are expected to shift a significant chunk of activity away from traditional physical locations and onto the Web. Although a good deal of that business will flow into established electronic brokerages, the profound shift in where, when, and how stocks are bought and sold is creating enormous opportunities for you. Online brokerage firms often change the dynamics of the investing game so that investors themselves make the markets the old-fashioned way—again, with no middleman. Sure, brokers are still involved in these transactions, but only to do the paperwork to officially transfer the stock from seller to buyer.

All the advancement in technology, however, does not mean you should throw caution to the wind and assume you are the panacea to your own good fortune. Many consumers still need assistance with not only understanding which investments to buy, but also *when*. This chapter will help you determine how to select the right investment advisor to help you make the most of your portfolio.

Who's Got the Goods?

An easy way to get started with your financial planner search is by asking family members or friends for references. Another source for referrals could be professionals with whom you work, such as an attorney or accountant. A third option is to call one of the many financial trade organizations.

The Institute of Certified Financial Planners and the International Association for Financial Planning in Atlanta, Georgia, are two groups that offer referral services. They will send you a list of consultants in your area and background information on each advisor.

Click Here

Looking for a financial planner in your area? Contact the International Association for Financial Planning (IAFP) at its Web site at **www.iafp.org** and click on "Consumers Click Here" to find your advisor.

If you are looking for investment analysis, there are several groups can turn to that rate advisor performance. The Directory of Registered Investment Advisors is the mother of all advisor sources, with more than 6,000 registered firms listed. It doesn't provide performance data, however.

The truth is that anybody can call themselves an investment advisor. Telling the experts apart from the phonies is just a matter of studying their credentials. Each of the titles attached to their names requires varying levels of experience and coursework—something to consider when choosing a professional. Some of the most common designations are as follows:

➤ **Certified Financial Planner (CFP).** A professional with a CFP designation should have a broad knowledge of all aspects of financial planning. Subject areas studied include securities, estate planning, insurance, and taxes. The CFP is certified by the International Board of Standards and Practices of the Institute of Certified Financial Planners, located in Denver, Colorado.

➤ **Registered Investment Advisors.** All financial planners and investment advisors are required to be registered with the Securities and Exchange Commission; however, this is a paper-registration process and no accredited schooling is involved. Therefore, although the SEC recognizes Registered Investment Advisors, it does not use the acronym *RIA* (like you would see with a CFP) to avoid the implication that mere registration equals financial expertise.

➤ **Chartered Financial Analyst (CFA).** CFAs earn their designation by undergoing a three-year independent study course run by the Association of Investment Management and Research in Charlottesville, Virginia. CFAs are most likely to work for mutual fund companies, institutional asset management organizations, or pension funds.

➤ **Chartered Investment Counselor (CIC).** For those advisors who have already earned their CFA, the CIC program focuses on portfolio management and is offered through the Investment Counsel Association of America, located in New York City.

➤ **Certified Public Accountant (CPA).** The CPA designation is given to those who have completed a 150-hour program and passed the CPA exam. Although a CPA does not manage money per se, he or she is involved in the tax implications of your investment decisions. The American Institute of Certified Public Accountants is the national association for CPAs.

As you begin to assemble your financial advisory team, consider what a stockbroker can do for you—or whether you need one at all.

And Now a Word About Stockbrokers

You want the real scoop? Here goes: Recognize that your stockbroker is a *salesperson*. Most investors pay for the services of their broker based on a commission on each transaction. Since different products can carry very different commissions, that type of arrangement can influence the recommendations your broker makes. A good stockbroker proposes investments that are tailored to your goals and financial position. However, a broker's earnings usually derive from how often and how much you buy and sell, not from your investment's success.

In other words, brokers make money even if you don't. Although your stockbroker has a long-term incentive for you to succeed and to gain the referrals of your family and friends, he or she also has a short-term incentive to earn commissions, just like any other salesperson. Don't confuse a sales pitch with impartial advice. Consider any recommendation to buy or sell stock just as you would any other commercial solicitation—ask questions.

Here's what you can do if you do decide to choose a full-service broker. Keep the following questions by the telephone and every time your broker recommends an investment, ask him or her:

➤ Why are you suggesting this?

➤ Does it meet the goals I outlined?

➤ What are the commissions and other transaction costs involved?

It's also important to make it your business to learn about commissions; they come in every shape and size.

Depending on the investment product, there are up-front commissions, commissions spread out for as long as you hold the product, or both. Commissions paid at the time you invest are called *up-front fees*, or *loads*. Commissions paid when you take your money out of the investment are called *back-end fees*, or *deferred loads*.

For some investments, such as municipal bonds, brokers don't levy sales commissions. Instead, the broker is paid from the *mark up*—the difference between the price the brokerage firm pays to buy the investment and the price it charges you. You can depend on one thing, however: Your broker earns a commission or a fee on almost every transaction you make. The critical point here is that the commission (sales fee) reduces the value of your initial investment.

Bet You Didn't Know

The Securities and Exchange Commission changed everything when it eliminated fixed commissions on May 1, 1975, known as "May Day." That is when the introduction of discount brokers came to be and investors had the option of using a full-service broker and paying top dollar in commissions for advice or a discount broker and saving a bundle on commissions.

For example, if you put $10,000 into a mutual fund and your broker earns a 5 percent commission on the transaction, $500 would go to the commission and, as a result, only $9,500 would be invested. Another factor to keep in mind is that because the size of commissions and fees varies greatly from product to product, brokers may have an incentive to recommend products that pay them a higher percentage over products that may be more suitable for you but pay them lower commissions.

This is of particular concern because, in general, the lowest-risk investments earn the broker the least in commissions. The more risky or complex the investment product, the higher the commission generally earned by your broker. At the same time, some brokerage firms pay their brokers more to sell *house brand* investment products—products created or managed by the firm (sometimes called *proprietary* products). These incentives may encourage your broker to sell you a particular investment product. These may or may not pay as well as non-proprietary alternatives that pay the broker a more modest commission.

The Fine Print

Watch for notices in the mail that confirm your buy or sell order. They are called *confirmation slips*, and they indicate the product, the price, and the broker's commission. Sometimes the commission reads *zero*.

Don't be misled; this does not necessarily mean the broker has not been paid to sell the product. In some transactions, the compensation to the broker isn't disclosed. This could happen, for example, when you buy new issue stocks and bonds and the commission is paid by the issuing company.

Also, stocks and bonds sold out of the brokerage firm's inventory may not include a commission, per se. Remember, however, a broker makes money on each of your transactions. In fact, your broker may earn more on these *zero-commission* sales than by selling other investment products. Be sure to ask what the broker is getting paid, and make a note of it on your confirmation slip. Keep track of your confirmation slips. They will come in handy when tallying what you paid in fees and commissions each year.

Each month, your brokerage firm sends you an account statement. Don't throw it away or toss it in a drawer! Force yourself to sit down and review it. Get smart about what they say and how to use them to your advantage. For starters, set up a system to track two important items: how you're doing and what it's costing. (You may want to do this in combination with your confirmation notices.) Keep a running total of the commissions and fees you have paid for your investments. If any unauthorized transactions appear on your account statement, or if your broker appears to be engaged in excessive trading, contact your broker's supervisor immediately to have the situation corrected. Don't wait to see how the investments perform; waiting may be viewed as giving tacit approval to the unauthorized trades.

Don't Tell Miss Manners

So, do you know what you are paying for your investments?

It may seem impolite to ask, but you have the right to full disclosure of all costs of any investment, including all commissions, markups, and fees. Ask your broker about commission rates, annual fees, transaction costs, and any other expenses. No fee should show up on any confirmation slip or account statement that you haven't been told about in advance. Put it this way: Buying an investment without considering the sales commissions is like ordering off a menu without prices. You may know what you're getting, but you don't know what it will cost.

You should also be aware of any sales contests, up-front bonuses, and other practices that may influence the conduct of your broker.

Your broker may encourage you to buy certain stocks, bonds, mutual funds, or other investments that bring extra income to him or her through higher commissions, bonuses, or points toward a vacation or other contest prize. When a product is sold as part of a contest or because it earns the broker and the firm additional compensation, you run the risk that the broker's interest in the contest or extra compensation may be placed ahead of your interest. Understanding that makes you a smarter investor. Don't be afraid to ask your broker if he or she is participating in any sales contests or receiving any other form of special compensation for the products he or she recommends.

Can You Get Me a Deal?

Some brokerage firms offer accounts with no commissions. Instead, the investor pays an annual fee based on a fixed percentage of assets, in return for which he or she gets a certain number of trades each year. Presumably, such a fee arrangement removes the broker's incentive to sell high-commission products or to increase the frequency of trades in order to earn commissions.

Under a fee arrangement, brokers are paid regardless of what you buy, and their income rises only if your assets do. Ask your broker whether it makes sense for you to pay by the transaction or whether a flat-fee arrangement may be more appropriate. If you do choose a commission arrangement, try negotiating for lower percentages. After all, the lower the fee you negotiate, the less you have to earn before you start making a profit on your investments.

Money Meaning

The **National Association of Securities Dealers** is the regulatory agency that operates under the guise of the Securities and Exchange Commission to uphold the ethical standards in securities trading.

When all is said and done, check out your broker's training and disciplinary record.

The National Association of Securities Dealers (NASD) and your state securities agency can provide extensive background and disciplinary information on any broker you are considering. Take the time to check it out; it could help you spot a broker with a history of abusing client trust before you hire him or her. If you are working with a broker with whom you have a long-standing relationship, this may not be necessary. It is essential, however, before placing your confidence in a stranger. Too many people have lost their life savings because they were too polite, or too trusting, to check out their broker's credentials.

So, How Do They Get Paid?

No part of the client/financial planner relationship is more important than understanding how you will be paying for their services. Knowing how each compensation plan works will help you decide which of them fits your goals and needs. There are five primary ways in which advisers get compensated, as follows:

➤ **Commission-only.** This type of billing plan receives a lot of criticism for the obvious reason that it creates a major conflict of interest for those who sell investments or other products. The more things you buy, the more money they make. On the other hand, commission-only planners argue that you can walk away without paying if you do not accept their advice.

➤ **Fee-only.** Fee-only planners are compensated solely through fees paid by their clients. Supposedly, this method eliminates the conflict of interest associated with commission-based services.

➤ **Fee-and-commission.** This is the most popular compensation plan. These planners claim they are more objective than commission-only salespeople. Critics say that having to pay once for counsel and then again to act on it is just too costly. This type of service makes it more affordable for clients with smaller accounts.

➤ **Fee-based.** This term is similar to fee-and-commission financial planning. The only distinction is that planners let you choose whether you want to work on a fee-only or on a commission-only basis if you want to implement the plan through them.

➤ **Fee-offset.** Under this unusual arrangement, planners charge a fee for developing an investment strategy, and then reduce that fee if the client buys products from the planner. Commissions or asset management fees are deducted from the initial fee. While this option doesn't totally eliminate the conflict of interest dilemma, it does prevent consumers from having to pay for both advice and products.

No matter which planner you choose, make sure you understand his or her compensation method to see where and how your dollars for their advice is being spent.

Financial Planners Versus Investment Advisors

A *financial planner* is a person who helps you organize your specific financial objectives and gives you a customized plan that addresses your individual concerns. *Investment advisors* (also known as *money managers*), on the other hand, manage assets and suggest portfolio changes. They are not as all encompassing as financial planners and typically do not deal in areas such as taxes or insurance.

Planners and advisors come with all kinds of titles and backgrounds, but one thing's for sure: They want to make your money grow. To determine whether you should consult one of these financial gurus, the first thing you need to do is to define your financial goals. Are you looking to save for retirement? A child's college education? Defining your goals will help you develop a financial *strategy*. To make sound investment decisions, you also need to review all information concerning your income, mortgage, tax returns, banking, employee benefits, and outstanding debts.

Not everybody has the time or energy to do the proper research necessary to make wise investment decisions. One circumstance in which you may be better off paying for advice is when you already have a hunk of cash in savings. At that point, hiring a financial advisor makes a lot of sense, especially if you have a lot of money.

According to a 1998 IAFP/Dalbar survey, the use of paid professionals increases as assets increase. For example, 48 percent of individuals with an initial $25,000 investment seek the help of a professional, while 70 percent of those with over $500,000 already work with a professional.

Choices, Choices

By now you've decided that you need some good counseling, but how do you choose a financial planner? Well, a quick glance through the Yellow Pages reveals a gazillion names under the listings of *financial planner* or *investment advisor*. Many of those listed carry fancy but uninformative titles, such as certified financial planner, chartered financial analyst, or chartered financial consultant. What makes choosing even more confusing is that stockbrokers, insurance agents, accountants, bankers, or attorneys can all offer investment advice, but that doesn't necessarily make them financial planners.

Know What Questions to Ask

First, what to ask? Most investment advisors offer a free initial consultation, which they use to determine whether they want you as a client. You, too, can interview the advisor without being obligated to hire him or her.

Next, what is their financial strategy? You must understand *how* the planner is going to help you reach your goals. Ask the advisor to describe how you will work together and how often you will receive reports and follow-up. A good idea is also to get their track record. You can do this through getting a copy of their ADV form, which is a form they are required to fill out when registering with the SEC or the state. Part II of the form provides useful information about the planner's background, methodology, and compensation. Financial planners are required to give clients this form or a brochure containing the same information. If the planner holds a federal securities license, check their record with the NASD to see if any complaints have been lodged.

What company do they keep? That is, what sort of clients do they have? Common sense suggests that if you have only modest resources, you don't want to hire someone who has limited experience with small accounts. Likewise, if you're a millionaire, why go to someone who normally deals with small investors? Here's a situation where you should ask for references. Of course, planners would never send you to anyone who is going to trash them, but it will give you the opportunity to see how they've dealt with other clients in your category.

Get their credentials. The general guideline is that *all* planners and advisers must be listed as Registered Investment Advisors by the SEC. The exception to this rule is if the person you're dealing with is primarily a stockbroker, insurance agent, attorney, or accountant who is *not* required to register because the investment advice they give is only incidental to the other services they provide.

Find out how they get paid. There are several compensation methods that advisors can use. You should know about any existing conflicts of interest before deciding which payment plan suits you. Checking their ADV will reveal those possible conflicts. This is a crucial step in determining whether you're dealing with an independent advisor, or whether they receive extra compensation for recommending certain products or services.

The Least You Need to Know

➤ A financial planner is a person who helps you organize your specific financial objectives and gives you a customized plan that addresses your individual concerns. Investment advisors (also known as money managers), on the other hand, manage assets and suggest portfolio changes.

➤ When discussing your investment portfolio with your financial planner or investment advisor, ask him why he is suggesting the particular investment product, how does it fit in line with your investment objectives and how much will he earn from the sale of the product.

➤ There are five different ways an investment advisor can get paid: fee only, fee-and-commission, commission only, fee offset and fee based.

➤ Find out as much as you can about your investment advisor from the National Association of Securities Dealers, also known as the NASD, including his or her financial strategy, how they earn their fees and what types of accreditations he or she has.

Chapter 11

Online Financial Resources—Your Power Tools

Imagine stumbling across some prohibited government financial data on the Internet a day before it was to be released. After you uncovered this information, you realized that not only could you profit from it but that you weren't the only online surfer who read the data.

Well, it really happened. On November 6, 1998, financial markets were rocked briefly after a government worker posted a key figure from the October employment report on the Internet—a day early. A financial consultant in Princeton, New Jersey, noticed the posting—the number of jobs created in October 1998—and began to alert clients. As word got out, investors deluged the Bureau of Labor Statistics with phone calls.

Within the hour, the Bureau of Labor Statistics announced it would release the full report earlier than usual because—and here's the key—investors had been eagerly awaiting the number as a clue to whether the Federal Reserve might cut interest rates.

America embraces the Information Age; the rush to access financial data is over-whelming. Phrases such as "real-time," "up-to-the-minute," and "now," are spread throughout financial Web sites, seeking to entice Netizens to read, learn, and stay.

A question remains: With the World Wide Web offering thousands of pages and pub-lishing financial data and facts to help you make better investment decisions and plan for your future, how do you know *which* Web sites will help you?

As you learned in Chapter 2, using specific, personalized criteria in a search engine narrows the hunt. This chapter will help you extend your online reach by offering you a chance to review essential and potentially profitable online financial resources before you click. This chapter is similar to the Yellow Pages ad campaign: It's like phoning first.

The Big Kahunas

Search engines are one of the primary ways that you find Web sites. That's why a Web site with a good search engine listing may see a dramatic increase in traffic. Everyone wants that good listing, but you want the information. Unfortunately, many Web sites appear poorly in search engine rankings or may not be listed at all, because they fail to consider how search engines work.

No matter what you find in each search engine or—we'll use the term loosely—online service, understand that when you're searching for online financial information, each service is set up with channels. For example, if you want to find information on business and personal finance, online services most likely have a "Business & Economy" or "Personal Finance" channel.

What does each offer? Let's take a peek.

Excite's Money & Investing Channel

Excite is a free, personalized online service that gives Web users just about everything they want in one place. The service offers 18 programmed channels of Web content, including the Money & Investing channel, along with state-of-the-art technology, private Web-based email with MailExcited, chat rooms, and online shopping.

Simply by logging on to www.excite.com and clicking on the Money & Investing channel, you can find a number of financial features that help you stay on top of the day's financial events. You can create and track your own personal investment portfolio, track the market, find quotes, and perform research. Excite's strategic partnership with Intuit's Quicken.com provides the content. Little, if any, original content from Excite exists within this channel. The content provided by Quicken, however, including how to find a mortgage, small business issues, and investment how-to's, is helpful reference material. You can also get tax answers and insurance quotes.

Excite's business relationship with the Charles Schwab Company allows visitors to review market index data, such how the S&P 500 or NASDAQ is performing. Note that data is delayed at least 20 minutes, with the exception of the NASDAQ quotes, which are delayed 15 minutes. Amazon.com, an online bookseller, offers its personal finance bestsellers on a weekly basis, along with the opportunity for you to buy books online.

Overall, Excite is one of the most popular search services on the Web. It offers a medium-sized index and integrates non-Web material such as company information and sports scores into its results.

Yahoo! Finance

Stay in touch with the latest financial and business developments with this channel of the online portal, Yahoo! (www.yahoo.com). In addition to delayed stock quotes, this comprehensive financial news source includes a number of (free!) newswire feeds from worldwide respectable media organizations, such as Reuters Financial News, PR Newswire, Standard & Poors, Business Wire, and Zacks.

Click Here

Keep track of your stocks and more with Yahoo! Pager. It provides instant stock alerts when prices reach a certain limit. You can view your portfolio and get immediate access to news, profiles, quotes, and insider trades. Log on to **http://pager.yahoo.com/pager/stocks.html**.

At Yahoo! Finance, you can look up stock prices and company news by ticker symbol, track a group of stocks with constantly up-to-date (but not up-to-the-minute) portfolio values, search for news by keyword, and browse business and financial news by specific industry.

In the end of 1998, Yahoo! Finance launched the following new features:

➤ **Tax Center**. The Tax Center enables you to estimate your refund, get the latest tax tips, and prepare and file your state and federal taxes.

➤ **IPO**. The IPO area offers a complete overview of the current IPO market as well as functionality to track hot IPOs from their registration to their post-offering performance.

➤ **Charts**. Charts allow you to look for historical quote data. It provides links to daily, weekly, and monthly historical prices. You can download the data to your favorite charting program.

➤ **Stock and Fund Screeners**. Stock and Fund Screeners help you find stocks and mutual funds that meet your investment objectives. You can analyze companies or mutual funds by applying a filter of one or more criteria.

➤ **Insider Trading**. The Insider Trading area allows you to follow the trading activity and planned sales of insiders for publicly traded U.S. companies.

➤ **Weekly Poll**. The Weekly Poll area, in conjunction with Marketplace Radio, enables you to vote on business issues and check out opinions of other Netizens.

➤ **Day Charts**. Day Charts let you track the weekly performance of a security.

➤ **S&P 500 Comparison Charts and Moving Average Charts**. These Charts give you the opportunity to compare a security's performance against the S&P 500 index or plot its price movement against its 50- and 200-day moving averages.

AOL.com's Personal Finance Channel

Log on to AOL.com's Personal Finance channel at www.aol.com and click the Personal Finance channel. You will find that it mirrors Excite's Personal Finance channel, complete with all information from Quicken.com. You will find news provided by worldwide media organizations, including CBS Marketwatch, and get investment opinions from Jim Cramer of TheStreet.com.

AOL.com is a branded version of the Excite search engine in the United States and Canada. It has a different name and look but is basically Excite underneath.

Microsoft's Money Central

Microsoft's personal finance center, Money Central (http://moneycentral.msn.com), gives visitors a daily dose of well-rounded content and financial news from MSNBC, Microsoft's 24-hour cable network partnership with NBC.

Money Central provides helpful information on investing, money and banking, taxes, insurance, and real estate, giving you essential strategies for making the right financial choices. In addition, a Quotes and Research button is available to get delayed quotes as well as follow major financial indexes, such as the Dow, S&P, and NASDAQ. Investing highlights include the ability to create a personalized portfolio, obtain information on the top funds and most actively traded stocks of the day, as well as search a mutual fund directory.

Financial service providers, such as Merrill Lynch, offer Money Central's visitors the chance to read daily market summaries, follow the stock market, and obtain free stock research through their partnership with Microsoft.

Money Meaning

Real-time quotes are stock quotes that are provided online as buy and sell transactions occur. Delayed quotes, however, provide the same information but the quotes are delayed 15 to 20 minutes.

Netscape's Personal Finance Center

Like AOL.com, Netscape Search is a branded version of the Excite search engine.

Reuters is the biggest supplier of real-time financial news to Netscape's Personal Finance Center (http://personalfinance.netscape.com). Like other online services, Netscape offers customized investment portfolios, market index pricing, and 20-minute delayed quotes.

S&P Personal Wealth provides a special feature, dubbed "Stock of the Week," to all Netscape Personal Finance Center visitors. You can learn about the stocks picked by S&P equity analysts each week and get the latest information about equities. S&P Personal Wealth also gives helpful advice about investment strategies, tax planning, saving, and borrowing. In addition to S&P Personal Wealth, the Motley Fool, a Web site geared toward finance and folly, also provides Netscape visitors with the chance to look up their favorite acronym in a glossary and get answers to investment questions.

Morningstar is also a major content contributor to Netscape's Personal Finance Center. The Morningstar Fund Selector enables you to find a mutual fund that fits your investing needs.

Since Excite competes with Netscape, it is ironic that Excite provides the bulk of the editorial content to Netscape—from banking and borrowing to investments and retirement information. Remember, however, that Excite gets its content from Quicken.com.

Snap Finance

Ever become overwhelmed by all the information not just on the Internet but also on a search engine? Don't call a librarian, just boot up and log on to www.snap.com for a look at its Business and Money section. You can read up on the latest U.S. and international market information and find exactly what you need. It makes the Dewey Decimal system look like binary code.

www.snap.com.

Snap Finance offers visitors an easy-to-read menu of financial information, features and up-to-date market activity. Snap.com is a free Internet portal service from NBC and CNET. It boasts that it offers the most powerful methods to find anything on the Internet. Its directory of personal finance and investing Web sites are provided to visitors of Snap Finance in a well-organized manner. Featured content is also provided from dozens of leading Web publishers, including Bloomberg, Quicken.com, and Business Wire.

125

You can search through the following categories on Snap Finance to find helpful Web sites that provide exactly what you're looking for:

➤ Accounting	➤ Law
➤ Banking & Finance	➤ Management
➤ Business Software	➤ Marketing & PR
➤ E-commerce	➤ News
➤ Economics	➤ Personal Finance
➤ Education	➤ Publications
➤ Employment	➤ Real Estate
➤ Home Office	➤ Small Business
➤ Insurance	➤ Statistics
➤ International	➤ Taxes
➤ Investing	➤ Top Corporations
➤ Labor & Guilds	

As with all other top search engines and portals, you can also get stock quotes, chart the DJIA hourly, and review the market summary of all major financial indexes. There is even a personalized stock tracker that allows you to create your own online investment portfolio, with positions updated every 20 minutes.

AltaVista's Business & Finance Channel

Rich in content but lacking in eye candy, AltaVista's LookSmart area (www.altavista.com) allows you to explore a number of finance-related Web listings by category. Categories include:

➤ News & Guides

➤ Business Professionals

➤ Data & Statistics

➤ Finance & Investment

➤ Industry & Trade

➤ Int'l Business

➤ Jobs & Careers

➤ Quotes & Profiles

➤ Regulation & Govt

➤ Small Business

➤ U.S. Regional Business

There is also a section where you can access a mortgage finder, search for a lower rate, and get cash by signing up through one of AltaVista's advertisers.

Interestingly, AltaVista is consistently one of the largest search engines on the Web, in terms of pages indexed. Its comprehensive coverage and wide range of power searching commands make it a particular favorite among researchers. It also offers a number of features designed to appeal to basic users who are not familiar with the Internet or using a search engine. For example, it's "Ask AltaVista" feature enables visitors to email the AltaVista "customer service" department with whatever query they have about the information they are seeking.

Extra! Extra! Read All About It!

The days of trekking down to the corner newspaper stand are long gone. Of course, curling up with the business section of Sunday's *New York Times* is always a pleasure after orange juice and an English muffin—but who has time for that anymore?

Instead, get your financial news 24 hours a day, 7 days a week—that's right, any time *you* want. By using the Internet's online financial news resources, you can:

➤ Follow the Malaysian Malay Business Conference to keep on top of business developments that may affect your investment in emerging market funds

➤ Track the U.S. economic statistics that follow the housing market, such as housing starts, to determine if now is the right time to buy or sell a home

➤ Read the latest report on computer sales and how they affect the Morgan Stanley Technology Index and, possibly, your small-cap mutual fund portfolio

If you want to spend only a few minutes reading the latest headlines from Wall Street, you can do that, too. The following are a few online news resources that enable you to stay on top of the business world and financial markets.

Money Meaning

The **Morgan Stanley Technology Index** is a basket of technology stocks grouped together and used as an indicator of the performance of the technology sector.

theStreet.com

If you want objective financial news written by unbiased journalists, log on to www.thestreet.com. The *New York Times* calls it "The Web's best for investment analysis." With the up-to-the-minute-publish-it-now approach the editors take, it's easy to see why.

www.thestreet.com.

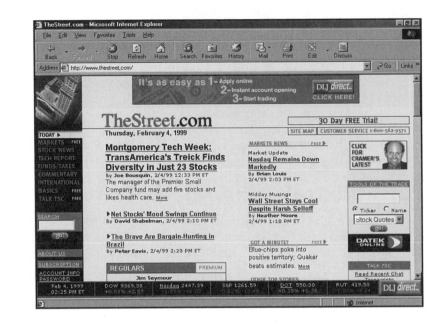

theStreet.com is an online forum ripe with market commentary and stock trading information provided by a team of independent financial journalists headed by noted editor Jim Cramer.

The Market section provides dozens of new stories on a daily basis, all posted with published times to the exact minute. TheStreet.com prides itself on its reports of what's happening in the markets and around the globe. Categories covered in the Market section include the following:

➤ **Market Roundup.** A lengthy yet informative review of the day's trading and news events.

➤ **Today's Market.** Several stories dedicated to specific market reports, such as what happened in the technology sector, a morning "wake up call" that reports on any overnight market activity or business news, midday musings, and an evening update.

➤ **Today's Bond Market.** Keep on top of the bond market with this educational inside look.

➤ **Yesterday's Market.** On a cloud yesterday? TheStreet.com keeps its news available a day later.

➤ **International Market News.** Find out what is happening in foreign markets with several stories from around the world.

➤ **Markets Features.** Not so much up-to-the-minute in nature, these stories give you an in-depth look at a variety of finance-related topics.

Other news sections are available in addition to the Market section of the Web site, but they come at a premium: You must be a subscriber to get this information. Online subscriptions cost $9.95 per month, although theStreet.com does offer a 30-day free trial.

CBS MarketWatch

Formerly known as DBC Online (Data Broadcasting Corporation), this online news Web site joined forces with CBS News to create a financial supersite at http://cbs.marketwatch.com.

Click Here

Watch TV converge with the Web...well, sort of. When CBS acquired MarketWatch.com in 1998, in exchange for promoting the MarketWatch.com name on the CBS network, MarketWatch.com was able to use the CBS acronym in its name. Check it out at **http://cbs.marketwatch.com**.

CBS MarketWatch caters to the mass market by using DBC's real-time quote and news operations with CBS News—one of the oldest and most recognized news brand names in history. MarketWatch.com's worldwide reporters provide individual investors with headlines, stories, and analysis throughout the trading day—and sometimes overnight, depending on foreign market events. The Special Reports give investors exclusive news stories that, according to its editors, you won't find on Dow Jones, Reuters, Bloomberg, or other newswires. Topics include IPOs, technology stocks, bond reports, and even taxes.

In addition to financial news coverage, CBS MarketWatch offers multiple personal portfolios, market and company research, intraday and technical charting, mutual and money market fund data, direct brokerage access, and delayed quotes—all for free.

The following features are also available for a fee:

➤ **CBS MarketWatch RT**. CBS MarketWatch RT is a $34.95 per month service that offers real-time snapshot quotes and historical and fundamental data and research tools for the active investor.

➤ **CBS MarketWatch LIVE**. CBS MarketWatch LIVE is the branded version of DBC's StockEdge Online that, for $79 a month, gives you a virtual trading desk on any or all of your computers. Using proprietary active *push* software, CBS MarketWatc LIVE allows you to set up dynamically updating charts, tickers, and quote screens.

Money Meaning

Push software, also known as push technology, is a technological feature that Web sites utilize to drive information directly to your computer screen without having you log onto their sites. You initially must sign up for this feature on their Web site to work. For example, if you wanted market news delivered or "pushed" to your computer screen without having to log onto the Web, you would sign up for this technological feature.

➤ **Reuters.com**. Dubbed as "the business of information," Reuters provides more than 457,000 users in 58,000 organizations with a wide range of information, including real-time financial data, historical databases, news and video for print and television. These users and organizations are companies like major daily newspapers and TV stations. How you get access to Reuters information is by reading these newspapers or watching TV news.

Reuters is the source of many of the financial stories you read in a newspaper or listen to on the radio. This information is also available at its Web site (www.reuters.com). The coverage there is quite extensive—and intensive—with a broad array of financial news on topics such as commodities, the Euro, and the treasury markets.

CNNfn.com

The 24-hour cable network comes alive on the Web with its round-the-clock financial news coverage at www.cnnfn.com. Stay on top of hot stories, such as company mergers and acquisitions, the world's business and economy, and "Washington unwrapped"—a section on CNNfn.com's hot stories category devoted solely to politics and its affect on the financial markets.

The financial market news coverage is broad; you can follow the U.S. stock market, world markets, currencies, interest rates, and commodities. In addition to this news coverage, you can get stock quotes and perform an interactive trading simulation.

The Motley Fool

Available at www.fool.com as well as on America Online (keyword: fool), The Motley Fool demystifies the world of finance and presents users with the basic tools to understand the financial world.

It does so with its mid-day and evening news, keeping users updated on the markets and stocks. In addition, it offers *conference calls* and StockTalk interviews, in which you can read the transcripts of discussions among company executives making headlines.

The Wall Street Journal Interactive

Taking cues from its print publication, The Wall Street Journal Interactive Web site (www.wsj.com) maintains a wealth of worldwide business, economic, and financial market news. Read the latest news headlines, follow the market indexes, or even obtain online quotes on this comprehensive Web site.

There is a slight monetary catch: In order to get any information from www.wsj.com, you must subscribe. Subscribers to the print edition of the *Wall Street Journal* can get the online version for $29 a year. Non-print subscribers pay $59. When you subscribe to wsj.com, you also get access to Barron's Online, the weekly newspaper full of financial data and expert commentary.

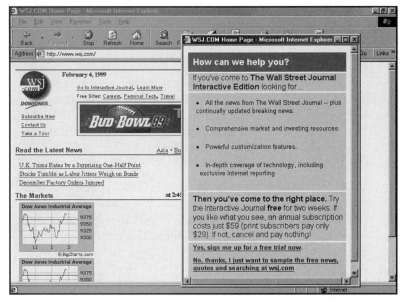

www.wsj.com.

The Wall Street Journal is available online at a discount to its newspaper subscribers.

Investors Business Daily

Originally launched on America Online in the mid 90s (keyword: IBD), the *Investors Business Daily* (IBD) is one of America's fastest-growing newspapers, touting 850,000 daily newspaper readers—not counting its online readers.

You can read the latest financial news at IBD online as well as editorials and commentary pieces about current business happenings around the globe. IBD also keeps you in the know with what's going on in the computer and technology sector and provides information on key economic data reports released by the government.

ABC News.com's Business Channel

ABC News.com's Business channel (http://abcnews.go.com/sections/business) provides small business, personal finance, and detailed market news to online readers. You can look up stock quotes, read wire reports on trading activity, and even check out tutorials on how to buy and sell stocks.

Online Financial Newsletters

Many Web sites offer free trial subscriptions to newsletters in the hopes that you'll sign up and remain a subscriber. Several of them, however, require you to give your credit card information before you get a free trial subscription to ensure that your subscription is uninterrupted. If you opt for such an online newsletter, make sure there is a customer service center available via email, fax, or telephone so that you can cancel your subscription should you wish to do so.

DRIP Investor

This newsletter, *DRIP Investor*, along with its Web site www.dripinvestor.com, gives information to help investors build a stock portfolio with few investment dollars by investing directly with the company—no brokers, no brokerage fees. Nearly 1,000 of the world's best companies offer dividend reinvestment programs, known as DRIPs, including such household names as McDonald's, Coca-Cola, Merck, Intel, General Electric, and AT&T, along with up-and-comers such as Paychex, Equifax, and Home Depot.

A DRIP is a program that hundreds of publicly-traded companies offer that allow you to purchase fractional shares of stock directly from the company without having to purchase them through a broker. However, in a DRIP, you must own at least one share of a company's stock prior to going to the company to enroll in the DRIP program.

For example, to enroll in General Electric's dividend reinvestment program, you would initially purchase your one share from a discount broker—as a way to reduce commissions on the stock trade—and then have the stock certificate mailed to you. Next, you would contact the shareholder services department at GE to enroll in their DRIP program, complete any paperwork they send you, and mail it back to them along with your stock certificate. Then, you will be paid dividends—remember, stocks pay dividends?—that are used to buy additional, fractional shares. The amount depends upon the current stock price. Plus, you can also purchase additional shares directly from the company.

But what if you don't want to go through the hassle of purchasing one share, paying a commission and then mailing in your certificate to a company? Then No-Load Stocks™ are your answer as several hundred companies offer this program that allows you to bypass purchasing your initial share of stock from a broker; you can buy it directly from the company.

DRIPs and No-Load Stocks™ are ideal for converting small dividend checks into a portfolio of compounding equity investments in blue chip stocks. Most of these plans provide the flexibility of adding to your portfolio on a regular basis—with no brokerage commission—often with as little as $10.

It's difficult to get information on DRIPs and No-Load Stocks®; the Securities and Exchange Commission (SEC) forbids companies from advertising these plans. Investors need to get this information themselves, which is why Chuck Carlson publishes a monthly newsletter on the topic: DRIP Investor.

Each month *DRIP Investor* brings you the latest news on Dividend Reinvestment Plans, including their many commission-free investment options, changes in existing plans that may affect your strategies, model portfolios that use DRIPs, and more.

Changes occur every day in the DRIP field. Many companies are adding DRIPs, while others are modifying their plans. DRIP Investor keeps you informed of these changes and helps you to make the most profitable investment decisions while eliminating the hassle of a broker and outrageously high commissions.

Subscription rates for *Drip Investor* are $7.95 per month, with a 30-day free trial subscription available. You can always cancel by email or telephone. Subscribe at www.dripinvestor.com.

Independent Investor Digest

Editor Greg Spear's model portfolio of "A" ranked stocks has outperformed the market consistently in each of the previous three years—by 34 percent in 1996, 46 percent in 1997, and more than 60 percent in the first nine months of 1998. These figures represent an annualized compounded growth of 82 percent—three times the gain of the S&P 500. Every week you can receive a portfolio of his best stock picks based on a consensus of 1,200 recommendations by the nation's top investment advisors.

Once you subscribe to this online newsletter, you will also receive hotline updates. For the $16.95 monthly subscription rate, you receive immediate online delivery with unlimited access to every issue, email notices when new issues are available, and a free portfolio workshop. Order the Independent Investor Digest at www.investools.com.

UnDiscovered Stocks

The best place to get stock ideas is to observe the changes taking place around you. For example, have you noticed how many teens are opting to wear Reebok gym shoes rather than Nike? Hey, Mom and Dad, that's a sign for you to do some investment research. Or the fact that every two minutes a personal computer with an Intel microprocessor is sold, according to Intel Corporation. And, as the 77 million baby boomers age, the amount of money spent on leisure products is rising, up 8.5 percent in 1997 from 5.4 percent in 1995.

What do these statistics mean for publicly-traded companies that either manufacture goods or provide services to consumers? For one thing, the aging of Americans is one trend that is bound to have a direct impact on Wall Street as companies aim to cater to this market.

How to stay on top of this? One financial newsletter, UnDiscovered Stocks, available in print and on the Web, focuses its stock picks on the demographic changes and aging population around the world. For example, baby boomers have environmental and infrastructure building and repair concerns, especially those boomers who want an environmentally-sound future for their children. A December 1996 stock pick of American Water Works at $19^3/4$ yielded a 62 percent gain in April 1998 at $31^7/8$.

One stock per month is selected for subscribers with in-depth analysis as well as performance information on previous month's picks. Subscription rates as of March 1999 are $99 a year for 12 monthly issues. Log onto www.undiscoveredstocks.com to subscribe.

NoLOAD FUND*X

If you invest in no-load mutual funds, consider a subscription to the NoLOAD FUND*X newsletter. This newsletter provides complete performance information on more than 720 funds and maintains its Fund*X's star system to quickly identify leading funds.

Fund*X's margined portfolio gained a total return of 17.4 percent for 1995, 30.5 percent for 1996, and 27.1 percent for 1997. According to the Hulbert Financial Digest (April 1997)—an independent service that monitors the performance of over 160 investment newsletters—NoLOAD FUND*X ranked among the top five newsletters based on both risk-adjusted and total-return performance over the past 15 years. This newsletter is available at www.investools.com.

InvesTech Market Analyst

In 1987, editor James Stack won national financial press recognition for leading his readers out of the market before Black Monday. He also alerted readers to the bull market with his famous "Toro Toro" issue, published ten days before the January 1991 blastoff.

With the InvesTech Market Analyst newsletter, you get stock and mutual fund recommendations as well as advice on when to switch or how to time your mutual fund purchases and redemptions. Your subscription also includes InvesTech Special Reports.

The newsletter maintains a widely diversified model portfolio based on risk allocation strategy. Stack clearly explains and documents the research behind specific stock recommendations and turns his strategy into a specific to-do list for readers. He provides commentary that answers not just where the market is heading but why. In addition, you'll get coverage of the bond market with Stack's proprietary Bond Barometer.

Subscribe for $13.95 per month by logging on to www.investech.com.

Dick Davis Digest

The Dick Davis Digest online newsletter (www.dickdavis.com) gives a concise view on a variety of investment-related issues by reviewing hundreds of financial publications and trying to spot investment trends. The subscription rate is $15.95 per month. In the Digest, you will find the following features:

➤ **Spotlight Stock.** After reviewing more than 400 financial publications, the Digest singles out the most compelling and promising stock and features it along with others positioned for growth.

➤ **Where's the Market Going?** Forecasts by top advisors are summarized in concise, non-technical language to give you the broad market direction you need for proper buy/sell timing.

➤ **Short and to the Point.** Concise insight on investment ideas and money-making suggestions taken from hundreds of publications, always bringing you right to the heart of the message.

➤ **Personal Note.** Thought-provoking insights emphasize the Digest's long-term investment approach. Commentaries and recommendations by such insightful investors as Peter Lynch, Sir John Templeton, Warren Buffett, and many other top market experts.

➤ **Follow-ups.** Updated opinions on stocks that were recommended in previous issues, with emphasis on former "Spotlight" and "Last Word" picks.

➤ **Mutual Funds.** Recommendations from top market newsletters dealing solely with mutual funds, including the latest positions of leading switch fund advisors.

➤ **The Last Word.** A special situation or outstanding group of stocks is featured, with emphasis on the key selections of leading market analysts.

Investment Research

Many of us spend countless hours searching for the perfect place to stay on our vacation. Why, we wouldn't be American if we didn't stress about which airlines to choose, why we can't get two double beds in the hotel, and, most certainly, what to pack.

Why don't we take the same exhaustive measure in researching our investments? After all, it's only *money*.

The following are a few online candidates that can help take the sting out of researching your stock or mutual fund picks.

Morningstar.net

Morningstar.net is considered by some as an online magazine rich with mutual fund news and resource information. Others laud it as the premiere live source of information on thousands of mutual funds and stocks. You can access its Quicktake reports, which contain detailed performance, portfolio, news, and management information from their homepage and from the Learn, Plan, Research, Invest, Monitor, and Socialize cover pages of the Web site. If you need to look up a ticker, select "Ticker Lookup."

To get stock quotes, click the "Quote" button on the home page. You can obtain quotes on up to 30 stocks and/or funds simultaneously by separating the tickers with a space.

You can also retrieve updated quotes on all the stocks and funds in your portfolios at the same time. Go to the Monitor area and log in. The current prices of all your holdings in your default portfolio are displayed on the right side of the screen. The names of all your saved portfolios are listed underneath the current price table. To switch among portfolios, just click the name of the portfolio you want to view.

Most of the information and features on Morningstar.net are free, although it does offer a premium service for $9.95 a month. You do need to register online to obtain all Morningstar mutual fund data even if you do not sign up for the premium service.

Zacks/Wall Street Source

Zacks Investment Research combined all its research efforts with Wall Street Source, another investment research firm, and together they bring the individual investor comprehensive and up-to-date delivery of critical market data and research on the Web at www.zwss.com. This partnership combines over two decades of delivery and research experience into a state-of the art Web site designed to empower individual investors to trade on their own.

Log onto their Web site to get the following market information to help you make more informed decisions:

➤ **Market Overview.** Live market analysis, breaking news from leading news services, proprietary company news updated live on your screen, leading economic indicators, and an economics calendar showing when economic data will be released to the public are all provided throughout this section of the Web site.

➤ **Daily Monitor.** The Daily Monitor provides the latest stock news, earnings releases and surprises, after-market activities, and conference calls. You can also set up a portfolio and monitor stock activity, earnings expectations, stock split announcements, and corporate buybacks. Plus, the guts of it all, the overviews, news, charts, earning snapshots, filings, short interest and insider information on all publicly traded corporations are also provided to visitors.

➤ **Value Line.** One of the world's most widely read investment information services, Valueline.com provides news and information to help you research mutual funds and stocks. Check it out at www.valueline.com.

Click Here

Want to join a club online? The National Association of Investors Corporation enables you to learn about investment clubs and get investing ideas through its Web site at **www.better-investing.org**.

Value Line Investment Survey is available on the Internet to help you get the financial information you need on thousands of companies and mutual funds. Value Line publishes widely acclaimed research reports, including the Options and Convertibles Surveys, the OTC Special Situations Service, The Value Line Mutual Fund Survey, The Value Line No-Load Fund Advisor, and the Value Line Investment Survey Expanded Edition. Value Line also provides electronic data services for individual and institutional clients.

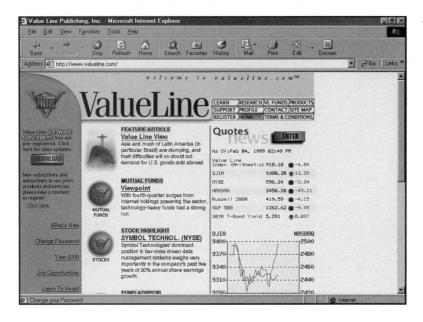

www.valueline.com.

Calculate This!

What will it take to become a millionaire? How long will it take to pay off your $5,000 Visa balance? Is it better to file your taxes jointly with your spouse or separately?

The World Wide Web has the answer. That is, several online calculators have the answer. Toss aside your Hewlett Packard or Texas Instruments calculator you've been saving since college; the following are a few Web sites that can do the trick:

➤ **Kiplinger.com**. Noted for its personal finance and investment magazine, Kiplinger.com provides several easy-to-execute calculators to help you with investment, stock, mutual fund, retirement, saving and borrowing, home, insurance, and tax calculations. The calculators are available at www.kiplinger.com/calc/calchome.html.

➤ **Smartcalc.com**. Smartcalc.com's collection of calculators enable you to compute anything and everything, from credit card debt to calculating investment returns and projecting retirement savings to mortgage costs. In fact, if you really want to find out exactly how long it would take to become a millionaire, the calculation would look like the following figure. How long would it take? Enter your information and click away!

Find out what it takes to become a millionaire with smartcalc's online calculator.

> **What will it take to become a millionaire? - Microsoft Internet Explorer**
>
> File   Edit   View   Favorites   Tools   Help
>
> Back   Forward   Stop   Refresh   Home   Search   Favorites   History   Mail   Print   Edit   Discuss
>
> Address   http://www.smartcalc.com/cgi-bin/smartcalcpro/sav1.cgi/kiplinger
>
> financenter.com
> click▶calcs™
>
> autos | homes
> insurance | credit lines
> credit cards | investing
> retirement | saving
> budgeting
>
> about us | contact us
> feedback
>
> **Tips for Using
> This Calculator**
>
> ### What will it take to become a millionaire?
>
> inputs   results   graphs   explanation   deals
>
> View Single-Page Format
>
> | | |
> |---|---|
> | Your Current Age | 35 |
> | Desired Age To Be a Millionaire | 65 |
> | Amount You Now Have | $ 20000 |
> | Amount You Can Save Monthly | $ 300 |
> | Return You Can Earn | 6 % |
> | Your Federal Tax Rate | 30 % |
> | Your State Tax Rate | 8 % |
> | Predicted Inflation Rate | 3 % |
>
> Calc**Builder**
> ©1995-99, FinanCenter, Inc.
> including libraries
>
> NOTE:
> The accuracy of this calculator and its applicability to your circumstances is not guaranteed. You should obtain personal advice from qualified professionals.

➤ **Bloomberg Online.** This information powerhouse has calculators that enable you to determine how much you can borrow on a house or whether it's a good idea to lease or buy a car. You can also compute the difference between a dollar and a drachma. It's all available at www.bloomberg.com/cgi-bin/efc2.cgi.

Bet You Didn't Know

As you learned in Chapter 4, several online discount brokers can help you execute trades either directly on their Web sites or by using proprietary software. For information on how to contact such online brokers, refer to Appendix C.

The Least You Need to Know

➤ Search engines are one of the primary ways that you find Web sites. Those such as Yahoo!, Snap.com and AltaVista provide their own personal finance and investing channels to help you perform research.

➤ Newspapers also provide business and financial news in their online sites. They include *The Wall Street Journal, Investors Business Daily* and *The New York Times.*

➤ There are hundreds of online financial newsletters that provide investment recommendations. Look for those online newsletters that offer free or low-cost trial subscriptions.

➤ Research firms, such as Morningstar and Value Line, have provided data to investors for many years through its newsletter subscriptions. They now provide this information on the World Wide Web and require you to create an account to access their data.

Part 3
The Future of Your Money On and Offline

When you think about where you're going to get the money to live on in the future, what is the first financial resource that comes to mind? If you're like most Americans in the 20th century, Social Security is the answer.

But that's all about to change. Reports indicate that the Social Security Trust Fund will be insolvent *by the time today's 20-year-olds hit retirement age, thereby putting all the pressure on you to think about your golden nest egg on the day you graduate from high school.*

That's why contributing to a 401(k) plan is a key investment strategy. While they shift the burden to you to save for your future, you control how you want your investment pie divided.

Of course, not everyone has access to a company retirement plan. You may instead prefer to build assets through investments such as real estate. Home ownership, if you play your cards right and understand mortgage rates, is brimming with financial benefits. When you know which areas of the country will fare better in the millennium real estate market than others, you have got a home-sweet-investment.

Your money is safe online, too—at least, for now. Whether you're buying, selling, or trading on the Internet, the government is working to keep it secure and tax-free.

Let's take a look at the future of your money, shall we?

Chapter 12

The Future of Social Security

In This Chapter

➤ Why it's important to learn about Social Security at any age

➤ Getting a grasp on the Social Security debate and its future

➤ Figuring out how much you're due when you retire

Have you seen the newspaper headlines or listened to television reports about your financial future—or perhaps, financial ruin?

Plan to shore up Social Security is stalled! Social Security privatization less costly to administer than critics claim! And one of our personal favorites: *Social Security is doomed!*

The people who manage the Social Security Fund, known as the Board of Trustees, project that beginning in the year 2013 the annual benefits paid to retirees will exceed payroll tax revenues. In other words, the amount of money they will shell out to Social Security recipients will be over and above what they collect in taxes, which is how they derive their revenue. This is largely attributed to the upcoming retirement of the baby boom generation and current demographic trends. And, from 2021 to 2031, it would have to tap into the principal cash to make Social Security payments to retirees; by the year 2032, the funds would all be depleted.

What many newspapers don't report in the headlines but reserve for the flyspeck type at the end of a story—if at all—is that the system will not become bankrupt or insolvent when the Trust Fund runs out. The taxes collected will be sufficient to pay 75 percent of the obligations to Social Security recipients at the time.

Social Security will always be in the news, from possibly being the recipient of surplus dollars in our Federal budget to privatizing the Fund. Still, we're not here to paint a rosy picture of the future of Social Security but rather to give you information about what Social Security is, how it came to be, and the possibilities for its future. After all, some day you will retire. Unlike your predecessors, one thing is certain: Social Security will not be the panacea to pay all your bills as it used to be.

Social Security: No Longer a Panacea

There is no doubt that the Social Security system frequently reaches a state of crisis in which predictions of its demise abound. Indeed, since it was enacted in 1935, Social Security has been amended often, most recently in 1983, when Congress imposed a tax on the benefits of high-income retirees, raised the retirement age, and revised the tax-rate schedule.

On January 27, 1998, in his State of the Union address, President Clinton recommended that the projected federal budget surplus be used to save Social Security. He said, "Tonight I propose that we reserve 100 percent of the surplus—that's every penny of any surplus—until we have taken all the necessary measures to strengthen the Social Security system for the 21st century." Social Security was also a major highlight of his State of the Union address in 1999, in which he proposed that surplus monies be allocated to shore up the Fund.

The reason Social Security is of such concern is that the extremely high number of citizens born in the post–World War II period—the much-discussed baby boom generation—is heading toward retirement. The generation that will take its place in the workforce is far smaller in proportion to the number of retirees, raising fears about the sustainability of Social Security.

Bet You Didn't Know

By law, the Social Security Board of Trustees is required to look 75 years into the future to determine whether, according to the best demographic and economic forecasts, Social Security will be able to obtain enough money through the payroll taxes of current workers to continue paying benefits to retirees. If the forecasts indicate a problem, a solution must be found.

In the past, the proposed solutions to the various problems facing Social Security aroused great debate. Yet each time, the arguments were stilled, repairs were made, and the system continued to fulfill its mandate.

Things are different now as the aging baby boomer generation takes a financial toll on the system. Obviously, this is an issue that concerns every American. It's important for you to understand both the economic and social sides of the system. If only, like Ebenezer Scrooge, we could visit with the ghost of Christmas future to see just what will happen. In the meantime, take a primer on a few Social Security basics.

Social Security Boot Camp

Knowing the facts is the only way to cut through all the hoopla that's permeated the media in recent years regarding Social Security—especially since this is such a hotly debated issue that many individuals and groups have proposed reforms to help solve the funding problems.

Social Security is a contributory social insurance program that provides benefits to millions of Americans. Workers contribute financially to the system during their careers and earn entitlement to family benefits upon retirement, disability, or death. Currently, nearly 44 million Americans receive benefits under the Old-Age and Survivors Insurance and Disability Insurance (OASDI). These are types of programs that make up Social Security. This group includes some 30 million elderly retirees and their dependents, 6 million disabled workers and their dependents, and more than 7 million survivors of deceased workers. More than 3 million of those receiving OASDI benefits are children.

That's what Social Security is and does. Where does it get the money to pay the benefits? Social Security is largely funded on a pay-as-you-go basis. Social Security is not a *piggy bank* that employees put money into and then take out of when they retire. The benefits that today's Social Security retirees receive are paid out of taxes collected from today's workers earmarked for the payment of these benefits. From this tax money, the government writes Social Security checks and mails them to beneficiaries. Any money left over is put into the Trust Fund, which is invested in U.S. government securities to provide funds for future use.

Bet You Didn't Know

If you are self-employed, be prepared to shell out a few bucks to Internal Revenue Service to help pay for Social Security taxes. The IRS slaps you with a 15.3 percent tax on your income to help pay for Social Security benefits for today's recipients.

From where does this pay-as-you-go money come? Well, about 96 percent of all workers in the United States contribute to Social Security, paying a flat tax of 6.2 percent of their wage income up to $68,400. Employers contribute an equal amount.

While the payroll tax is by far the largest source of funding for Social Security, a small amount of additional revenue is raised through the taxation of the Social Security benefits of high-income beneficiaries. That's right—if grandma and grandpa are high-income Social Security recipients, listen to this.

Single elderly taxpayers who receive Social Security benefits and have a combined income (that is, adjusted gross income plus non-taxable interest plus one-half of their Social Security benefits) between $25,000 and $34,000 may have to pay taxes on 50 percent of their Social Security benefits. Up to 85 percent of Social Security benefits of those whose combined income is over $34,000 may be subject to taxation. (The thresholds are higher for married couples filing joint tax returns.). These tax revenues are channeled into both the Social Security and Medicare programs.

The Debate Heats Up

There has been discussion of employers shifting the cost of Social Security taxes onto workers in the form of lower wages. As a result, workers, in effect, may actually bear a substantially larger share of the tax burden than employers. Self-employed people pay both their own and their employer's share. Yikes!

Still, lost in all the rhetoric surrounding the issue this time have been the numbers underlying the debate and the context in which those numbers must be viewed. The uncertainty about the future has resulted in suggestions for change that range from minor adjustments to the complete privatization of the system.

Bet You Didn't Know

In January 1996, the Social Security Trust Fund provided nearly 44 million Americans (primarily retirees and their spouses) with an average monthly benefit of approximately $745. At the end of 1996, the latest year for which published data is available, the accumulation in the Social Security Trust Funds was about $567 billion. Social Security took in about $424 billion and paid out more than $353 billion in 1996; the remainder went into the Trust Fund.

Eligibility

As your paycheck can attest, you are required to contribute to the Social Security program. All citizens and legal aliens who work and pay contributions for the required number of years (ten) are eligible for pension benefits when they reach the minimum retirement age. To qualify as disabled, individuals must have a prolonged or terminal condition and may not earn more than $500 per month. Under certain circumstances, a worker's spouse, children, and parents may qualify for Social Security benefits based on the worker's contribution history.

Who else is eligible? Unmarried children under age 18 (or over 18 if severely disabled), elderly spouses, and spouses caring for young children are generally eligible for benefits if a worker retires, becomes disabled, or dies. The elderly parents of a deceased worker may be entitled to survivorship benefits if they were financially dependent on the child for at least half their support.

And I Get How Much?

Retirement benefits are based on average earnings during a 35-year career. Higher lifetime earnings result in higher benefits up to an inflation-adjusted cap. Here's a breakdown of how the benefits are doled out:

➤ Workers who retire at age 65 receive full benefits.

➤ Workers who retire at age 62 receive reduced benefits based on the likelihood of their collecting benefits over a longer term.

➤ Workers who postpone retirement beyond age 65 up to age 70 and beyond get more than the full benefits.

➤ Recipients of retirement and survivorship benefits who continue to work have their benefits reduced if they earn above a certain threshold. In 1997, beneficiaries under age 65 lost one dollar of benefits for every two dollars of earnings above $8,640. For individuals between 65 and 69 years of age, one dollar in benefits is withheld for every three dollars of earnings over $13,500. The benefits of individuals aged 70 and older are not subject to any earnings test.

Bet You Didn't Know

About 92 percent of individuals age 65 and over receive Social Security benefits. An additional 3 percent of individuals who continue to work and have not yet claimed benefits are eligible to receive benefits upon retirement.

All the benefits are adjusted annually to keep pace with inflation, as measured by the Consumer Price Index (CPI). This means that during periods of high inflation, such as the 1970s, inflation-adjusted benefits protect Social Security recipients from having the real benefits of their Social Security check eaten away by a higher cost of living. Most private pensions do not make similar adjustments for inflation.

So How'd We Get into This Problem Anyway?

Imagine that your washing machine isn't operating as well as it used to. Sure, when you first bought it, your clothes were clean and colors remained bright. As the years passed, however, you noticed the washing machine making funny noises and collecting more lint in the lint catcher; your bright red shirts are now a dull pink.

What do you do? You assess the situation depending on how much money you have in your bank account. You can either call a repairman to come and put a Band-Aid on the problem or get a new machine.

While the Social Security Fund's problems reach far beyond a $500 Kenmore washing machine, the analogy is the same: A decision has to be made based on financial projections; that's exactly what the Board of Trustees do.

The Social Security Trustees' rate projections about the Trust Funds are based on assumptions about demographic and economic trends over the next 75 years. There is no magic 8 ball to determine future conditions, so the Trustees make 3 sets of predictions based upon optimistic, intermediate, and pessimistic assumptions. Social Security's finances look dramatically different depending which assumptions are used.

Under the more optimistic set, the Trustees estimate that Social Security will be adequately funded through 2035, at that point having more than $50 trillion (in 1998 dollars) in the Trust Funds. In contrast, the pessimistic assumptions yield a shortfall amounting to 5.4 percent of taxable payroll over the 75-year period. Under the intermediate projection, the shortfall would amount to about 2.2 percent of taxable payroll.

A large part of this equation is that most elderly Americans have received Social Security benefits far exceeding what they contributed in payroll taxes during their working years (plus accumulated interest). The actual benefit-to-contribution ratio depends, of course, on one's work history and age of retirement.

According to the Congressional Research Service in Washington D.C., an average-wage employee retiring in 1997 would regain his or her Social Security tax contribution with interest after 6.2 years of retirement; a minimum-wage earner would earn back his or her portion of the tax (with interest) in 4.4 years; and a maximum-wage earner would regain his or her tax contribution in 8.1 years.

Back in 1935, when the system was first designed, contribution rates were very low. In fact, the total tax rate was 2 percent in 1937! The earliest retirees paid low taxes for a short period of time—less than their entire career—and received sizable benefits upon retirement. As a result, they reaped substantial returns on their contributions. Over time, as Social Security benefits became more generous and the number of individuals receiving benefits grew, the payroll tax was increased. The difference between the amount of money that has been paid into the system compared with the amount of money collected in benefits is the *benefit-to-contribution ratio*.

The benefit-to-contribution ratio for future generations of retirees is declining. Let's see what can happen with benefit payments with the following examples:

➤ In 2029, a 65-year-old single man with low earnings is expected to have an average annual real rate of return from the OASI program amounting to 2.4 percent, slightly higher than the 2 percent average real return on government bonds.

➤ A couple with one worker who earned an average income would receive a substantially higher average real rate of return, 3.75 percent, upon turning 65 in 2029.

➤ A single male with high earnings would receive a much lower rate of return (0.72 percent).

Money Meaning

The **benefit-to-contribution ratio** is the amount of money that has been paid into the system compared with the amount of money collected in benefits. The ratio has declined for each new cohort of retirees because later generations contributed to the Social Security system for the duration of their careers and were subject to higher payroll tax rates.

Where else can we point the finger for today's Social Security funding problems? Over the past 50 years, older Americans have been retiring at a progressively younger age. In 1950, 83.4 percent of men aged 55 to 64 were employed. By 1990, only 67.8 percent of men in this age group were working. Today, most men and women retire before age 65. In fact, almost 60 percent receive Social Security benefits at age 62, when reduced benefits for early retirement first become available.

On the one hand, earlier retirement is a trend that benefits individual workers, allowing them to enjoy a longer retirement than in the past. Most Americans say they would rather retire sooner than later. Furthermore, if individuals continue to retire earlier, this might increase the demand for younger workers. On the other hand, some economists are concerned that earlier retirement, combined with increased longevity, exacerbates the problem of economically sustaining an aging population. If the trend toward early retirement continues as the population ages, an even smaller share of workers will be supporting a larger proportion of retirees.

An examination of the ages at which most Americans retire suggests that how the Social Security program is structured completely affects all your retirement decisions.

What's on the Table

You would think that with 144 million workers making payroll tax contributions to the Social Security system and building credits toward future benefits, there would be enough dollars in the system to provide a substantial number of workers and their families with benefits.

Not so, but there is a positive side to the problem. In 1996, for example, the benefits paid by Social Security exceeded $347 billion. These benefits, in combination with Medicare health insurance, have dramatically reduced poverty for the aged in America. In 1959, the U.S. Census Bureau estimated that more than 35 percent of elderly Americans were poor. During the 1960s, elderly Americans experienced twice the poverty rate of all other Americans. By 1996, in large part because of changes in the Social Security and Medicare systems, the poverty rate among senior citizens was 10.8 percent. This is slightly lower than the rate for other adults.

Several measures, however, have been adopted that modify the Social Security system so that is provides more incentives for older Americans to continue to work.

➤ Benefits will be increased for workers who retire after age 65, adding to the financial incentive to work longer.

➤ The amount that individuals age 65 to 69 can earn without benefit reductions is gradually being raised over time.

➤ The standard retirement age is scheduled to rise gradually from 65 to 67 for individuals who will turn 62 in the year 2022, though individuals will continue to be eligible for reduced-retirement benefits at age 62.

As impressive as a 70-year-old's resume may be, getting hired by Corporate America may be a tad challenging, don't you think?

Obviously, there are problems; a number of individuals and groups are working hard at solving the financial crisis of the system.

The Suggestions

There are numerous proposed reforms of the Social Security system that would bring the system into long-run (75-year) balance. They include preserving the basic structure with a few minor modifications or making more dramatic transformations by shifting part of the system from today's pay-as-you-go insurance plan to an arrangement more like 401(k) retirement plans and IRAs.

The 1994–1996 Advisory Council on Social Security suggested the following proposals that would reduce—but not eliminate—the projected deficit:

➤ **Increasing the working period over which a retiree's benefits are computed from 35 to 38 years.** Adding three years to the wage history that is taken into account when formulating a retiree's benefits would include a worker's earlier, lower-paid employment years, thereby reducing benefits. This change would close about 12 percent of the projected gap.

➤ **Changing the way in which Social Security benefits are taxed so that any benefits a retiree receives beyond what he or she contributed to the system as a worker would be taxed as ordinary income.** Other retirement plans, such as some individual retirement accounts (IRAs), already are taxed in this manner. Currently, only beneficiaries with incomes above certain annual thresholds owe taxes on their benefits, and just a portion of their benefits is subject to the tax. This change would close about 14 percent of the projected gap.

➤ **Extending Social Security coverage and participation to 3.7 million state and local government employees who are currently excluded from the program.** Subjecting government workers to Social Security payroll taxes would bring more revenues into the system. This change would shrink the estimated shortfall by about ten percent.

➤ **Accelerating the scheduled increase in the retirement age so that it becomes 67 by 2011; the retirement age would be indexed to longevity thereafter.** Advocates of raising the retirement age for Social Security point to the fact that Americans are living longer than before. Indexing it to longevity would reduce how much the system pays out and improve the long-term financial picture for Social Security. This change would eliminate about 22 percent of the gap.

➤ **Adjusting the Consumer Price Index (CPI).** The Bureau of Labor Statistics, which is studying possible adjustments to the CPI, announced in 1996 that it is putting in place measures that are expected to decrease the CPI by 0.21 percent per year; this change will take care of an estimated 14 percent of the gap. There is substantial controversy among economists about whether the index, even after the change, would continue to overstate inflation.

These incremental changes would eliminate more than 70 percent of the projected long-term shortfall.

A variety of reforms have been suggested to deal with the remainder: investing the Social Security Trust Funds in the stock market and privatizing Social Security. The last of these ideas would entail switching from a system of social insurance, in which everyone is guaranteed an inflation-proof benefit for his or her retirement, to a system of individual retirement accounts resembling 401(k)s, in which individuals' benefits would no longer be guaranteed by the government.

A Recipe for Disaster?

One proposed reform is to invest some of the Social Security Trust Funds in the stock market to prevent future shortfalls. Under current law, the Trustees of the Social Security Trust Funds may invest the surplus that the fund accumulates only in U.S. government securities, the debt the government issues to finance its borrowing.

Because these securities are the safest investments available, they pay a relatively low rate of interest. Under one proposed plan, part of the Trust Funds would be invested in stocks through an unmanaged index fund holding a diversified portfolio of shares. (More than half of the Trust Funds would remain in Treasury securities.)

What happens next? An independent investment board nominated by the President and approved by the Senate would oversee the investments and would be allowed to invest the Trust Funds' money. Because stocks have generated higher investment returns in the past than treasuries, diversifying might leave the Trust Funds with greater assets over time.

Of course, with any situation, there are advantages and disadvantages. First, this proposal preserves the current system of benefits, leaving the safety net unchanged. The system would remain progressive, with lower-income seniors receiving a higher proportion of their past earnings than upper-income retirees. And, if stock market returns continue to match past performance, it could leave the system healthier.

But having the monies in the Social Security Fund invested in stocks can also be a disadvantage. Stock markets are risky—remember Chapter 7? Investing the Trust Funds in stocks implies taking a bet that returns will be high enough to make up the short-fall. If returns are not high enough, or the stock market falls, future generations will be left facing the bill because the value of the money invested will go down with no money left in the Fund to pay Social Security recipients.

Furthermore, all this plan does is change the form in which Trust Funds investments are held. It does not increase national saving or otherwise change the system in a way that might encourage future economic growth. And then enters Uncle Sam as a major stockholder in many American companies. Though reformers advocate an independent investment board, the threat of political interference in corporate governance has raised concern. Can you say *un-deregulation*?

No matter if any of these privatization plans pass, most of them would entail significant tax increases or newly generated borrowing to maintain current benefits for workers who will be retiring in the next 10 to 20 years. If you're in your 50s, you already know that you have relatively little time remaining before your retirement. The younger generation may have to cough up and pay taxes for both current retirees' benefits and for their own future benefits. That's why getting started as early as possible to save for your own retirement through company-sponsored retirement programs or funding your own Individual Retirement Account is an integral part—if not the only part, some day—to making money in the new millennium for your retirement.

You know, you could always go back to work.

Would You Like Fries with That?

You've retired from the conundrums of corporate life and working again is the furthest thing from your mind. But then again, you might have to. Or maybe you just want to.

Either way, the financial impact of returning to work after you retire depends on when you do it. If you're younger than 62 years of age, your job will increase the ultimate benefit you will receive when you opt for your Social Security payments because the Social Security Trust Fund calculations use the best 35 of the 40 highest years' earnings.

If you're 70 years or older, you don't have a thing to worry about. Younger retirees, though, may see a reduction in their Social Security checks, depending on how much they earn in wages during the year.

From ages 62 to 64, if you receive a Social Security check, you must forfeit one dollar of that check for every two dollars you earn above a certain maximum earnings limit. The limit moves upward each year with inflation. In 1999, the limit was $9,600. If you're age 65 to 69, you could have earned up to $15,500 in 1999 without penalty. Above that amount, though, youu would have forfeited one dollar for every three dollars of the excess. Over age 70, you basically have no worries in these circumstances.

Working after retirement has its good points and its bad points—just make sure you evaluate both scenarios!

A Few Last Minute Secrets

Whether Social Security is here or not, don't consider benefits to be your only means of paying for your living expenses. Studies indicate that average-wage earners can expect Social Security benefits to replace 42 percent of their income—and those are today's figures. What about tomorrow?

As you work and pay FICA taxes, you earn Social Security credits. The number of credits needed for retirement benefits depends on your date of birth. If you were born January 2, 1929 or later, you need a total of 40 credits. In 1999, workers earn one credit for each $740 in wages, or four credits for earnings of more than $2,960. Extra credits, however, do not increase your benefits.

To learn the secrets of the Social Security system—and to make the most of your benefits—be informed, but don't let Social Security be the end to your means. The following are a few tips to help you get the most out of your Social Security benefits when the time comes:

> ➤ **Find out what your Social Security benefits are now**. Call the Social Security Administration's toll-free line (800-772-1213) and ask for a *Request for Earnings and Benefit Estimate Statement* (REBES). The SSA will send you a form asking you how much you earned last year, your estimated earnings for this year, the age you plan to retire, and your estimated future annual earnings.
>
> Based on this information, you'll get a complete earnings history, along with estimates of your benefits for retirement at age 62, 65, or 70. It includes estimates of disability or survivor's benefits and lists total Social Security taxes you have already paid.

➤ **Verify your Social Security records every three years.** Make sure all the taxes you have paid are credited to your account. Errors identified early are easier to correct. If you happen to run across an error, have your past tax returns and pay stubs available for proof.

➤ **Consider delaying your retirement.** You can increase your benefits if you do so. Currently, age 65 is considered to be full-retirement age for receiving full benefits. Benefits are reduced if you retire sooner and collect them; they are increased if you delay retirement. You can start collecting benefits at age 62, but it does pay off to retire later.

The Least You Need to Know

➤ Social Security is a contributory social insurance program that provides benefits to millions of Americans. Workers contribute financially to the system during their careers and earn entitlement to family benefits upon retirement, disability, or death. Currently, nearly 44 million Americans receive benefits under the Old-Age and Survivors Insurance and Disability Insurance (OASDI).

➤ The *benefit-to-contribution ratio* is the amount of money that has been paid into the Social Security system compared with the amount of money collected in benefits. Forecasters use this data to determine if the Social Security Fund will run out of money.

➤ To stay on top of how much you have paid into the system, verify your Social Security records every three years. Make sure all the taxes you have paid are credited to your account.

➤ Call the Social Security Administration at 800-772-1213 and ask for Form SSA-7004-PC, *Request for Earnings and Benefits Estimate Statement.* When you get it in the mail, fill it out and return it. In about 4 weeks, you will have your PEBES for review.

Chapter 13

The Lowdown on Your Retirement Plan

In This Chapter

➤ Calculating how much you need for retirement

➤ Determining whether your 401(k) plan makes the grade

➤ Learning about the retirement products available to you

If you had the chance to retire early, would you?

In the late 1960s, the notion of leaving a 30-year career before age 65 was practically unheard of. But workers are retiring younger, with the average retirement age in the United States at 62.2 for men and 62.7 for women, according to the U.S. Labor Department. That is down from 64.1 for men and 65.3 for women between 1965 and 1970.

The enigma is that while you may desire to retire early, life expectancies are increasing dramatically as people take better care of themselves through exercise, vitamins, and other proactive health-related programs. As a result, what was thought to be a 20-year retirement is now looking like a 40-year retirement.

Hey, it's an equation with variables that work for us, especially after slaving for the first 40 years in school and at a corporate desk. We say: Why not enjoy our golden years surrounded by tropical breezes, filled with foreign travel itineraries, and loaded with grandchildren?

It's doable, but only if you get the variables to the equation right. That means implementing and constantly reviewing your retirement investment plans. Today, questions such as the following beg answers to help you live as well, if not better, during your retirement:

➤ How much will it cost?

➤ Will you have enough to retire on?

➤ How much should you have taken out of each paycheck?

Forty years of retirement is a long time. This chapter will help you get answers to the questions you're asking about retirement now, enable you to learn about the retirement products you have available to you, and provide important elements you should remember as you create your plan.

Take This Job and...

Of course you like your job. Maybe it's the fact that you're 100 percent vested in your company's employee stock option plan or maybe it's all that paperclip art you've been making the past ten years that graces your credenza.

Company loyalty aside, it's time to start thinking about not being there. We don't mean getting a new job or starting your own business, although you can learn how to do both later in this book; rather, what you would do when you retire. You don't have to go fishing, play shuffleboard, or take up golf, although those are favorite past-times of retirees. You can volunteer to teach English as a second language to foreign elementary students here in the States, write that novel you always said you would, or even take up skydiving.

The idea is to enjoy your retirement exactly as you imagine it now. The best way to do so is to get answers to the following questions *today*.

If you were to retire today:

1. What would you do?

2. Where would you live?

3. Do you have enough money to live on?

Funny. The answers to questions number 1 and 2 all depend on how you answer number 3. Eeek! Does that mean its back to your faux leather office chair and fluorescent overhead lighting in the cubicle farm with Dilbert as your neighbor until you drop?

Nope. But it is time to figure out how much your retirement will cost. Use the following table to determine what your expenses will be after you retire.

Table 13.1   Calculating Your Monthly Expenses in Retirement

Costs That May Decrease At Retirement	Current Living Expenses	Estimated Expenses for Retirement
1. Housing (mortgage, rent, homeowner's insurance, property taxes)	_____	_____
2. Life insurance	_____	_____
3. Transportation	_____	_____
4. Clothing and personal care	_____	_____
5. Taxes	_____	_____
6. Business and entertainment	_____	_____
7. Miscellaneous expenses	_____	_____
8. Loan repayments and interest	_____	_____
9. Education	_____	_____

Costs That May Increase During Retirement	Current Living Expenses	Estimated Expenses at Retirement
10. Medical	_____	_____
11. Food	_____	_____
12. Recreation and entertainment	_____	_____
13. Auto insurance	_____	_____
14. Other	_____	_____
15. TOTAL MONTHLY EXPENSES: (add lines 1–14)	_____	_____
16. ANNUAL COSTS AT RETIREMENT* (12 times MONTHLY EXPENSES ON LINE 15)	_____	_____

Does not adjust for inflation.

You should also keep in mind what inflation does to your dollar's purchasing power. Like the Atlantic Coast shoreline, it slowly erodes the value of your money each year. Sure, your current $55,000 annual salary looks good now but will certainly have to be much larger to buy the same things in the future as it does today. The scary thought is not what's inflation going to be through the years until you retire but what is it going to be after you retire and beyond? As you learned in Chapter 9, the yardstick by which we measure our inflation rate is the Consumer Price Index.

Click Here

As for the future, however, you're going to have to determine what today's savings will be worth years from now. Go to **www.financecenter.com** and select the retirement calculator.

Once you determine how much your savings will be worth years from now, you'll be able to decide the starting portfolio you need at retirement to support you and your spouse for the rest of your lives.

During your retirement, you're going to need someplace to live—yes, even if you haul off in an RV and travel the back roads of America. (Have you seen the price of a campus cruiser lately?)

Most likely, your mortgage will be paid off so that all you have to worry about is property taxes. Maybe you'll even sell out and move into a smaller place in a sunnier climate—sure beats having to shovel snow at age 70. Don't worry, you know the kids will visit.

Above all, retirement planning entails far more than just picking an age to do so and beachfront property to do it upon. It requires a hard look at your lifestyle, resources, and a whole host of factors that we tend to take for granted while we're working.

Living in the Lapse of Poverty?

Many retirement experts say you will need 70 to 80 percent of your current income to maintain the same type of lifestyle after you retire. That means if you make $50,000 a year, you will need to earn at least $35,000 per year. This money most likely will come from a few income-producing investments you have made during the latter portion of your pre-retirement years. (We're disregarding Social Security at this point because of its bleak future.)

How are you going to get that $35,000 a year paycheck for 40 years? Why, that would mean you need $1.4 million dollars—and that's in today's dollars. Basically, you want a retirement income that equals your gross income today less all savings and all FICA taxes.

What about those expenses? You could sit down to a long, drawn-out process in which you look at your expenses and try to anticipate what they would be in retirement. Retirement may be a long way off, however, and you probably have no real idea of what those expenses will be then.

The solution? Don't laugh, but you're going to have to guess at your expenses and then determine what income you will need in retirement to live the way you want. Hmmm, sounds like a budget, doesn't it? What you will need is a way to determine what you need to do to get started.

Consider the following example as a primer. Let's say you have $50,000 saved for retirement, but that this savings earns no return now or after retirement. And now let's say you want an annual income of $35,000 in today's dollars after you retire, that you will retire in 30 years, and that you will live 30 years during your retirement. Based on these variables, you need to figure out how much you'll need in your golden years and how much you'll have to save each year between now and then.

Time to plug in the numbers. You need $35,000 a year for 30 years, which comes to $1.05 million needed in the first year of retirement. Because you already have $50,000, you're only $1 million short. Divide the shortage by the 30 years you have to save it, and you discover you have to save approximately $33,333 annually between now and the time you retire to hit your goal.

Uh, hello? Save almost $34,000 annually *now*? It seemed like such a simple equation that nets a difficult-to-achieve result—especially when you consider that some factors were omitted, such as the inflation rate. That was just for the sole purpose of understanding this example, however. Furthermore, the example assumed that you would earn no returns now or after retirement. In order to really get there from here, you must take an objective look at your desired income, plug in a few assumptions, and then perform detailed calculations.

You need to determine the following:

➤ How much income you want in today's dollars

➤ How much your lifetime average inflation rate will be

➤ How much you expect to earn on your investments on average each year—before and after you retire

➤ How much money you currently have in all your investment portfolios, including IRAs and 401(k) plans

➤ How much you'll receive in future Social Security benefits (as you learned in the preceding chapter)

➤ What date you will retire

Plugging the answers to the preceding questions into helpful software packages, such as Quicken Financial Planner, will enable you to conclude the annual savings required to enjoy the good life. Learning how to maximize those savings each year comes from the investment and simple wealth-building strategies you learned in Part Two.

Recall learning about assessing your risk tolerance and the reward of taking on that risk. It couldn't be more true than with the stock market. In exchange for that risk, however, there have been some pretty handsome rewards over the long haul. Take the S&P 500 index, for example, which is composed of 500 companies. In 1998, the S&P 500 returned more than 28 percent, and over the previous 100 years averaged almost ten percent per year. You won't have 100 years to save for retirement, but you do have an element working in your favor, especially if you invest in equities or equity mutual funds: long-term growth. You should shoot for the best growth investments that you can get.

The idea is to avoid overly conservative investing and opt for long-term growth with products such as equities. You can do this by monitoring the performance of the S&P 500 index, for example, and selecting a fund that comes closest to the S&P 500 average (as you learned in Chapter 8).

Ready to Retire (Not!)

Many Americans are not ready for retirement, according to a nationwide poll of 401(k) investors by *Money* magazine and Lincoln Financial Group—ready with their wallets that is, not with their mindset.

According to the December 1998 survey, participants in employer-sponsored 401(k) retirement savings plans have a fair knowledge of investing fundamentals but aren't taking the actions that will enable them to reach their goals.

In fact, the survey found that 82 percent of 401(k) investors said they understood most or all of their investment options. Seventy percent (and 72 percent of the self-described knowledgeable group) tended to pick funds based on past performances—an unreliable gauge of future returns—rather than on an understanding of how the portfolios work.

Approximately one-third of the respondents said they didn't know where to start, that the subject was too complicated, or that the topic was too frightening.

You don't have to go it alone, however. Many companies offer a retirement savings program, such as the 401(k) plan, that can help you invest for your retirement future.

Are you contributing? The *Money* magazine and Lincoln Financial Group poll revealed that 40 percent of 401(k) investors surveyed said they are contributing the maximum allowed in their 401(k) plans up to what their employers match. Why aren't they maxing out? At least 73 percent say they would contribute more if their companies made a larger match. Our rebuttal to this: Where else can you earn a specific and guaranteed fix percentage on your money? Take advantage of company plans to the maximum extent that you can. It will help you reach that financial goal you calculated in our earlier example. The following table shows you how much more money you can make in your 401(k) if you were to contribute the maximum 15 percent allowed above and beyond your employer's match.

Compare how much more money an employee in his early thirties can save if he contributes the maximum amount possible to his 401(k)—including an employer 6% match on his $30,000 annual salary—over a period of 25 years assuming an average annual rate of return of five percent.

Table 13.2 Save Now or Save Later

Number of years	Contributes $2,700/year	Contributes $7,500/year
1	2,835	7,875
2	5,812	16,144
3	8,937	24,826
4	12,219	33,942
5	15,665	43,514
6	19,283	53,565
7	23,083	64,118
8	27,072	75,199
9	31,260	86,834
10	35,658	99,051
11	40,276	111,878
12	45,125	125,347
13	50,216	139,490
14	55,562	154,339
15	61,175	169,931
16	67,069	186,303
17	73,257	203,493
18	79,755	221,543
19	86,578	240,495
20	93,742	260,394
21	101,264	281,289
22	109,162	303,229
23	117,455	326,265
24	126,163	350,453
25	135,306	375,851

Source: Employee Benefits Research Institute

We're here today to show you how to begin, how to untangle the complications and not be scared by this little three-digit number with the letter "k" in parentheses.

How Does Your 401(k) Plan Compare?

There are now more than 142,000 401(k) plans of all asset sizes nationwide, according to the Department of Labor. With 401(k) plans becoming the employer pension plan of choice, plan participants can now find out how their plan stacks up against the *average* 401(k) plan.

Click Here

If you would like to compare the features of your 401(k) plan to others across the nation, log onto **www.the401kwebsite.com** for details.

Most mid-sized and large employers have a retirement plan in place for their employees. Many have two, and some three or more. The plans come in a wide variety of flavors, some offering more features than others. All of these, though, can help you achieve your retirement desires if you fully understand them and integrate them into your planning.

In fact, according to the Ninth Annual Merrill Lynch Retirement and Financial Planning survey, defined contribution plans (for example, 401(k) plans) remain the most popular kind of retirement plan, with 44 percent of all employers offering them and 71 percent of large companies—those with 2,000 or more employees—sponsoring them. Many of these employers believe that if they didn't provide some type of matching program, employees would contribute less to retirement savings accounts.

Bet You Didn't Know

Six out of ten employees report that their employer provides them with financial education materials, a slight increase from 56 percent in 1996, according to the 9th Annual Merrill Lynch Retirement and Financial Planning Survey.

The 401(k)...Explained

It all goes back to that employee handbook you received on the day you were hired. Buried in those pages you will find a summary of the retirement plan(s) available to you. Those pages tell you what kind of plan you have, when you become eligible to participate, and the ultimate benefit you will receive.

The 401(k), named for the relevant section in the tax code, is a tax-deferred investment and savings plan that acts as a personal pension fund for employees. The plan lets you defer taxes on a portion of your salary until you retire. Taxes on investment gains are deferred until you withdraw money from the plan. You can begin withdrawing from a tax-deferred investment account without penalty at age 59$^1/_2$. Unlike pensions, which shift the burden of funding to the employer rather than the employee, 401(k) accounts are portable; that is, you can *rollover* the account, take it with you, and continue building it at your next employer with no penalty.

Because you can deduct a portion of your earnings—before taxes—and put the money into various investment options, the money that comes out of your paycheck is in pre-tax dollars and grows tax-deferred until you take it out at retirement. Also, you usually can make changes to how you allocate the percentage of money you contribute to each investment option every quarter. Some companies offer the chance to do so every month.

In fact, according to data in the 1996–1997 Standard Directory of 401(k) Plans, an average plan offers the participants six investment options, allows the participants to take out a loan against their account balance, provides daily valuation, and has an employer matching contribution. The most common employer match rate is 50 percent of the first six percent a participant elects to defer.

Bet You Didn't Know

According to the 1996–1997 Standard Directory of 401(k) Plans, the top five investment managers for 401(k) plans were: Fidelity Investments, The Vanguard Group, Cigna. T. Rowe Price, and Merrill Lynch. Each plan in the study had a minimum of $5 million dollars in total assets.

In terms of asset size, 401(k) plans far outweighs other types of defined contribution plans, such as profit-sharing, 403(b), SEPs (simplified employee plans), and stock ownership plans.

In recent years, employers have expanded the range of employee investment options, offering five investment types in nearly half of all plans. By comparison, only three investment types were offered in the early 90s. In fact, companies now appear to offer employees the option of more frequent investment selections, with 53 percent of large firms allowing their employees to change investment selections on a daily basis.

Click Here

Want to see how other 401(k) plans are doing? Log on to The Hewitt 401(k) Index, the first online barometer of daily 401(k) investment activity of employees at large U.S. companies, at **www.hewitt.com/401kindex**. This Web site tracks the daily transfer activity of 1.4 million employer plans with more than $62 billion in collective assets.

Many 401(k) plans offer a wide range of investment choices, the most common being money market funds, index-based stock funds, and actively managed growth funds. Typically, corporate bond funds, government securities funds, and balanced stock and bond funds are offered. Company stock, although offered, is the most infrequent type of investment option offered to plan participants, according to the Merrill Lynch Retirement and Financial Planning Survey of Employers.

The money you sock away in a 401(k)plan is in pre-tax dollars. Couple that with the market growth in the 90s and you could find you and your friendly 401(k) sitting on a slight windfall of money for your future.

Let's say you have saved $9,000 a year in a taxable investment account. Well, you have to pay taxes on the contribution first. Depending on your tax bracket, that means you really invest only about $6,000. If you put the $9,000 in a 401(k) plan, however, you get to invest all $9,000 and reap the earnings of that tax-free contribution until you withdraw the funds. Plus, when you factor in the matching contributions that some companies kick in, you have guaranteed returns for your investments—no matter what the stock market does. Check with your employee benefits or human resources department to see if your employer offers a matching program.

What You Should Look for in Your Company's Plan

Take out your 401(k) summary plan description and look for the following:

➤ When you may participate

➤ The types and perhaps the risks of the investment options within the plan

➤ How often you can switch among those options

➤ Whether early withdrawals for hardships or personal loans are permitted

➤ Which distribution options are available when you leave the company or retire

➤ How much your employer will contribute to the plan on your behalf

➤ When you will be vested in those contributions

As you now know, your contributions to a 401(k) plan help reduce your tax bill because they don't count against your taxable income for the year. Of far more importance, though, is an employer's contribution on your behalf—the *matching* we spoke of earlier.

With the common employer match rate at 50 percent of the first 6 percent you elect to defer, why not jump at the chance to earn a guaranteed, risk-free 50 percent return on your money?

Bet You Didn't Know

One of the most generous match rates, 200 percent up to the first 6 percent of compensation deferred by the participant, is given to employees of Pemco Financial Services in Seattle, Washington, according to the 1996–1997 Standard Directory of 401(k) Plans. Now that sounds like a match made in retirement heaven!

Advantages...

There are many advantages to saving in a 401(k) plan. Take a look:

➤ **Pre-tax investing.** Your 401(k) contribution is deducted before taxes are taken out. That helps in two ways. You are taxed on a smaller sum of money, so your initial tax hit is lower. If you elect to contribute 6 percent of your gross salary to your 401(k), you'll notice your take-home pay is reduced, but by far less than the 6 percent. In fact, if you earn $30,000 per year, are taxed at a rate of 28 percent, and contribute 6 percent to a 401(k), your tax hit is reduced by more than $500.

Pre-tax investing also increases your investing power. By putting up a chunk of your money before taxes, you will be investing a larger amount of money. That 6 percent of your $30,000 pre-tax annual income amounts to $1,800. But 6 percent of your post-tax income comes to less than $1,700. If you wanted to match that $1,800 through post-tax investing, you'd have to cut into your own take-home pay.

➤ **Tax-deferred growth on your investment.** You accumulate savings faster in a 401(k) plan since you don't pay taxes on any return you make. That's called *tax-deferred growth*. If you are 40 years away from retirement and begin contributing a fairly modest $2,000 a year to a 401(k), that money grows quickly. Say your investment options offer an annual return of 10 percent, and you contribute faithfully each year. At the end of 40 years, you will have contributed a total of $80,000, but your 401(k) account will be worth $973,684. Remember when we said you would need $1 million to retire in the example at the beginning of this chapter? That's because the growth on your investment each year has not been subject to tax.

...And Disadvantages

You should be aware of some things before investing in a 401(k) plan. First, your money is off limits until you turn 59$\frac{1}{2}$. Remember that this is a retirement investment. If you withdraw it before age 59$\frac{1}{2}$, you will face some stiff expenses. For starters, you will be taxed on all your investments and earnings. Furthermore, most plans impose a financial penalty for early withdrawals.

You also are responsible for deciding how to invest. There are added levels of risk and more complex investment issues to consider when you are making your investment plan. It's important to know what you're buying, and there's one way to find out: Ask your plan administrator to explain all the details and make sure to review all your paperwork.

Being Cautious Does Not Win Out

Despite the increase of investment options in 401(k) plans, the most frequent investment choice is a money market fund—a vehicle typically used as a safe haven during turbulent market conditions.

Big mistake!

Here's why. If the goal for investing in a 401(k) is long-term growth, why do most participants choose these overly cautious investments for the long haul? Chalk it up to getting the nervous nellies when dealing with nickels and dimes. Over the short term, Americans are optimistic about their financial future; there is deep-seated apprehension about long-term prospects, however.

Even armed with the belief that their retirements will be financially more difficult than their parents, the typical Baby Boomer fears outliving the money they have put away or plan to put away for retirement. A 1994 report by AARP, *Aging Baby Boomers: How Secure is their Economic Future?*, details that the aging of this demographic will take place during a period of substantial economic uncertainty. There is a major restructuring of the job market and indications that future worldwide economic growth may be substantially slower than in the past. These factors raise serious questions about the future economic security of Baby Boomers during the remainder of their working lives. Remember, by the year 2030, the 56 million surviving Boomers will be 66 to 84 years old and will form the largest elderly cohort in United States history.

Even still, with longer life spans and workers retiring earlier, it does not pay to be too conservative with your retirement strategy. With the large majority of 401(k) participants putting 60 percent or more of their contributions into bonds or money market funds, the wake up call on retirement day will require more than earplugs.

Yes, stocks are riskier, but over the long run they have far greater growth potential than money market funds. Even small stocks have outperformed large-company stocks over the years, and, depending on which time frame you look into, foreign markets beat U.S. markets in some periods—as they did in 1993. Unless you expect to retire in the next five to seven years, many money managers advise you put almost all your 401(k) money into stock funds.

The bottom line? Ideally, your 401(k) plan should have at least half a dozen investment options. Unfortunately, some employers still limit you to three or fewer—although that is changing. If your plan falls short, complain to your employee benefits department.

What Happens If I Have an Emergency?

You must leave your contributions in the plan (or roll it over into an IRA if you leave the company, or take it with you to a new employer's plan) until age 59^1/$_2$. You can withdraw money under certain hardship cases, such as purchasing a home, emergency medical expenses, or college tuition.

What constitutes a hardship? The withdrawal must be made on account of the participant's (that's you) immediate and heavy financial need, and the withdrawal must be necessary to satisfy such need. Check with your employer to find out exactly what your company's plan allows.

Off to a New Watercooler

What happens if you leave your job and want to take your money with you? If you are one of the millions of people who will leave their jobs this year, either due to a career move, a layoff, or retirement, you must decide what to do with your 401(k) monies.

You do have several options: You can keep the money invested in your former employer's plan, transfer it to a new employer's plan, roll it over into an Individual Retirement Account, or take a lump sum distribution.

Unfortunately, many people are unaware of their options, as well as the tax consequences involved with each. In 1996, for example, only 40 percent of job changers rolled over their retirement distribution into an IRA or other qualified retirement plan, according to the Employee Benefits Research Institute. The rest took their distribution in cash.

That can be a costly strategy. Lump sum distributions are subject to a 20 percent withholding for prepayment of any federal taxes owed, and additional federal taxes may be due depending on your tax bracket. If you are younger than age 59^1/$_2$, you may also owe an additional ten percent tax penalty for early withdrawal of your retirement savings.

Because every company's policy is different, it is important to ask the following questions *before* you leave your job:

➤ **Should I stay with my current employer's 401(k) plan?** While you can avoid taxes and penalties by doing this, it may limit your investment and distribution options. Does the plan meet all your needs? Are you satisfied with the investment choices you have for your money? Be aware that some plans pose certain restrictions if you are no longer an employee.

➤ **How much money do I have invested?** If you have at least $5,000 invested in a workplace savings plan, the company must let you leave the money in the plan if that's what you want to do. Even if you have less than that amount in your company plan, your company may allow you to leave it there.

➤ **When can I get access to my money?** The company may give you between 60 days and up to one year after you leave to reinvest the money. If you choose not to reinvest, you may have to wait until you are 65 years old to get access to your retirement money. Other companies let you obtain your distribution at any time once you terminate employment. Check with your 401(k) plan administrator.

➤ **Should I move my assets to a new employer's plan?** This strategy avoids having to pay current taxes and penalties. However, because some companies require you to work for a certain length of time before you can participate in their plan, you may need to leave your assets in your former employer's plan or transfer the eligible assets temporarily to a rollover IRA.

A Quick Word About Fees

When you contribute to a 401(k) plan, your account balance will determine the amount of retirement income you will receive from the plan. While contributions to your account and the earnings on your investments will increase your retirement income, fees and expenses paid by your plan may substantially reduce the growth in your account. The following example demonstrates how fees and expenses can impact your account.

Assume that you are an employee with 35 years until retirement and have a current 401(k) account balance of $25,000. If the returns on investments in your account over the next 35 years average 7 percent, and the fees and expenses reduce your average returns by 0.5 percent, your account balance will grow to $227,000 at retirement even if there are no further contributions to your account. If the fees and expenses are 1.5 percent, however, your account balance will grow to only $163,000. The 1 percent difference in fees and expenses reduces your account balance at retirement by 28 percent.

In recent years, there has been a dramatic increase in the number of investment options typically offered under 401(k) plans as well as the level and types of services provided to participants.

These changes give today's employees who direct their 401(k) investments greater opportunity than ever before to affect their retirement savings. As a participant, you may welcome the variety of investment alternatives and the additional services, but you may not be aware of their cost. The cumulative effect of the fees and expenses on your retirement savings can be substantial.

You should be aware that your employer also has a specific obligation to consider the fees and expenses paid by your plan. There are laws that require employers to follow certain rules in managing 401(k) plans. An employer must:

➤ Establish a process for selecting investment alternatives and service providers

➤ Ensure that fees paid to service providers and other expenses of the plan are reasonable in light of the level and quality of services provided

➤ Select adequately diversified investment alternatives

➤ Monitor investment alternatives and service providers to see that they continue to be appropriate choices

To know how fees affect your retirement savings, you need to know about the different types of fees and expenses and how each are charged. Generally, fees and expenses in 401(k) plans fall into the following three categories:

➤ **Plan administration fees.** These are the day-to-day operational fees of a plan for basic administrative services, such as plan recordkeeping, accounting, legal, and trustee services—basically, what is necessary for administering the plan as a whole. Plus, today there are plans that offer a host of additional services, such as telephone voice response systems, access to customer service representatives, educational seminars, retirement planning software, investment advice, electronic access to plan information, daily valuation, and online transactions.

➤ **Investment fees.** By far the largest component of 401(k) plan fees and expenses is associated with managing plan investments. Generally, fees for investment management and other investment-related services are assessed as a percentage of assets invested. You should pay attention to these fees! You pay for them in the form of an indirect charge against your account, because they are deducted directly from your investment returns. Your net total return is your return after these fees have been deducted.

➤ **Individual service fees.** In addition to the overall administrative expenses, there may be individual service fees associated with optional features offered under a 401(k) plan. Individual service fees are charged separately to the accounts of individuals who choose to take advantage of a particular plan feature. For example, individual service fees may be charged to you for taking a loan from the plan or for executing participant investment directions.

169

If you have questions about the fees and expenses charged to your 401(k) plan, contact your plan administrator. Your plan administrator should be able to give you information on the following:

➤ If your plan permits you to direct the investment of assets in your account, the plan administrator should provide you with copies of documents describing investment management and other fees associated with each of the investment alternatives available to you (for example, a prospectus).

➤ The plan administrator should also provide a description of any transaction fees and expenses that will be charged against your account balance in connection with the investments that you direct.

➤ Your account statement will show the total assets in your account, how they are invested, and any increases (or decreases) in your investments during the period covered by the statement. It may also show administrative expenses charged to your account. Account statements are provided once a year upon request, unless your plan document provides otherwise.

➤ Your 401(k) plan's summary plan description (SPD) tells you what the plan provides and how it operates. It may tell you if administrative expenses are paid by your plan rather than by your employer, and how those expenses are allocated among plan participants. A copy of the SPD is furnished to you when you join a plan, every 5 years if there are material modifications, or every 10 years if there are no modifications.

➤ The plan's annual report contains information regarding the plan's assets, liabilities, income, and expenses, and shows the aggregate administrative fees and other expenses paid by the plan. However, it does not show expenses deducted from investment results or fees and expenses paid by your individual account. Fees paid by your employer also are not shown. You may examine the annual report (for free) or request a copy from the plan administrator (for which there may be a charge).

And Then There's the IRA

Up to this point, we've mostly discussed the 401(k). That's not a green light, however, to overlook another type of retirement account available to you should you not have the option to contribute to a 401(k): the Individual Retirement Account (IRA).

An IRA is available for you to make an annual contribution of $2,000 or 100 percent of earned income that year, whichever is less, up until the year you reach age $70^{1}/_{2}$. In other words, your contributions must come from a salary, wages, or self-employment income. Even alimony counts.

So what will an investment in an IRA look like over time? Check out Table 13.3 to see how advantageous tax-deferred investing can be.

What an investment in an IRA looks like over specific number of years.

Table 13.3   What Contributing $2,000 a Year into an IRA Could Yield

Annual Rate	5 years	10 years	15 years	20 years	25 years
1%	$10,304.00	$21,134.00	$32,516.00	$44,478.00	$57,050.00
2%	$10,616.00	$22,337.00	$35,279.00	$49,567.00	$65,342.00
3%	$10,937.00	$23,616.00	$38,314.00	$55,353.00	$75,106.00
4%	$11,266.00	$24,973.00	$41,649.00	$61,938.00	$86,623.00
5%	$11,604.00	$26,414.00	$45,315.00	$69,439.00	$100,227.00
6%	$11,951.00	$27,943.00	$49,345.00	$77,985.00	$116,313.00
7%	$12,307.00	$29,567.00	$53,776.00	$87,730.00	$135,353.00
8%	$12,672.00	$31,291.00	$58,649.00	$98,846.00	$157,909.00
9%	$13,047.00	$33,121.00	$64,007.00	$111,529.00	$184,648.00
10%	$13,431.00	$35,062.00	$69,899.00	$126,005.00	$216,364.00
11%	$13,826.00	$37,123.00	$76,380.00	$142,530.00	$253,998.00
12%	$14,230.00	$39,309.00	$83,507.00	$161,397.00	$298,668.00
13%	$14,645.00	$41,629.00	$91,343.00	$182,940.00	$351,700.00
14%	$15,071.00	$44,089.00	$99,961.00	$207,537.00	$414,665.00
15%	$15,508.00	$46,699.00	$109,435.00	$235,620.00	$489,424.00
16%	$15,955.00	$49,466.00	$119,850.00	$267,681.00	$578,177.00
17%	$16,414.00	$52,400.00	$131,298.00	$304,277.00	$683,525.00
18%	$16,884.00	$55,510.00	$143,878.00	$346,042.00	$808,544.00
19%	$17,366.00	$58,807.00	$157,700.00	$393,695.00	$956,861.00
20%	$17,860.00	$62,301.00	$172,884.00	$448,051.00	$1,132,755.00

What if you're a non-working spouse? If you are part of a couple with one spouse working and the other not working, the working spouse may contribute an extra $250 (for a total of $2,250). The contributions must go into separate accounts, however: one bearing the name of the working spouse and one bearing the name of the non-working spouse. The account held by the non-working spouse is called a *spousal IRA*. Spouses who work part time and have no company benefits can open their own IRAs. The same rules apply.

IRAs cause a lot of confusion. Many people ask, "Should I invest my money in a mutual fund or in an IRA?" The truth is that you should invest your money in a mutual fund *inside* an IRA. An IRA is an account that shelters your contributions from current income taxes. The contribution you make should be made by your tax-filing due date.

Bet You Didn't Know

An IRA is precluded from investing in collectibles, which are defined as any work of art, rug or antique, metal or gem, stamp, alcoholic beverage, musical instrument, historical objects, and most coins. Certain gold and silver coins and bullion are exempt per the Taxpayer Relief Act of 1997.

And then there's the Roth IRA. The Taxpayer Relief Act of 1997 provides a unique opportunity to those of us who have reached the maximum contribution we want to make to our employer plans. A Roth IRA enables you to make a non-tax deductible deposit of up to $2,000 per year, allow the earnings to accumulate tax-free through the years, and ultimately withdraw all of the proceeds tax-free. This is an excellent vehicle for monies to be invested outside of an employer-provided plan.

Click Here

For more information about the Roth IRA, go to **www.RothIRA.com** where you can find links and calculators to help you determine if a Roth IRA is for you.

What Can You Do If You're Self-Employed?

You can create your own retirement savings program! Plus, you can contribute much more than the $2,000 IRA maximum. There are *Keogh plans*, which fall under two types: *defined benefit* and *defined contribution* plans. The choice is yours, but make sure you review the paperwork about requirements, especially if you have employees, in which case you *must* include contributions for them as well.

There's a lot of legal mumbo-jumbo in the paperwork when you set up a Keogh plan, but most mutual fund companies and brokerage firms (full-service, discount, and deep-discount) just need you to fill out the basic paperwork. A Keogh plan must be set up by the end of the year, and contributions must be made by the tax-filing due date.

As a self-employed individual, you also can open a Simplified Employee Pension IRA (SEP-IRA). A SEP-IRA is easier to understand and administer successfully than a Keogh. Sometimes dubbed an "easy-to-manage retirement plan for individuals," an SEP-IRA can be opened and contributions can be made up until the last day of your tax filing deadline, including extensions. You can contribute up to the lesser of the following: 15 percent of your compensation or $30,000.

401(k) Versus IRA

The name of the game is tax-deferred growth, and both contenders—the 401(k) and IRA—offer both. Is one better than the other?

It depends on your tax situation. However, there are several benefits to investing in a 401(k). Even with the new tax laws, you can still contribute more tax-free dollars to your 401(k)—up to $9,240 a year, depending on your salary. Also, many employers will contribute (match) to your 401(k) plan, which is free money to you. Having an employer pay 20 cents on the dollar is like earning a 20 percent *guaranteed* return. Where can you get that these days?

Other benefits of a 401(k) versus an IRA include the following:

➤ Investing in a 401(k) is done with pre-tax dollars; with an IRA, your contributions are with after-tax earnings.

➤ You can borrow money from your 401(k). There are rules you must follow, however, as you've learned in this chapter.

➤ You can invest in a variety of products, such as a stock fund, an index fund, a money market fund, a bond fund, and even company stock.

It takes time—and a little bit of discipline—to plan for your retirement. By understanding what types of products are available to you and implementing investment strategies that meet your objectives, you can save enough money to live and enjoy your retirement.

The Least You Need to Know

➤ Many retirement experts say you will need 70 to 80 percent of your current income to maintain the same type of lifestyle after you retire. That means if you make $50,000 a year, you will need to earn at least $35,000 per year.

➤ A 401(k) plan is a retirement program sponsored by an employer that enables employees to invest for their future. Many employers match employee contributions, typically fifty cents for every dollar contributed up to a certain percentage.

➤ An IRA is an individual retirement account that you can contribute up to $2,000 of earnings per year and invest in a variety of products, such as stocks, bonds and mutual funds.

➤ An IRA is precluded from investing in collectibles, which are defined as any work of art, rug or antique, metal or gem, stamp, alcoholic beverage, musical instrument, historical objects, and most coins.

Chapter 14

How Real Estate May Play a Role in Your Future

In This Chapter

➤ Boomers, busters and millennium kids

➤ Minimizing investment risk

➤ What's in a loan

➤ The virtual house hunt

➤ Emerging markets

Baby boomers will want vacation homes; baby busters will want first time homes; and the millennium kids will be looking for apartments and townhouses. One thing you can count on in real estate in the next century is location, location, location—mainly, that people will be moving to new ones.

Like all other sectors of business, the real estate industry doesn't know what will really happen in 2000 and beyond, but they're speculating all over the place. The forecast is a steady demand for housing and growing home sales. What did you expect them to say? Stay home? But really, the population is shifting and so are their needs. Demographic changes will keep the real estate market hopping for a few years to come.

Not only that, but home buying will be easier and faster thanks to new technologies. With the Internet at your fingertips, you can educate your realtor about what you want and need, instead of the other way around. You can shop for bids on your mortgage interest rate, online. You can even arrange for a loan, online, and probably get it, thanks to more flexible lending rules.

Will it be a smooth transition into the next century? Probably not. Experts are calling for a cyclical decline in housing, although it should remain steady, and a slight decrease in construction. Economic cycles will always dictate short-term activity. A few years into the millennium, however, and the population transformation will cause niche markets to bloom.

Can you, an average American citizen, make money in real estate? Yes, and it's one of the easiest, least painful ways we know to make money. Even though stocks have outperformed home equity in recent years for providing household riches, home ownership remains the cornerstone of financial security for most Americans. Although not without risk, it has many advantages as a vehicle for creating wealth.

The Economy Has Been Very, Very Good to Me

For eight strong years, the U.S. economy grew and thrived. The 90s brought us an unusually long and stable period of economic expansion. The last time there was such sustained growth in housing sales was in the late 60s. But that boom was cut short in 1972 when growth surged and inflation soared.

Inflation and growth have remained incredibly stable, however. At no time in 50 years has there been such non-inflationary growth for so long. Not surprisingly, the housing market thrived. Existing home sales in 1997 set new records, and new home sales hit 19-year highs.

What other factors fueled the 90s housing boom?

➤ **Consumer confidence.** When the economy is strong, employment rises. If you feel secure in your job, or job prospects, you'll be more confident about the future and your ability to pay the price of owning your own home. The 90s saw huge gains in employment.

➤ **Lower interest rates.** Lower interest rates also encourage people to buy homes. Mortgage interest rates reached near 30-year lows, hovering near 7 percent for much of 1998. Economists expect the rate to stay between 6.5 and 7 percent well into the next century.

➤ **Flexible financing options.** Even an economic downturn can be tempered by changes in mortgage lending. Market and regulatory forces pressured financial institutions to make home buying more accessible to everyone. So, they changed their underwriting standards for more flexible lending. And several new products made it easier for the cash-strapped to qualify for a mortgage.

But then home sales started to slow toward the end of 1998. Asian markets began to falter, causing a worldwide ripple of fear that shook the stock market. The Federal Reserve dropped the central bank's interest rate three times in three months to improve market stability and to help businesses get credit. Economists began muttering the "R" word—recession.

Bet You Didn't Know

Between 1994 and 1997, the number of homeowners climbed by 4 million. This raised the national home ownership rate to an all-time high of 65 percent.

Reasons to Invest in Real Estate

Anyone involved in the stock market joined millions of other investors in the roller-coaster ride of a lifetime. Deep dips and rapid gains left the most stalwart investor reeling. On top of the news of failing Asian markets and fluctuations in world economies came the sobering secrets of the Millennium bug. Although the market had created massive wealth for many, there began a move toward less risky investments—a so-called "flight to safety."

Only about 40 percent of the American population own stocks. Over 70 percent have purchased homes. Why? Because there are so many financial advantages. Similar to playing the market, buying real estate is not without risk. However, there are several simple factors to consider when purchasing a home that help you make money.

Bet You Didn't Know

The rising cost of rent can make it cheaper to buy a house than stay in an apartment. Apartment dwellers nationwide paid 4 percent more in rent in the last quarter of 1998 than they did in 1997. The average national monthly rent was $811.

Advantages of Home Ownership

If you own a home already, you know the advantages. You may even be considering buying more property for investments. (We'll get into that a little later on.) Not only is your new investment your castle, which you can paint, polish, and decorate the way you like, you get tax benefits. For those of you still renting, it's time to wise up and start paying yourself, not someone else.

The following are some of the things independent home ownership can buy:

➤ **Equity.** When you make mortgage payments, you're paying for principal and interest. The principal is going toward the final cost of your home. It's called *building equity*. Pay rent, and you're building equity for your landlord.

➤ **Deductible interest.** Interest is the way your lender makes money. You pay them to borrow cash. But more importantly, interest is also how you lower your taxable income. Mortgage interest payments on first and second homes can be deducted from gross income. Property or real estate taxes (those levied by state and local government to pay for public services) are also deductible. Certain loan fees, points, and pre-payment penalties can all be deducted from your gross income.

➤ **Fixed mortgage rates.** Mortgage rates have hovered near a 30-year low in 1998. Guarantee a lock-in of low rates at today's property price, and you've insured against rising rents and property values.

Money Meaning

Leverage is the use of credit to enhance one's speculative capacity. If you make a down payment of 20 percent or less on your home, you still reap the 100 percent benefit of price appreciation when you sell.

Money Meaning

PITI is one way to describe your monthly house payments. You total the monthly principal, interest, taxes, and insurance.

➤ **Appreciation and leverage.** Hopefully, your property value will increase. The chances of that grow the longer you own the property and offset transaction fees. By leveraging your investment, staying a few years can bring a very decent return on investment.

➤ **Borrowing power.** You can borrow against your home equity for special needs like home improvements, medical emergencies, or education advances. The interest on these loans to yourself may also be tax deductible.

➤ **You have a nice place to live.** Where we live, it costs more to rent than it does to buy, when you figure out the monthly mortgage payment. That's not always the case though, so carefully weigh the transaction fees and monthly *PITI* with rents in your area. Don't forget to factor in the good feelings you get from being king or queen of your own castle and from being a member of a community.

➤ **Capital gains tax.** Sell your house and the profit you make gets favorable tax treatment, thanks to revised tax laws. Not so when you sell a boat, car, or shares of stock. But check the current tax laws; the amount of profit that can be deducted or the time you have to "roll-over" your gain into new property can change.

We're not saying to sell all your stocks and buy property. Far from it. Stocks and mutual funds should continue to hold an important place in your portfolio. Home ownership, however, will always be one the biggest investments of middle income Americans. It's also becoming easier to do—and do profitably.

Investing in Property

Some of the conditions that spurred record home sales are already showing signs of trouble. Well, it would be unrealistic to expect them to last forever. But the demographic trends alone in this country should keep realtors, buyers, and sellers very busy for the next decade or longer—not to mention investors.

The changing needs of three generations are at work in shifting the population. You can take advantage of these shifts by buying the kind of property that people will be looking for.

➤ **Baby boomers (born between 1946 and 1964).** The 45- to 65-year-olds are the fastest growing age group, and they want more house. They're looking at second homes for vacations, or larger, more luxurious homes. The senior market will also be growing as boomers age, and most prefer to own their own homes. They do want low maintenance, though. Good properties for seniors are well-appointed single story, single family homes near recreation and services.

➤ **Baby busters (born between 1965 and 1979).** Also known as Generation X, the children of the baby boomers are all grown up and starting their own nests. They'll be looking for three bedroom, single family homes with garage and minimal yard work. Also, multi-family housing and manufactured housing may get a lift in the new construction area to take care of this group's needs.

➤ **Millennium kids (born after 1979).** These kids will reach prime first-time home buying age in about ten years, and will be looking at single-person homes, apartments, condos, and townhouses. Vertically stacked "company-towns" and loft-like living spaces will become commonplace.

The buster and millennium groups may be smaller than the boomers, but the rise in the immigrant population will fill in the gaps in housing demands.

If you want a steady return on your investment, look at this: The price of a home has been increasing annually at the rate of inflation plus one or two percent. That's according to the National Association of Realtors, who has been tracking home prices since 1968. Okay, so your investments may not skyrocket overnight like some of your stocks may have done, but they don't drop so quickly into the abyss, either. Real estate trends tend to move a lot slower.

So, what does the average house cost? The median price of an existing single-family house in the second quarter of 1998 was $131,100, 6 percent above the year before. The median price of new homes during the second quarter of 1998 was $147,900.

By 2010, expect the median existing home price to range between $210,000 and $252,000. New home prices should be between $261,000 and $302,000 for the same time.

Click Here

Curl up and do a little reading first at **www.relibrary.com**, an educational resource site for beginners and professionals alike.

How Do You Get Started in Real Estate?

Go digital. Really. The Internet is the perfect place to start your research as a potential real estate investor. Even if you're just chewing on the idea of a first home, log on. Calculate how much house you can afford, then look online for what's selling in your area. You'll be joining thousands of others who do. Between 1995 and 1997, online house hunting increased ninefold. As more realtors set up Web sites and buyers get more Net savvy, online real estate sales could lead the way in e-commerce.

Before you boldly launch yourself into a cyber house hunt, let's take a look at some of the basics in real estate. We'll show you the online shortcuts as we go.

But I Have No Cash

No one expects you to pay for the property up front; very few people have that kind of cash hanging around. That's where financing and mortgages come in, and that beautiful concept of leveraging. A down payment of about 10 to 20 percent of the purchase price plus closing costs is all that's usually required by the bank. Several types of first-time home loans need less, and some people swear they make money in real estate with no money down. We're sure you've heard the claims.

Can it be done? Yes. Millions of people have bought real estate with no money down through the VA loan program. Can you make money? Yes, if you buy property that can produce a positive cash flow and/or can be sold at a profit. How much you put down is really a financing negotiating issue, not a factor in making money.

Today's robust housing market owes some of its vigor to innovations in mortgage financing. The financial institutions bowed to the pressure to make it easier for the cash-strapped and lower-income earners to buy a house. So, along with more flexible lending standards came some new products that everyone can enjoy.

Bet You Didn't Know

Wired? Why not make automatic electronic payments on your mortgage and shave interest rates by a quarter to a half percent. By keeping your loan and checking account at the same bank, your discount rate could save you hundreds of dollars on interest payments.

➤ **Flexible lending**

Lower down payments ease the burden of upfront cash to buy a home.

Ratios of mortgage maximum to income levels can be flexible. In other words, you can qualify for more loan with less income than before.

Sellers are allowed to contribute to often steep *closing costs*.

Borrowers can use timely rent and utility payments to establish a credit record.

➤ **New mortgage products**

Loan terms vary from 15 to 30 years, depending whether you need lower monthly payments or want better interest rates.

Adjustable Rate Mortgages provide a way to initially obtain a lower interest rate.

Adjustable Rate Mortgages (ARM) offer a lower initial interest rate that can fluctuate as interest rates rise and fall. The lower initial rate of an ARM makes it possible for many buyers to qualify, especially those who expect their incomes to increase. ARMs can be configured with a wide variety of initial adjustment periods, interest rates, and adjustment indexes.

Lenders have streamlined operations, reducing the time and cost of transactions and passing the savings on to us. This means it's easier to find a loan that suits your needs and switch it when the time comes to something more desirable. They've also set up digital offices.

Money Meaning

Closing costs are all costs incurred before the loan is closed, and can sometimes be wrapped up in the loan itself. Many are negotiable, including the appraisal fee, credit report, attorney fee, survey, termite inspection, and the bank loan origination fee and/or discount points.

Bet You Didn't Know

The interest rate on a 15-year mortgage is typically half a percent lower than on a 30-year mortgage. Because there are fewer years of interest payments, the overall interest paid is less. If you want to save money over the long term, pay it off in 15 years. In the short term, however, 30-year loans make monthly payments more affordable.

Bet You Didn't Know

Real property is often described as a *bundle of rights*: the right of possession, the right to control the property within the law, the right of enjoyment, the right of exclusion, and the right of disposition. The phrase came from old English law when common sellers and buyers couldn't read or write. They passed on a bundle of sticks cut from a tree on the property.

The following sections discuss the basic steps to buying a house.

How Much House Can You Afford?

Start here so that you don't waste time ogling properties out of your reach. You'll suffer less heartache with a realistic approach. Buy what you can handle; sell it later for a profit. This is also important if you're buying property to rent. If the rents in the area go for $850 a month and your payments are $800, great. You'll have a positive cash flow of $50 a month as well as having someone else building up your equity; that's the way to make money.

Here is a financing rule of thumb used by lending institutions: The monthly cost of buying and maintaining a home should not exceed 28 percent of gross (pretax) monthly income. For example, say your monthly gross income, combined with your spouse's, is $4,500. You can probably qualify for a monthly mortgage payment of $1,260.

$4,500 × 28 = $1,260

Of course, several other variables affect where that $1,260 will be spent. It's not all just principal. There is a price to pay for borrowing money, and it's called interest.

The higher the interest rate, the more you pay for the same amount of money borrowed than if the rates were low. Higher rates mean you can afford less house. The housing market tends to freeze up in times of high interest while buyers wait for them to drop. Lower rates means you can buy more house for your money. Of course, the housing prices will fluctuate with interest rates to compensate, because an increased demand for housing for any reason can make it a seller's market. Over the long run, however, you want a lower interest rate. Check the current rate with daily updates on sites like www.bankrate.com. Even slight adjustments by the Federal Reserve can impact the mortgage market.

Bet You Didn't Know

Lower interest rates caused many people to refinance their homes in the third quarter of 1998 when mortgage interest rates hit their low. Over 40 percent of conventional mortgage loan applications in 1998 were for refinances. Even the cost of refinancing is worth the price when you can shave a point or two off of a 15- or 30-year mortgage.

When buying something as valuable as a piece of property, you want to insure it. If you're borrowing money to buy it, the lender will insist on it. So, you must include the insurance premiums as well as the real estate taxes charged by your city into the monthly cost of owning a house. Taxes are often, but not always, included in the mortgage. Utilities and maintenance fees are not factored into your mortgage either, but you want to make sure you can meet these expenses after the PITI has been paid. Many communities have associations that require monthly or quarterly fees for upkeep of pools, gardens, and other amenities.

Relieve your math headaches by logging on to the many calculators available online. Intuit's quicken.com and Microsoft's homeadvisor.com are two good places to start. Or just do a search criteria of the words "mortgage" or "financing" and you can choose from many sites. Go one step beyond just knowing what you can afford. Get a pre-qualification letter instantly and free online. This means that a lender has reviewed your financial situation and is offering to loan you money. You don't have to accept the loan offer, but you'll have a good idea of what you can borrow. Having a pre-qualification letter also presents you as a strong buyer when you make an offer on a house. Both quicken.com and homeadvisor.com offer online pre-approval and pre-qualification.

Finding an Agent

Real estate agents have access to a very important news source: the Multiple Listing Service (MLS). The MLS is a database of houses listed by all cooperating agencies. You want immediate access to the newest listings, and here's where the agent can be very valuable to you. If they know what you're looking for and what you can afford, the agent can keep you informed on new properties.

The agent has access to many of the other people and papers that will be involved in your real estate transaction: the inspectors, warranty companies, and even local trades people. They also have knowledge of local laws, and have the contracts ready. If you're ready to make an offer on a house, the agent can provide the contract and the escrow to hold the earnest money that shows you're serious.

Of course, you have to choose your agent carefully. Make sure they know the area, are enthusiastic about what you want to do (buy the best house at the lowest price), and willing to help. An agent does receive a commission, on average 6 percent of the purchase price. It's almost always paid for by the seller. The commission is then split between the two agencies involved in the purchase. The agent also splits part of the commission with their house broker, so a good agent earns the money.

Always keep in mind that unless you specify otherwise, the agent represents the seller. They do not represent you unless you have a contract with them that says so. They do owe it to you as a customer, however, to deal fairly with you and follow all aspects of their license law.

Click Here

The Fair Housing Act prohibits an agent from discriminating against buyers or sellers in any way, including refusing to show, sell, or rent a house to someone on the basis of race, color, religion, sex, national origin, handicap, or family status. If you feel you've been treated unfairly, contact the Housing and Urban Development Office or file an online complaint at **www.hud.gov**.

Finding a Property

Now that you know what you can afford, you can narrow down the search, saving time and money. If you know that you want to buy an investment rental property in the upscale center of town in the $150,000 dollar range, you can plug in the facts and see what shows up. You can search the MLS by price as well as many other criteria.

Bet You Didn't Know

One New York City real estate broker said "Webheads" who buy after online research have spent about one month searching and looked at five different properties. Non-internet users take about four months and see more than 20 homes!

If you're not ready to talk to a realtor, try one of the online sites with limited versions of the Multiple Listing Service. Several offer homes by email services. Rather than repeating your search criteria, you can set up a search, enter an email address, and get electronic notices of new listings. For complete local listings, however, you have to contact a real estate agent. The following are some places to look online:

➤ **Cyberhomes.com.** This site offers interactive street level mapping and a homes by email service. While they claim to offer the entire MLS database in your area, they report that agents and brokers may choose not to post some listings.

➤ **Realtor.com.** More than one million homes nationwide contributed by 516 MLS's.

➤ **Homeseekers.com.** An updated list daily of more than 650,000 homes nationwide. Includes virtual tours.

➤ **Homeadvisors.com.** The Hometracker section has more than 500,000 listings.

If you buy an income property, advertise it! One of our friends had a vacation rental property in the Florida Keys that was losing money until he listed it online. Now it's booked solid!

Finding a Loan

The first thing you'll find out about home financing when you go to secure a loan is that there are hundreds of different loans and loan arrangements. You can ask your lender to design one that fits your needs. Two loan types that you'll hear a lot about are the VA and the FHA.

➤ **VA loans.** The U.S. Department of Veterans Affairs guaranties mortgage loans for veterans and service people. The loans usually have very favorable terms, such as: no downpayment, a loan maximum up to 100 percent of the value of the property, flexibility of negotiating interest rates with the lender, no monthly mortgage insurance premium, and limitations on the buyer's closing costs.

185

➤ **FHA loans.** The Federal Housing Authority (FHA) assists first-time home buyers and others who may have trouble with down payment requirements for conventional loans by providing mortgage insurance to private lenders. To get a FHA-insured loan, you have to apply to a HUD-approved lender.

Online or off, you'll still be dealing with traditional sources of real estate financing to find your loan.

➤ **Savings and Loan Associations.** Traditionally, these have the most flexible mortgage lending procedures, and are local. They also have limited participation in FHA-insured and VA-guaranteed loans.

➤ **Mutual Savings Banks.** These are primarily savings institutions mutually owned by the investors. They are highly active in the mortgage market, particularly for low-risk loans.

➤ **Commercial banks.** Commercial banks are an important source for conventional real estate financing as well as VA and FHA loans. If you have personal or business accounts with a commercial bank, check with them first; you may get preferential treatment.

➤ **Mortgage Banking Companies.** These companies get money to loan through insurance companies, pension funds, individual capital, and their own bank funds. They make the loans with the intention of selling them to other investors and receiving a fee for servicing the loan. They are the largest source of FHA, VA, and conventional loans.

Click Here

Priceline.com, the online service that lets you bid on airfares and automobiles, is getting into home financing. You name the rate and terms, and Priceline will find a lender willing to agree. Would-be borrowers make a $200 good-faith deposit when they make an offer, with the sum credited toward closing costs.

Mortgage brokers can arrange and compare loans from many different institutions for you. They are a great way to save time and money. But so is mortgage shopping online. Mortgage loans originating on the Internet are expected to make up 20 percent of all mortgage volume within the next five years. Lenders are trying to simplify the process so that loans can be approved in 30 minutes or less! Be aware, however, that all loan applications charge for a credit report before processing your request.

The following are some online loan finders:

➤ **eloan.com**. Claims to save consumers up to 75 percent on brokerage fees.

➤ **Homeadvisor.com**. Track rates, calculate a comfortable monthly payment for you and find the best loan online.

➤ **Quicken.com**. Offers a $225 rebate for online applications. The loan must close for the rebate to apply.

Market Cycles

There has been a steady flow of traffic out of the cities and into the suburbs since the beginning of 1990. Only the number of immigrants that continue to settle first in urban areas has slowed the exodus from the cities. But even they eventually move away from the urban core once they've lived here for awhile.

What does that mean for the future of the residential real estate market? As long as the economy stays strong, the housing market is strong. As we've mentioned, however, the recent changes in mortgage lending can ease an economic setback.

Act Locally

The long-term growth trends in the country are likely to continue in the South and West. For the past 20 years, these regions have expanded faster than the Northeast and Midwest. They've also juiced up the infrastructures and beefed up the labor supply, making them attractive climates for business. Whether people follow jobs, or business follows people, look to California, Texas, Florida, Washington, Arizona, Nevada, Colorado, Northern Carolina, and Georgia as leaders in housing production because of population growth.

Niche Markets

We've talked about the housing markets that the generational shift will highlight. There are other spin-offs of a changing demographic population, however, as follows:

➤ **Health care facilities**. Health care systems are looking for multi-use office centers for primary care physicians, specialists, research, and temporary services.

➤ **Assisted living facilities**. There is a large and growing need for residential communities that suit the personal desires of an aging population. The Census Bureau shows that only 3 percent of retirees leave their home state, so nationwide there are opportunities to build sites with easy access to recreation, public transportation, and health care.

➤ **Suburban office centers**. The flight from the cities and the rise of telecommuting as a viable business tool have increased the demand for satellite offices.

➤ **Apartments**. Apartments were ranked in the West as being very attractive for development in the coming years.

Worldwide Real Estate

Ready to reach out and think globally? We are becoming an interdependent world as the ease and speed of transferring money and information around the world increases. The next frontier in real estate will go beyond the U.S. borders. According to industry experts at Price Waterhouse Coopers, the following four trends target emerging market investors:

➤ **Globalization of real estate services.** With across-the-border expansion of real estate brokers, information, data reporting, and all other processes will become standardized.

➤ **Public ownership.** U.S. public real estate companies are expanding into emerging markets.

➤ **Increased real estate market information.** The Asian crisis has a good side; disclosure from the bad loans is resulting in an explosion of data never before available.

➤ **Technological advances.** Advances in imagery, from satellites to aerial photography, provide research analysis tools.

The Least You Need to Know

➤ Even an economic downturn shouldn't dampen the real estate market too much or for too long. As boomers age, busters form families, and Generation X grows up, the shifting needs of three generations will keep the housing market busy for the next decade.

➤ Investors looking for low risk can turn toward real estate. Most people leverage their property purchase with a small downpayment so that the investment gives a return greater than stock market appreciation. The stability of the real estate market and the tangible investment evidence also make it attractive.

➤ The Internet can cut both search time for properties and financing fees. Millennium buyers are much more computer savvy, and the entire real estate industry is remodeling the way it does business for the digital age—to the benefit of the consumer.

➤ Real estate opportunities exist at home and abroad. While growth should continue at home, worldwide real estate is the next frontier. In a world where technology allows information and currency to move at lightening speed, a global real estate community will continue to build.

Chapter 15

Regulating Internet Commerce—Who's in Charge?

In This Chapter

➤ The early adopters and winners

➤ Uncle Sam loves the Internet

➤ The domain game—and the winner is?

➤ Information warfare—do we need more intervention than we'd like?

Imagine a world of flourishing commerce where competition is fair, and privacy and property are protected. Sound Utopian? Maybe, but it's the goal of the U.S. government to establish such an environment—on the Internet!

Attempting to pave the way for seamless electronic commerce is a lofty endeavor, especially in a burgeoning frontier town like the Internet. The real estate is global and endless, and nobody's sure who owns it anyway. So, who's minding the Internet, and where's the posse when you need them?

Look first to the federal government, which funded and developed the early versions of the Internet for national security and research. But don't look there for long. Although it will continue to pay for research and development on this and other high-performance computing technologies, it is stepping down from its early role as keepers of the Net.

In some ways, it's a similar story to the early growth of the United States. The government handed out grants and subsidies to private industry to stimulate growth of the country's infrastructure. The nation's rail network was built on land grants, and the highway system came from combined federal and state dollars. Both the communications and power companies were virtual monopolies. They are all still encouraged and regulated by officials in Washington.

The digital revolution, however, is changing the roles of government and the private sector. Most of the moohla for building out the Internet, in terms of telecommunications and computing hardware and software, has come from the private sector. Internet growth has far outpaced anyone's imagination. For development to continue in this borderless world, it's going to take a whole new set of rules as you'll see in this chapter.

Who's the Boss?

During the 1970s, the Department of Defense developed a computer "network of networks," later known as the Internet. Protocols, or rules, that allowed the networks to intercommunicate became known as Internet protocols (IPs). Responsibility for coordinating who was on the network was handed around to different departments, but there was always one guy involved.

Bet You Didn't Know

Every Internet computer has a unique Internet Protocol (IP) number. Blocks of numerical addresses are distributed to regional IP registeries—ARIN to North America, RIPE to Europe, and APNIC to Asia/Pacific. Internet Service Providers apply for blocks of addresses from the IP registry and reassign them to smaller service providers and end users like you.

The First Pioneer

Dr. Jon Postel took over the maintenance of a list of host names and addresses for the Defense Department while a graduate student at the University of California. Affectionately dubbed the pioneer of the Internet, he gradually developed the list of rules for protocols that became known as the *Internet Assigned Numbers Authority* (IANA). He was basically the keeper of the address book, so to speak, and assigned names to newcomers. He remained a key figure in the architecture of today's Internet until his death in October 1998.

By 1992, a tiny firm called Network Solutions won a million dollar government contract to take over managing the list of a few thousand Internet addresses, or domain names, because it had done some other computer jobs for Uncle Sam. It posted losses for the first three years. By 1995, however, the Internet was invaded by users outside of academia, and the owner sold the company complete with government contract for $48 million.

Bet You Didn't Know

According to a 1998 report by Network Solutions, there were only 26,000 registered domain names in 1993. Just four years later, there were over 1.3 million!

The Domain Name Game

Then the Internet got *real* busy; more than 17 million users worldwide logged on. Network Solutions still posted losses but then was granted permission to charge for domain name registration by a cash-strapped government agency that could no longer justify spending taxpayer dollars for all the work. The company was growing way too commercial. Network Solutions finally posted earnings over 4 million dollars in 1997, the same year they registered the one millionth domain name. They went public and scored again big time. The domain name game was raking in some real money for the winners. And it was a monopoly.

By the time Network Solutions' contract ran out in September of 1998, Washington was abuzz with the future of the Net and its next potential guardian. From its origins as a U.S.-based research vehicle, the Internet had turned into an international medium for commerce, education, and communication. There were a lot of complaints from the Internet community, however, about the way the domain names and IP addresses were being administered.

➤ There was dissatisfaction about the absence of competition in domain name registration.

➤ Cyberpirates took advantage of the first come, first serve system of domain name distribution. Trademark holders lost out, or had to buy their names from the pirates at premium prices. (This is not to be confused with disputes between two parties with legitimate competing interests in a particular market.)

➤ Commercial interests wanted a more formal management structure for a place in which they were staking large future interests.

➤ Internet names suddenly had commercial value, especially the top level of the hierarchy

Money Meaning

Domain names are easy-to-remember names for Internet computers that map to IP numbers serving as routing addresses. Computers known as **Domain Name Servers** (DNS) translate Internet names into the numbers so that the information can be transmitted across the network.

of *domain names*, like those ending in .com. Decisions to add new top-level domains must be made by entities accountable to the Internet community.

➤ As the Internet became more commercial, it became less appropriate for the United States to direct and fund its functions.

Now comes Uncle Sam's big challenge. Believing it would be irresponsible to just pull out altogether from its management role, the agencies involved formed a committee along with the World Intellectual Property Organization (WIPO) and the International Telecommunications Union (ITU) to decide the future of the Internet.

Bet You Didn't Know

Have a digital business idea? Take it to the Patent Office. More entrepreneurs have been sealing up their way of doing e-business, prompting the PTO to create a new classification called, "Data Processing, Financial, Business Practice, Management or Cost/Price Determination."

Money Meaning

A **cybersquatter** is someone who buys a domain name that is a well-known brand name, intending to resell it to a company who has a trademark on the name. A **typosquatter** is someone who buys up a domain name that is a simple misspelling of a well-known brand name.

Uncle Sam Bows Out

In 1998, after the committee meetings and a careful review of the complaints of the community, the government broadcast its decisions in a *Green Paper*, which, among other things, called for the creation of a new private, not-for-profit corporation to coordinate Internet domain names.

Where would it live? Well, that was bound to bring trouble no matter what the decision was. Uncle Sam proposed that while it would remain under the jurisdiction of all nations, it remain headquartered in the United States because of all the DNS expertise here, and just plain old stability. It landed in Los Angeles.

The paper then addressed the trademark problem by laying it on the WIPO to create a balanced process to resolve disputes of cyberpiracy and *cybersquatting*.

The Internet Gets a New Boss

Just say ICANN, or Internet Corporation for Assigned Names and Numbers. That's the new non-profit, big-daddy boss of the Internet that was officially named in the fall of 1998. The original keepers—the Internet Assigned Numbers Authority (IANA), headed by Jon Postel, and Network Solutions, run by Gabe Battista—worked together and came up with a set of bylaws for the new corporation.

ICANN's job is mainly an administrative one of setting policy and overseeing operations of domain names. That's expected to cost between $4 and $5 million a year. The money will not come from any one government but from regional registries and domain name registrations fees.

Who will govern ICANN? A committee diverse both in geography and outlook. The first Advisory Committee was appointed in December of 1998, and included men and women from the U.S., Canada, Brazil, India, France, German, Asia and the Caribbean. But it won't stop there: The public will also be invited to help ICANN achieve its goals. A new millennium world order of the Internet is born.

E-Commerce Blooms

Signals sent over the Internet do not stop at border checkpoints for passport stamps. People can work on the same project in several different places, different countries, and be in constant communication without ever physically changing location.

Let's say we are manufacturing a new widget for our company. You are overseeing production in Hong Kong while I run the sales and marketing end in California. My market research showed that people would never use a square widget, our original design. I send you my email at close of business on Tuesday. The next day you send back a brand new set of widget designs via attached email. We arrange an online video conference for that afternoon and approve the go-ahead.

Before the week is out, we've got the widget the world was waiting for, marching merrily off the production line. B.I, or Before Internet, it would have taken a week at the very least to get designs delivered, approved, and into action.

Information is deployed in seconds, from sharing new product introductions or corporate earnings to material lists. Large corporations have been sending and receiving shipping orders through cyberspace since the 1970s via *electronic data interchange* (EDI). But these were over private networks, called *value-added networks* (VANs), that were too costly for the small- and medium-sized businesses to install. The Internet now makes electronic commerce affordable to even the smallest home office.

Money Meaning

Electronic data interchange is a standard for compiling and transmitting information between computers, often over private communications networks called **value-added networks**.

Businesses use the Internet to buy, sell, distribute, and maintain products or services both locally and abroad. They're getting real cost savings as well as bottom line profits. Analysts predict $300 billion worth of commerce on the Internet by 2002. And that's just the business-to-business stuff. When we start to calculate the possibilities in world commerce that includes you, the consumer, the potential profits are anyone's guess.

Remember Mail Order Catalogs?

Of course you remember mail order catalogs; you probably get two or three a week and still use them. With all the demands on our time they're an easy way to shop. Especially with overnight and second day delivery services. We know they've saved our hides on a few forgotten birthdays in the past. Now, however, we use the Internet to order last minute gifts or flowers. And so, apparently, do a lot of you.

We shop the Internet for the same reasons we used to use mail order: convenience, ease of research, and good prices. Only online, we have a greater assortment of goods and choice of companies. You can compare prices between FAO Schwartz and eToys, Land's End and L.L. Bean, Dell and Compaq. A conservative estimate of how much money we'll actually spend online versus window shopping online (completing the purchase through private phone lines) adds up to about $7 billion dollars by the millennium.

Optimists say that that number is low and that we'll soon be extremely comfortable zapping our credit numbers into cyberspace. They expect that sales completed online will rocket to more than $100 billion in the next five years. That's a lot of dough. And a lot of people want a piece of it, including state and local governments. Whoa! That's where things get really sticky!

Preserving the Internet

A couple of things could stop the accelerated growth of the Internet dead in its tracks. Luckily, the founding father, the Federal government of the United States, recognizes these concerns. They have been loudly voiced by big business and small business alike, and they are:

➤ Lack of a predictable legal environment

➤ Government over-taxation

➤ Uncertainty about the Internet's performance, reliability, and security

Can I Trust You?

Governing the Internet is a little like making up the rules for a treasure hunt after the race has started. Issues crop up along the way, and someone tries to set policy. When you're dealing with a legal environment that spans the globe, it gets even more complicated. A lot of ideas are out there on who really rules; they'll just take time to develop. The following sections detail some of the major developments going on now.

Internet Security

The problem? Trust. To feel comfortable communicating with suppliers or customers, you want to know who's really on the other end. Then you want to be sure the agreement is binding.

The solution? Businesses use passwords, *electronic signatures*, and IP addresses. Everybody's got a schtick. Some type of internationally recognized digital authentication, however, is what's needed. The U.S. government is promoting that concept right now and passed the Government Paperwork Elimination Act, which will launch the adoption of a national plan.

They are also working with the United Nations Commission on International Trade Law to support the use of international contracts in e-commerce.

Money Meaning

An **electronic** or **digital signature** is the electronic equivalent to your written signature. It can be used by friends or businesses to verify your identity. It can also guaranty that the original message content was unchanged during transfer.

No New Taxes...At Least for Now

What about the tax bite? With so much money changing hands in e-commerce, companies and customers alike are afraid of excessive taxation. The U.S. government, however, has always said that no new discriminatory taxes should be laid on the Internet. It was a staunch supporter of unfettered growth of the new medium.

Bet You Didn't Know

Booz, Allen & Hamilton estimates that it costs about a penny to conduct a banking transaction using the Internet and more than one dollar if handled by a teller at a branch bank.

On October 21, 1998, the government backed up its words with a bill. The Internet Tax Freedom Act (HR4105) was signed into law by President Clinton, banning the following for three years:

➤ Any Internet access taxes, with the exception of eight states that were already charging Internet access tax. They were given one year to enact a law stating they wanted to continue to collect. Those states are: Connecticut, Iowa, New Mexico, North Dakota, Ohio, Tennessee, South Dakota, and Wisconsin.

➤ Bit taxes on data flowing over networks.

➤ Multiple or discriminatory taxes on electronic commerce by state or local governments. Existing taxes, such as sales, would be unaffected.

Commercial Web sites that give minors access to "harmful" material could face new taxes under an added provision. Sites that give underage Net users access to any communication, image, or writing that contains nudity, actual or simulated sex, or that "lacks serious literary, artistic, political, or scientific" value will get no economic incentives. The provision also requires Net access providers to offer customers products to screen out this material.

The reason for a three-year moratorium was to give everyone time to figure out this new form of commerce. The new law authorized an Advisory Committee on Electronic Commerce to lay out a fair taxation regime for the Internet. At this writing, the committee members were still being discussed but were to come from the following areas:

➤ Secretaries from the Treasury and Commerce Departments

➤ The U.S. Trade Representative

➤ Eight representatives from industry

➤ Eight representatives from state and local governments

The blue ribbon panel was given 18 months to come up with a proposal. The bill also promotes global free trade on the Internet, however, and calls on the Administration to demand that foreign governments keep the Internet free of taxes and tariffs. So, the jury is still out on Internet tax.

Point of Sale

If you're an Internet shopper, you know that sometimes you pay sales tax and sometimes you don't. It depends on the tax laws of the state where the company selling goods resides. How can you tell what the tax policy is before you load the stuff in your virtual shopping cart? Click the Customer Service button or the Help button. Most cybermerchants will have their sales tax policy listed. Here are some examples of how tax policies read in early 1999:

➤ The Gap

Gap has stores in all 50 states. We are required by law to charge sales tax except in Connecticut, Massachusetts, Minnesota, New Jersey, Pennsylvania, and Rhode Island, which exempt apparel merchandise under certain circumstances. There is no sales tax for orders delivered to addresses in Alaska, Delaware, Montana, New Hampshire, or Oregon.

Some states tax shipping charges as well as the purchase total. Those states are: Arkansas, Colorado, Georgia, Hawaii, Kansas, Mississippi, Nebraska, Nevada, New Mexico, New York, North Carolina, Oklahoma, South Dakota, Texas, Washington, West Virginia, and Wisconsin.

➤ eToys

State laws require companies to collect sales tax from residents shipping merchandise to states where the company has established offices. The eToys main office and warehouse operations are in California; we are, therefore, required to collect sales taxes on orders shipped to locations in the state of California.

➤ NetMarket by Cendant Publishing

State tax is applied to an item if our company, the vendor, or the manufacturer conducts business in the shipping address state.

➤ Amazon.com

Sales tax is charged only on orders sent within the state of Washington and Nevada. Washington State and Nevada State law requires that we charge a sales tax on the full amount of the order. Because charges for gift-wrap and shipping and handling are considered part of the product, by law these charges must be included when sales tax is calculated.

No sales tax is charged when buying gift certificates; purchases paid for with gift certificates, however, will be charged sales tax if shipped to addresses within the states of Washington and Nevada.

Click Here

Under siege from worldwide cyber-attacks, the Pentagon ordered the removal of sensitive data from Department of Defense Web sites in September 1998. Pentagon officials realized that users could access data about operations, military capabilities, and personnel. For a list of Federal agencies, try **www.lib.lsu.edu/gov/fedgov.html**.

Some Other Laws That Effect High-Tech

On the same day that he penned an "okay" on the Internet Tax Freedom Act, President Clinton signed a $500 billion spending bill for fiscal 1999 that included several technology industry-backed provisions and some other controversial Net content regulations. That brought the number of high-tech bills from the 105th Congress, and signed by the President, to eight. These included:

➤ The Child Online Protection Act, which calls for commercial Web site operators who offer "harmful" material to check visitors' identifications or face up to $50,000 in fines and six months in prison for each violation.

197

➤ The Child Protection and Sexual Predator Punishment Act, which increases penalties for and protects children from sexual predators and computer pornography.

➤ The Government Paperwork Elimination Act, which requires government agencies to put more forms online and then set up systems to accept digital certificates within three years. These certificates verify the accuracy of a person's digital signature and are protected by public-private key encryption. This would go a long way toward creating a national framework for authenticating people's identities when they shop online or send documents over the Net.

➤ The Digital Millennium Copyright Act, which creates criminal penalties for anyone who tries to circumvent high-tech anti-piracy protections, such as encryptions, used to block illegal copying. It implements the provisions of two international treaties adopted by WIPO at a Geneva conference on digital information and copyrights in 1996.

The bill also:

➤ Forbids the manufacture, import, sale, or distribution of devices used to evade protective systems.

➤ Frees ISPs from liability for copyright infringements by their customers.

Bet You Didn't Know

The Russian state police, FSB, formerly known as the KGB, has a plan to monitor every piece of data sent over Russian bandwidth. All ISPs would have to install a snoop device in their main computers. One service provider noted that the Russian language has no adequate translation for the word "privacy."

More Freedom of Speech

In 1994, the idea of regulating content on the Web would have been laughable. There was no content, really. By 1999, however, the Internet was swamped with pornography, hate literature, and just about anything an imagination can muster, sick or sane. So, where's the posse?

While government is backing away from Internet involvement by handing over much of the administration to private industry, it keeps trying to pass laws on pornography. And the courts keep blocking them. The Communications Decency Act took aim at killing smut but was later snuffed out in 1997 by the Supreme Court as restricting free speech.

In October of 1998, President Clinton took another swing and signed the Child Online Protection Act (COPA), also known as CDA II. The new law made it a federal crime to knowingly communicate material considered harmful to minors for commercial purposes. Penalties included fines of up to $50,000 for each day of violation, and up to six months in prison.

Is it destined for the same fate as the earlier CDA? In February 1999, Philadelphia Judge Lowell A. Reed, Jr. blocked the law by granting a preliminary injunction on behalf of the American Civil Liberties Union. CDA II could easily go the way of the other anti-smut amendment.

Meanwhile, another U.S. judge ruled that libraries cannot install filtering software on Web-browsing computers available to the public. The ruling was based on the right to free speech guaranteed by the First Amendment but applies only to adult browsers and says nothing about restrictions to minors.

Bet You Didn't Know

According to a U.S. National Fraud Information Center report, the Internet is rife with fraud, most of which occurs offline. Over three quarters of the scams involve personal sales through online classified ads, newsgroups, and online auctions, where decoys up the bid or goods are not delivered.

A Private Place

Overall, the government approach to policing the Internet is to encourage private industry to self-regulate, even when it comes to copyright and privacy, both that of our personal information and of our transactions. Encryption codes to protect credit card and financial information seem to work for now. We don't often get the opportunity, however, to block the gathering of information that takes place when we enter it in some online site. What it's used for and how widely it can be disseminated are questions we'd like answered.

The best you can do for now is to be wary of what you reveal of yourself and where you reveal it. Also, look for the graphic image of a lock at the bottom of your screen when performing online transactions. If the lock is missing or broken, stop sending information.

The critics say that industry self-regulation isn't enough, but right now, the Internet is still in the early stages of architecture. Any detailed rules enacted by government bodies may soon prove outdated, impractical, and, worst of all, uneconomical.

Click Here

The Electronic Privacy Information Center (**www.epic.org**) surveyed 100 top Web sites and found that 49 percent of them collected personal data through online registration, surveys, and profiles. Only 17 percent posted easily accessible policies explaining how the data would be used.

Bet You Didn't Know

Don't sign away your E-rights. Literary agent Richard Curtis is launching a campaign called *E-rights* to protect the rights of authors. Many have already signed away their rights to electronic publishing royalties.

The Least You Need to Know

➤ The federal government started the Internet as a tool for research and national security. It funded the development of the new medium much as it funded the growth of the country when it was new.

➤ The first organizations to manage the Internet address system were government funded. It gradually grew into a lucrative commercial concern with over one million addresses and $4 million in income. When the government contract ended in 1998, a new non-profit corporation was named to take over, with worldwide approval.

➤ The 105th Congress passed a number of high-tech bills, the major law being the Internet Tax Freedom Act that banned any new taxes on Internet commerce and access for three years.

➤ The federal government has declared its role in the Internet to be one of encouraging mentor and guide, facilitating global cooperation. It plans, however, to let the commercial industries self-regulate in these early stages of growth.

Part 4

Thriving in Tomorrow's Workplace

It sure would be nice to be your own boss. No one to tell you what to do or when to do it. No bi-annual performance reviews. No paycheck. What? Wait! Don't let the fear of success keep you from taking control of your career. There are so many ways to build and grow a business today—especially with entrepreneurship thriving in the United States. Plus, the Internet levels the career field for all us sports fans. Even you can have a store in the mall open 24 hours—a virtual mall, of course. And you don't even have to hire a salesperson!

Even if you're not ready to become a captain of industry just yet, you can learn which are the next hot job markets and how to get there. You may find yourself joining the force of telecommuters, the next best thing to being your own boss, and maybe the next step. Time to figure out where you are on the career path, and how to take the right turn toward success.

Let's take control of your career and determine how you, too, can thrive in tomorrow's workplace—and make money!

Chapter 16

Businesses and Industries for the Year 2000

In This Chapter

➤ Why the economy needs your small business

➤ Who's minding the store?

➤ The Internet's role in starting and building a business

➤ Waking up to the American dream of business ownership

➤ A look at the top growth industries

It's another beautiful day. You jump out of bed to the strident peal of the alarm clock, put on a suit you don't feel like wearing, grab some breakfast you don't have time to eat, drive your car to a place you don't want to go, and work with people you don't really like. That's your job, and somebody has to do it.

Let's rewind and try that again. It's a beautiful day. You wake up to the sun streaming in your windows and the smell of coffee brewing, and you stretch. You put on yesterday's shorts (still clean and they're your favorite) and a pair of tennis shoes. You enjoy breakfast at your kitchen table, and then stroll into the next room to your home office. Oh yes, you also put on your red baseball cap, the one that tells your family you are officially "at work."

Sound better? Sure it does. That's why 16 million Americans are doing some type of entrepreneurial activity, whether full or part-time, inside or outside the home. Okay, so being your own boss may not be just about wearing whatever you feel like to work, but it is about doing what you want, for yourself.

Owning a small business is all about taking risks and taking control of your own destiny. But it's so much more. Small businesses are also becoming the life's blood of our global economy. They provide the majority of new jobs and fuel economic growth through innovation and creativity.

Why Uncle Sam, and Everyone Else, Needs Your Small Business

In the 1992 elections, the chief concern in the United States was that we were losing ground in the global economic race. Banks and industries in other countries, such as Japan and Germany, were in better shape. Their trends in investment, as well as market share in high technology, seemed far superior.

By the late 1990s, however, the United States had turned around, clearly making the leap from an industrial to an information economy. The country has seldom seemed more balanced—unemployment is low, the economy is growing, the dollar is strong, and the Dow Jones Industrial Average is breaking records as a matter of course.

Why the change? Economists at the Small Business Administration's Office of Advocacy attribute a large part of our current success to **entrepreneurship** and new firm startups.

More than 23 million **small businesses** currently operate in this country, and interest in owning or starting a small business has never been greater. It's a fairly new phenomenon that small business is driving the economy. The corporate giants always had the upper hand because they could produce goods at lower cost than the little guy could. But that was during the industrial age…. Information has changed all that. Large firms have downsized and restructured. Meanwhile, small firms have sprouted and thrived. These small firms in turn have added millions of new employment opportunities.

Money Meaning

The Small Business Administration has page after page of tables and rules defining **small business**, which you need to read if you're trying to qualify for federal assistance programs. Basically though, the small business has no more than 500 employees and generates no more than $500,000 in annual revenue.

New Jobs

All the new jobs created from 1992 to 1996 came from small firms, and nearly 70 percent of those came from very small businesses (those with fewer than 20 employees). So these lean and mean companies are vital to creating new jobs that mean economic growth for the country. They also create an endless supply of diverse employment opportunities.

Imagine if we all had to go to work in the same type of office or factory. We punched the same clock and worked all day making up our similar products or reports. Then we all headed home with the same size paycheck. Boring! Enter small business and diversity, hello creative workplace.

How many times have you said, "Wow, wouldn't that be a cool job to have!" or, "I wish I had your job." From aquaculturalist to leisure consultant, small business has more than likely created that "dream" job you're talking about. Take *Complain To Us* (www.complaintous.com), a business started by a Massachusetts couple. They dog down and extract refunds from companies that you don't have time to fight. Imagine being paid to complain professionally!

Small firms not only add spice to the job market, they also provide an education not found on any college campus such as on-the-job training and an introduction to office politics.

Money Meaning

An **entrepreneur** is one who organizes, manages, and assumes the risks of a business or enterprise.

Training Grounds or Employee 101

Remember your first *real* job? You were probably 17 or 18 years old and may have only filed papers in an office or bussed tables in a restaurant, but you learned how business worked. You had to arrive on time, dress properly, and follow instructions. It was basic, but it was training.

Most of the initial on-the-job training in this country takes place in small business. These are the jobs more likely to be filled by the under 25 age set or the over 50s, and women. Often these people prefer to, or can only, work part-time. So as a small business owner, not only are you training the workforce, but you are also providing a valuable work situation for people who might not otherwise find a place in the larger, corporate world.

Not all small companies serve up food or documents, however. More than 75 percent of high technology firms in the United States have fewer than 20 employees, but these firms make the lion's share of new product innovations (according to Small Business Administration research). They are the firms that keep us on the global cutting edge.

Eureka! We've Got a Live One!

Who says bigger is better? Small firms produce twice as many product innovations as large firms. They also apply for more patents; so they apparently have more discoveries. And of all the federal research and development money (read: your tax dollars) that goes out to business, the small firm is four times more likely to spend that dollar on basic research than a large firm.

Some of these innovations have changed the global marketplace and life as we know it, dramatically. In the twentieth century, small U.S. firms have discovered the airplane, fiber-optic examining equipment, the heart valve, the optical scanner, pacemaker, audio tape recorder, double-knit fabric, the infamous personal computer, soft contact lenses, and the zipper. Let's not forget velcro, how did we live without it? Pretty impressive inventions! And to think, these companies probably started out as someone's need to be his or her own boss.

Of course the goal here is to make some money, right? And small business is profitable. The Small Business Administration reports that income is rising at a steady pace among small business owners and partners. Total personal income in 1996 alone rose 5.8 percent, to a grand total of $4.1 trillion.

Who's Running Small Businesses?

Take the needs of tomorrow, the characteristics of the labor force (they're older, experienced, and looking for more freedom), toss in the Internet, and you've got a recipe for a small business boom. Technological advances and big-business organizational changes will naturally lead workers toward their own small businesses.

Bet You Didn't Know

Nearly half of all small businesses used to be home-based, according to the Commerce Department's Census Bureau. Today more than four million people work from home in small businesses. Nearly six million self-employed people work from home, and that's expected to double in the next 10 years.

While the white male still dominates small business, women now represent 38 percent of business owners; and other minorities are nipping at their heels. The latest Census Bureau findings report certain similar characteristics among all these entrepreneurs. Do you recognize yourself here?

Characteristics of the small business owner include the following:

➤ They have prior work experience (10 or more years).

➤ They are educated (nearly half have a bachelors or a professional degree).

➤ Most used minimal startup capital, with more than 50 percent using less than $5,000 to get their business going.

➤ They are computer/technology-savvy. What is the area in which business owners say they are most likely to invest? Computers! Hmmm…maybe a small business computer sales operation would be a good small business?

Women in Small Business

We told you that the ranks of women in business are growing, but we didn't tell you how much. There are almost 8 million female-owned businesses in the United States, half of them home-based. Because these businesses make a significant impact on society, this is a true growth industry to watch. According to the National Foundation of Women Business Owners, these businesses:

➤ Employ nearly 18 million people, either full-time or part-time, which is more than are employed in the Fortune 500 industrial firms (according to Dunn & Bradstreet). They also generate more than $2 trillion in sales...a real boost for the economy.

➤ Are tech savvy—most have computers, nearly half have more than one. They also have faxes, modems, and some carry cell phones and have Internet access.

➤ Are even more optimistic about growth than other small business owners, because they think that their global activity will increase. That confidence is due in large part to the worldwide gateway opened up by the Internet.

Click Here

Share the entrepreneurial spirit online with the National Foundation of Women Business Owners at **www.nfwbo.org/**.

How the Internet Plays a Role in Success

Information technology is providing new business arenas and making it easier to start home-based businesses. The freedom of choice is exhilarating, thanks to the Internet and our new ability to reach out and connect with the world.

The low price of personal computers and the high speed of telecommunications helped tear down the barriers to the marketplace. To do business in cyberspace, however, you have to take some of the basic steps mentioned in Chapter 1:

➤ Sign up with a service provider.

➤ Secure a domain name and Internet address.

➤ Create a Web site, either on your own or with the help of a designer.

You can spend anywhere from $50 to $5,000, fairly inexpensive when compared to the price of, say, building an office site. And the value is unbeatable, offering a flexible, low-cost, global reach.

There are also plenty of online web-hosting services that will take care of all your e-commerce needs, like online ordering and credit card transactions. We'll get into those specifics in Chapter 19, "Setting Up Shop Online."

Bet You Didn't Know

It took radio 38 years to get the full attention of 50 million people. It took television 13 years to grab that same number. Once it was opened to the public, it took the Internet less than four years.

Click Here

If you don't yet have an Internet "presence" for your business, you're about to get left behind. Half of all business owners now have access to the Internet, 35 percent maintain their own Web site, and one in three transact business on it. (D&B)

You can do the following things with your Web site:

➤ Build an electronic *store*—heck, build a whole mall without having to get permission from your local zoning board or buy a single sheet of plywood.

➤ Distribute product catalogs nationally and internationally with no print or mailing costs.

➤ Cross time zones and international borders without blinking an eye.

➤ Take orders and payments, reducing time and paperwork.

➤ Advertise globally on a low budget.

➤ Service large numbers of customers with a very small sales force; it may even just be you alone.

➤ Get feedback from customers and stay in touch with surveys and emails.

Click Here

Domain names are disappearing at the rate of 30,000 a week. If you are considering registering your business name, check today with Network Solutions (**http://rs.internic.net**), the company that manages the naming system. Your name may already be taken.

Hello American Dream!

The latter half of the 1990s showed the highest formation of new small businesses ever in the United States. And why not? The economy is robust and the U.S. dollar is strong. But if you think consumer confidence is high (and it is), then small business owner confidence is soaring.

Entrepreneurs nationwide report to Dunn & Bradstreet—a leading research-based business information provider—that they expect their businesses to grow and revenues to increase in the future. It's that positive attitude that generates a more aggressive approach to finding, and *getting*, new customers—a kind of self-fulfilling prophecy.

So what about your interest? Maybe you have the desire or the driving passion it takes to start up a business of your own, but you just don't know where to begin. Without some background knowledge of the businesses and industries making money now, you're like a traveler with no direction, let alone a map.

Let's take a look at the growth areas predicted into the future by the Bureau of Labor Statistics and the Department of Commerce. With these directions in mind, you can begin to build your own map of what you could do and how to do it. If you want to get on the fast track for growth in 2000, try computers, information technology, healthcare, and service. These are the fields of the future, and they span all industries. Let's break it down and see where you fit in.

Technology and new innovations are forging the way for the millennium. From computer-repair companies to consulting firms, there's a lot of room for business. If your knowledge of computers is limited, now is the time to learn the lingo:

➤ **Information overload.** All companies will need to manage, store, track, and distribute information. Whether your business is in computer software, fashion, or public relations, you will be working with information.

➤ **Service, please.** We need help, and we need it now. Business, health, and education will be the fastest growing sectors in need of service. If you're looking for real estate, everyone will tell you, it's all location-location-location. Well, when looking for growth industries in the 21st century, think service-service-service.

➤ **How's my health, doctor?** In the pink, if you're in the healthcare field. Health services and care will be big business, with a growing customer base. The largest segment of the population, the baby boomers, is aging and they want good care. Most of them can afford to pay for it, too. Add that to the advanced technological breakthroughs in science, and the savvy entrepreneur cannot ignore healthcare.

According to the Bureau of Labor Statistics, the following are some of the fastest growing industries for small business:

➤ Medical and dental laboratories

➤ Residential care industries

➤ Computer and data processing services

➤ Restaurants

➤ Outpatient care facilities

➤ Physician's offices

➤ Special trade construction contractors

➤ Credit reporting and collection firms

➤ Day care providers

➤ Counseling and rehabilitation services

Whether you're out for yourself, or ready to launch a new business, it helps to know what's hot. Check out the following tables for a look at fastest growth and top industries in the United States.

Fastest Growing Industries for Small Business in United States

Industry	1993	1994	Amount Change	Percent Change
Total - All Industries	50,316,063	51,007,688	691,625	1.4
Nondepository Credit Institutions	165,111	195,655	30,544	18.5
Security & Commodity Brokers, Dealers, Exchanges, & Services	137,675	147,521	9,846	7.2
Special Trade Contractors	2,559,404	2,682,009	122,605	4.8
Automotive Repair, Services, & Parking	755,279	791,276	35,997	4.8
Social Services	1,712,372	1,782,961	70,589	4.1

Top Five Industries in the United States by Employment

Industry	SIC	Employment Total	Percent of Total	Percent Small
Total - All Industries	—	96,721,594	100.0	52.7
Health Services	8000	10,743,655	11.1	40.8
Eating & Drinking Places	5800	7,019,385	7.3	65.9
Business Services	7300	6,364,997	6.6	50.1
Wholesale Trade - Durable Goods	5000	3,701,376	3.8	71.4
Food Stores	5400	3,259,218	3.4	37.9

Top Five Small Business Industries in United States by Employment

Industry	SIC	Employment in firms with 0–499 employees	Percent of Total	Percent Small
Total - All Industries	—	51,007,688	100.0	52.7
Eating & Drinking Places	5800	4,625,040	7.3	65.9
Health Services	8000	4,385,299	11.1	40.8
Business Services	7300	3,191,279	6.6	50.1
Special Trade Contractors	1700	2,682,009	3.0	93.2
Wholesale Trade - Durable Goods	5000	2,643,265	3.8	71.4

Sources: Office of Advocacy, U.S. Small Business Administration. Latest date available: 1994.

Facing the Challenges of Tomorrow's Business Ownership

Once you start a small business, how do you maintain it? Keeping up with technology is just one of the obstacles you will face while trying to compete in the new millennium marketplace. Here are the top troubles that business owners of today say they are struggling with, and some possible solutions:

➤ **Keeping in touch with hi-tech.** Use technology to keep up with technology. The worldwide marketplace is chock full of information and people willing to share. Stay tuned in to Internet newsletters and sign up with discussion and chat groups. Netscape Communications Internet service provider launched its Small Business Source in May 1998. The Small Business Source includes Web site creating and hosting services, news and information retrieval, and a number of community forums for small business owners to join in.

➤ **Finding employees.** The labor force is growing at a slower rate than in past decades, and finding qualified workers is the number one complaint for business owners. The best solution for the cash-strapped entrepreneur is the temporary employee. Hence the rise in what is turning into another growth industry, staffing agencies. Don't you just love the economy in all this?

Bet You Didn't Know

Even if you have to shut your doors for good, you are not considered an actual failure by business standards if you pay off all your bills. So if things aren't going as you planned, pay up, and pat yourself on the back for making a good job of it. Of every seven businesses that close up shop for keeps, only one is considered a failure. (SBA–sponsored research.)

➤ **Rising insurance and healthcare costs.** The costs of insuring your business and your employees both keep going up. That's why small firms traditionally have been unable to provide health insurance and pension plans to their employees. Staffing agencies come to the rescue again, by offering group plans to the workers they hire out. Also, check with any professional and trade associations in your field; they too can offer group rates. The insurance industry online is expected to grow faster than any other online business, meaning that you will be able to get more competitive rates faster in the future.

➤ **Finding new customers.** Afraid you've tapped out your market? No way. A whole industry of mailing lists and marketing services is cropping up online, and it's a great way to keep your client list fresh and growing. You have to subscribe and pay a fee, but they do all the work.

So you know now that small business is a major driving force behind economic good times, now and in the future. You know there are exciting and enriching possibilities in small business. But is it for you? Chapter 17 will give you the chance to test yourself, and the knowledge you need to get started.

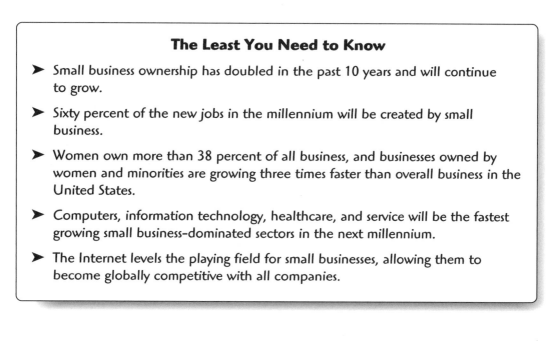

The Least You Need to Know

➤ Small business ownership has doubled in the past 10 years and will continue to grow.

➤ Sixty percent of the new jobs in the millennium will be created by small business.

➤ Women own more than 38 percent of all business, and businesses owned by women and minorities are growing three times faster than overall business in the United States.

➤ Computers, information technology, healthcare, and service will be the fastest growing small business-dominated sectors in the next millennium.

➤ The Internet levels the playing field for small businesses, allowing them to become globally competitive with all companies.

Chapter 17

Is Small Business Ownership for You?

In This Chapter

➤ Finding your personal motivations

➤ Testing yourself

➤ What will you do?

➤ Steps to starting up and what it costs

➤ Financing your business

➤ Marketing strategies on a shoestring

One out of every three homes in America includes a member who is involved in a startup or small business, according to the SBA's Entrepreneurial Research Consortium. Business ownership is practically an epidemic these days, and you may be catching the bug. But you have to ask yourself what are your motivations, skills, and level of commitment? The answers to these questions, and many more that will be explored in this interactive chapter, can mean the difference between reaching your goals as a business owner and getting stuck in another rut like your last job.

People start their own businesses for many reasons, including flexibility, independence, and freedom. Freedom from corporate limitations, freedom to take risks, and the independence to work at your own pace are the inspiring, pep-rally type cries heard from entrepreneurs. But it all boils down to just words without some solid planning. You'll also need a healthy dose of the following: knowledge of the area of business through training or on-the-job experience, a formal business plan, capital, and dedication (in other words, be willing to work long hours with little income, at first).

After all that comes the idea. Do you know what you want to do? If not, this book will give you some idea generators. We've already told you that service is the future—anything that relieves the everyday pressure cooker of our busy lives is likely to succeed. You might want to become a professional organizer, for example, whether it be for children's birthday parties, weekly meal planning and delivery, or a home maintenance scheduler and provider. You can help to lighten our workload and have some fun too. But first, are you ready to be a business owner? Here is where you face the tough questions. Sharpen your pencils, you've got some homework to do!

Is It for You?

You've been threatening to quit your job and start your own business for years. So what's holding you back? If you're just not sure you have what it takes and are harboring some self-doubts, it's time to find out the truth about yourself. If you can honestly answer "yes" to the next three questions, great! Then we'll move forward and dig a little deeper into your psyche and help you find your business niche. A *niche* is defined by Webster as a place, employment, status, or activity for which a person or thing is best fitted—a specialized market.

Are you:

- Flexible?
- Open to change in technology?
- Ready to trust yourself?

Bet You Didn't Know

According to a 1993 Small Business Administration research report by Richard Fullenbaum and Mariana McNeill, 53 percent of business owners who went bankrupt became owners of another business, and 13 percent left the labor force altogether; the rest went back to wage and salary employment.

If you answered yes to all these questions, you've cleared the first hurdle. Now let's test your risk quotient. This quiz was developed by the American Women's Economic Development Corporation in Stamford, CT, together with Women in New Development of Bernidji, MN. It should help you decide if the life of the entrepreneur is for you, or if you have potential (but that potential just needs a little polish). Remember, however, that you can't fail this test; it's just a tool, fun to take and fun to interpret.

Check off the answers to the following questions, and then total up the points and read the evaluation. You must answer all the questions for the test to be accurate. Have fun!

Answer			Statement
Yes ❑	Maybe ❑	No ❑	I'm persistent. I "stick to it."
Yes ❑	Maybe ❑	No ❑	When I'm interested in a project, I need less sleep.
Yes ❑	Maybe ❑	No ❑	When I want something, I keep the end results clearly in my mind.
Yes ❑	Maybe ❑	No ❑	I examine mistakes and learn from them.
Yes ❑	Maybe ❑	No ❑	I keep my New Year's resolutions.
Yes ❑	Maybe ❑	No ❑	I have a strong personal need to succeed.
Yes ❑	Maybe ❑	No ❑	I have new and different ideas.
Yes ❑	Maybe ❑	No ❑	I am adaptable.
Yes ❑	Maybe ❑	No ❑	I am curious.
Yes ❑	Maybe ❑	No ❑	I am intuitive.
Yes ❑	Maybe ❑	No ❑	If something can't be done, I find a way.
Yes ❑	Maybe ❑	No ❑	I see problems as challenges.
Yes ❑	Maybe ❑	No ❑	I take chances.
Yes ❑	Maybe ❑	No ❑	I'll gamble on a good idea even if it isn't a sure thing.
Yes ❑	Maybe ❑	No ❑	To learn something new, I dig into subjects I have no background in.
Yes ❑	Maybe ❑	No ❑	I can recover from emotional setbacks.
Yes ❑	Maybe ❑	No ❑	I feel sure of myself.
Yes ❑	Maybe ❑	No ❑	I'm a positive person.
Yes ❑	Maybe ❑	No ❑	I experiment with new ways to do things.
Yes ❑	Maybe ❑	No ❑	I'm willing to undergo sacrifices to gain possible long-term rewards.
Yes ❑	Maybe ❑	No ❑	I usually do things my own way.
Yes ❑	Maybe ❑	No ❑	I tend to rebel against authority.
Yes ❑	Maybe ❑	No ❑	I often enjoy being alone.
Yes ❑	Maybe ❑	No ❑	I like to be in control.
Yes ❑	Maybe ❑	No ❑	I have a reputation for being stubborn.

Test Source: http://onlinewbc.org, 4/97.

Now total up your score. Give yourself three points for each Yes, two points for each Maybe, and one point for each No. The results are interpreted as follows:

If you scored between 60 and 75, decide on a business and get going on that business plan. You have the makings of an entrepreneur.

If you scored between 48 and 59, you have potential but may need a little push. Try to work on skills in your weaker areas, or hire someone else to do them.

If you scored between 37 and 47, you may not want to start a business on your own. A partner can strengthen your position.

If you scored below 37, it doesn't look like self-employment is for you. You may be more successful working for someone else until you've developed more confidence.

Still feel you'd like to go into business for yourself? Okay, now you know you're comfortable taking risks, so you need to determine the business that's right for you. Skip the next set of questions if you already have a business idea in mind. Everybody else should answer them carefully—it's your future in the making.

Bet You Didn't Know

After making the effort to start up a new business, 9 percent of new entrepreneurs expected their business to survive 90 years or more, 13 percent estimated survival of 40 to 60 years and 78 percent thought their business would last 30 years or less.

Your Ideal Business

Hopefully you've kept your pen and paper handy, because you will refer back to these answers often while you read this book and write your business plan. This is the foundation from which you will build your enterprise, regardless of how big or how small.

It is now time to figure out what you can really do. This is a good time to assess your personal skills and education. No skimping on the praise here, but lay on what you do well. Listing everything will help you figure out what field you may want to do business in. If you know the field of interest, list your experience or what you know about the specific business.

Here is a simple worksheet to help you determine what you like to do, and what you have the aptitude to do. Too many people get stuck in businesses they don't like; they just thought it would make them money. It doesn't always work that way. Pin down your interests, and then look for a profitable venture in those areas.

Let's start with education, hobbies, and interests. Fill in the information in the following table to see for yourself.

Education: (B.S. Math, B.A. English)

_____

_____

_____

_____

Hobbies: (Internet, coins)

_____

_____

_____

Interests: (cooking, flying)

_____

_____

_____

Passions: (sports, boating)

_____

_____

_____

Talents: (words, wood)

_____

_____

_____

Aptitudes: (computers, math)

_____

_____

_____

By now, some common threads between interests and talents should be surfacing. If not, pick out some of the areas that you feel really positive about and imagine the possibilities of turning them into a business. To help you out, we've compiled a list of possible business ideas based on future trends, and where possible, listed a contact or resource in that field to get you started.

Finding the Right Business

There are somewhere between 23 and 34 million households with people who work at home, depending on whether you're reading statistics from the U.S. Department of Labor or the research firm IDC/LINK, respectively. Either way, that's a lot of work being generated from the home-sweet-home.

Click Here

The 1995 edition of the Catalog of Small Business Research provides a listing of the U.S. Small Business Administration's contracted research studies completed between 1978 and mid-1994. It also includes a back file of out-of-print publications and some technical reports published by other SBA offices. For a free copy of this catalog, call the National Technical Information Service (NTIS) in Springfield, VA 22161 at 703–605–6000 or 800–553–6847.

Perhaps the most interesting news about home workers, according to a survey conducted by America Online's Business Know-How Forum, was that despite the 40 to 50 hour week these people put in, they still claim to have more family time. Is that important to you? Let's look at the pros and cons of working at home first, and then look at some potential businesses.

The following are benefits of a home-based business:

➤ **Financial**. You can eliminate major overhead of an office by working from home. Also, most home-based business owners can partially write-off house payments, utilities, and maintenance. Check with your certified public accountant (CPA) to be sure. No CPA? Try TurboTax software; it walks you through every step of your eligibility.

➤ **Freedom**. The word explains it all. It's your life, your business, and all the decisions are pretty much yours to make.

➤ **Flexibility**. Need a last-minute dental appointment or want to offer your support at your child's first spelling bee at school? You don't need permission if you're the boss.

➤ **General**. Eliminating a trip to the office every day also saves wear on the car and gas bills. While every home worker has his or her own preferred attire, whether it be fuzzy slippers or designer jeans, the wardrobe savings can be substantial.

The following things need to be considered as well before you decide to break off on your own. You may not have the temperament, or the right location for a home-based business.

Money Meaning

Home-based business owners are self-employed individuals who operate a business or profession primarily from or in a home office.

➤ **Self-Discipline.** When you work at home, no one will be telling you what to do; but then again, no one will be handing over a weekly paycheck either. So keep your distractions to a minimum if you want to complete those projects and generate more work which translates into more income.

➤ **Isolation.** Most of us are used to the camaraderie and daily banter that takes place in the office, so a long stretch at home with no contact other than the cat can get lonely. Better decide now if you can live without the companionship of colleagues.

➤ **Boundaries (or the lack of them).** It's difficult to stay out of the kitchen or laundry room when you're supposed to be finishing up a work-related project. It's even harder to make friends and family understand that you can't be interrupted. Making your expectations clear can eliminate conflicts. The red baseball cap mentioned in the beginning of Chapter 16 is a good example of how a *uniform* can let family know you're on business time, even if you're in plain view.

➤ **Laws.** Depending on the type of business you'll be doing from home, you may need to check into state and local laws. Some states don't allow the production of certain items at home (fireworks, toys, or medical products, for example). You may also need a work certificate or license, if for instance you decide to become a day-care provider. Also, if you hire employees, you have to comply with employee health and safety laws.

With some of these considerations in mind, let's look at a sampling of home-based businesses:

➤ **Health home care services.** Chapter 16 mentioned an aging population and an increase in outpatient care in the new millennium. This adds up to a need for home care providers. The people in this profession would be caring for the sick, elderly, or disabled in their homes. So you may not be working in your home, but you won't have to report to a boss in an office, either. Contact the National Association for Home Care, 228 Seventh Street, SE Washington D.C. 20003, 202-547-7424, for more information (www.nahc.org).

➤ **Internet consulting.** If you know how to navigate the Internet or how to design and manage a Web page, people need your expertise. You can start small here, maybe by teaching an evening class at your local high school or computer center.

This is an excellent way to meet clients and grow your business base. If you need more training yourself, or just want information about the business potential, contact the Information Technology Training Association Inc., 8400 N. MoPac Expressway, Suite 201, Austin, TX 78759, 512-502-9300 (www.itta.org).

➤ **Professional organizer.** Do you drive your family crazy by neatly arranging their sock drawers and closets? You may have the earmark of a professional organizer. Contact the National Association of Professional Organizers, a non-profit association whose members include organizing consultants, speakers, trainers, authors, and manufacturers of organizing products. Their referral line is 512-206-0151, and they're located at 1033 La Posada, Suite 220, Austin, TX 78752 (www.napo.net).

➤ **Travel agent.** With more disposable income, but less free time, people want to make the most of their vacations. Travel is predicted to be one of the fastest growing industries in 2000 by the Bureau of Labor Statistics, and adventure travel is leading the pack. Want to send people on the vacation of a lifetime? Contact the Adventure Travel Society, 6551 S. Revere Pkwy., #160 Englewood, CO 80111, 303-649-9016 (www.adventuretravel.com).

Click Here

Get together with like-minded individuals by checking out the American Association of Home-Based Businesses at **www.aahb.org**.

➤ **Medical billing services.** A government General Accounting Office study estimates that 99 percent of hospital bills contain overcharges and errors. Filing claims electronically for doctors and surgeons can cut out errors and shorten the time it takes for them to be paid by as much as a month. Interested? Contact the Electronic Medical Billing Network of America Inc., P.O. Box 7162, Watchung, NJ 07060, 908-757-121, or http://webcircle.com/embn/letter.html.

Here are some more ideas based on future trends of an aging population, the population's concern for fitness, two career couples, corporate downsizing, fear of crime, and fear of environmental pollution. Some of these are good ways to make money working from home, and many can be worked into full-time businesses.

Auto detailing and repair	Catering
Cleaning services	Collections service

Commercial photographer	Computer consulting or repair
Construction management consultant	Daycare for adults or children
Desktop publishing	Editor/writer
Employment agency	Environmental restoration
Events planner	Fitness trainer
Food delivery service	Franchise consultant
Handyman services	Healthcare consultant
Information broker	Market research
Mystery shopper	Newsletter production
Pet care service	Pool cleaning service
Publicist	Referral service
Risk management consultant	Security consultant
Small business consultant	Tax preparation
Translator	Wedding consultant

Not all of these businesses need to be done from home. It might be difficult to detail an automobile, for instance, if you live in a second-floor condo. If you're the type of person who wouldn't want to live and work in the same dwelling anyway, maybe buying an already existing business is more your style.

Should You Buy a Business or Franchise?

You won't be the first entrepreneur who shudders at the thought of all the little details involved in a business startup. That's why buying an existing business or franchise looks so attractive. Beware though, you will gain some things, but you'll lose some things too.

Bet You Didn't Know

Like other businesses, you will need to register your business and get a sales tax number before you can officially start operation. Otherwise you may get shut down and even fined.

Buy a Franchise

There is no shortage of variety when choosing a franchise business, from fast food to auto sales to real estate. But the real attraction lies in the having someone else, the franchisor, provide the business expertise (marketing plans, management guidance, site locations, training, and so on). Here's a quick look at the pros and cons of buying into a franchise rather than starting your business from scratch.

The following are advantages:

➤ **Head start.** You buy an established product or service.

➤ **Technical and managerial assistance.** They've done it before, now they'll tell you how to do it.

➤ **Quality control standards.** You have to follow their standards—great if you don't know the product, a problem if you disagree.

➤ **Less operating capital.** Although nothing is ever free, many franchisors offer some type of financing. They have also spent the money on marketing and product recognition for you.

➤ **Opportunities for growth.** Once you get good at it, you may want to buy more franchises in other markets, or expand your existing territory.

The following are disadvantages:

➤ **Play by their rules.** There may be some restrictions on the freedom of owner-ship, including dress codes and hours of business.

➤ **Royalties.** Most franchisors require you to pay them a percentage of your monthly gross sales.

➤ **Failed expectations.** Did you really want to serve up frozen yogurt all day?

Click Here

The Better Business Bureau has an online area with tips on selecting a franchise (**www.bbb.org/library/busfranc.html**). BeTheBoss.com lists franchise opportunities world-wide, plus franchising basics, links, and a calendar of franchising shows and events (**www.betheboss.com**).

Here are some franchise fraud tactics the Better Business Bureau warns to be on the lookout for when considering a franchise opportunity. Be wary of franchisors that do the following:

➤ Demand that you act *immediately* before investigating so that you can get in on the ground floor.

➤ Fail to provide statistics on franchise sales, profits, or locations.

➤ Fail to identify company officers or principals.

➤ Promise large incomes from work-at-home or spare-time efforts.

➤ Offer to *trade you up* to a higher-than-advertised price franchise.

Buy a Business

You know you don't want to start your business from scratch, so you look around for one to buy. You'll save time and reduce risk by purchasing an established company. So far, so good. Here are some advantages:

➤ **Business is up and running**. Operational practices, supply, and distribution channels are already set up and key personnel are in place.

➤ **Planning**. With an existing cash flow, future projections are easier to make. That helps the business plan.

The following are some possible disadvantages:

➤ **Purchase price**. Your cash flow may be greatly hindered by the debt you incur to buy the business.

➤ **Business health**. How strong is the company you're about to buy? Why is the owner selling? There may be personal problems, or there may be marketplace changes that you're not aware of. Do your research.

Click Here

The Small Business Administration has a huge Web site devoted to the small business owner and the wannabe small business owner. Don't miss this site (**www.sba.org**) if you are in the market for business. If you're looking for a business to buy, start at BizBuySell. BizBuySell has a great QuickSearch feature, where you can enter your business interest keyword—*restaurant*, for example—and your desired location. They also have large databases of information for buyers, sellers, and brokers (**www.bizbuysell.com**).

Are You Ready Now?

How much time, planning, and cash can you commit to your business now? How much can your family afford this business if you were to start today? There are businesses to suit every lifestyle, so you need to figure out what your needs are before you commit. First you have to decide how your finances will survive a business startup.

More than 75 percent of small business owners use their own personal savings to start their own business, according to the SBA. Examine your savings and spending habits and see if you have the resources. If you don't, this may be the first obstacle to overcome. You can check other sources of income, such as bank loans, government loans, family, friends or partners, and mortgages.

Start off by using this worksheet to figure out where you stand right now.

Fixed Annual Expenses:

Insurance_____

Mortgage or rent_____

Car loan payments_____

Utilities_____

                        Total: _____

Flexible Annual Expenses:

Food_____

Entertainment_____

Clothing_____

Miscellaneous_____

                        Total: _____

Total Expenses: _____

Expected Annual Income: _____

Total Balance: _____

Subtract both totals from your expected annual income. If there is a good balance, or even some left over, that's a good thing. Keep this sheet handy to track your actual versus expected expense and income. One fool-proof way to keep on track is to lay out a plan and stick with it.

Bet You Didn't Know

The leading complaint among self-employed persons is not long hours or isolation, but the lack of health insurance. Make sure that you can cover medical expenses and possible disability before striking out on your own.

Planning It All on Paper

It's the blueprint (to give you structure) and the roadmap (to give you direction) of your company. You'll use it to make decisions, to track your progress, and to obtain investors or loans. What is it? It's the *business plan*. Don't launch your business without one. Lots of specifics are needed here, but overall you must know what your company does and does well. You must also know your customer and know your investor.

The business plan can be divided into four sections: the description of the business, the marketing plan, the financial-management plan, and the management plan. Sounds simple doesn't it? Well, it's not rocket science, but it will take time and thought.

Here's what the plan should look like and the elements it should contain. You can follow these steps and create your own outline, or you can log on to the SBA Web page and locate a Business Incubator near you. Counselors there will be happy to check your work. You can also find lots of small business plan software that will take you through step by step. Just make sure it contains at least some form of the following parts:

Page 1: (cover page)

My New Business, by Iman Entrepreneur

Page 2: (business statement)

To Build the Best Web sites on the Internet

Page 3: (organization)

Table of Contents

Page 4: (as follows)

Section I. The Business Description—contains who you are and why you want to be in business. Make sure to include the following:

1. Form. What form will your business take—proprietorship, partnership, or corporation? Also mention the licenses you will need.

2. Type. Are you in manufacturing, merchandising, or service?

3. Product description. What is your product or service?

4. Is it new, franchise, takeover, or an expansion?

5. Will it be profitable, and why? Examine the growth opportunities.

6. Location, hours, and days of business.

7. Your research on this type of business from publications, franchisors, trade suppliers, and others.

Section II. The Marketing Plan—Identifying and targeting your customers. This section should do the following:

1. Define your customer, age, sex, income, and educational level, their likes and dislikes.

2. Talk about the condition of your target market, growing? Steady?

3. Show how you will attract, hold, and build your market share. Who is your competition?

4. Give your pricing strategy.

Section III. The Management Plan—A good management plan will make success at business less stressful. Here are the four questions you need to answer.

1. Operating procedures. How does your background help, and what will you need to strengthen your weaknesses?

2. Personnel. Who will be on your management team and what are their duties?

3. What are your plans for personnel hiring and training?

4. What benefits, if any, can you offer?

Section IV. The Financial Management Plan—Sound financial management is the cornerstone of every business.

1. A startup budget addressing personnel, legal, and professional fees, licensing fees, equipment and insurance, supplies, utilities, and payroll.

2. Operating budget including any loan applications, capital equipment, balance sheet and breakeven analysis, profit-and-loss statement, and cash-flow projections.

Once you've created your business plan and used it to jump start your company and attract investors, don't leave it in the bottom of a filing cabinet. Look it over often so that you can stay on track and grow. That's why you are doing all the work now, so that later, you actually work less.

Key Leadership Traits

It's not really enough just to want to run a business. You have to have guts, talent, and persistence. You may also have the personality traits of a "born leader." There have been long-standing philosophical discussions about whether leaders are born or made, but many agree on the basic characteristics of leadership. Raymond Cattell, a pioneer in personality assessments, developed this list of leadership traits. Read them for a boost to your self-esteem, or just as a reminder of what it will take to succeed in your new business.

Good leaders are as follows:

➤ **Enthusiastic.** Leaders are often very optimistic and energetic. They're open to change, are quick, alert, and uninhibited. They set examples and use the power of intuition.

➤ **Emotionally stable.** Leaders must be well-adjusted and able to tolerate stress and frustration. They develop people and apply influence.

➤ **Conscientious**. A good leader has high standards of excellence and a desire to do his or her best. Order and self-discipline are strong driving forces.

➤ **Tough-minded**. Poised, practical, logical, and to-the-point. Comfortable with criticism.

➤ **Visionary**. They are experimental, flexible, and creative.

Ready to be a leader? Move on to the next chapter to learn about the care and maintenance of your small business.

The Least You Need to Know

➤ The first step in starting a small business is knowing what you want, and what you do well.

➤ Starting part time from home is an excellent way to plant the seed for growing your own business. More than 20 million Americans now work from home and make money doing it.

➤ One way to cut down on the details of starting from scratch is to buy a business, either from a business owner or buy the rights from a franchisor.

➤ A sound business plan is critical to success. It is both the roadmap for you and a tool to attract investors.

➤ Whether leaders are born or made, you can strengthen your own character traits toward a leadership role in developing your own business.

Chapter 1

Running a Small Business in the New Millennium

In This Chapter

➤ Business strategies for the new millennium

➤ Fundraising for your favorite cause—your business

➤ Make up the grocery list before you open the store

➤ Marketing on a shoestring

➤ Where to find help, online and off

"If you build it, they will come," was the advice actor Kevin Costner heard in a recurring dream in the movie *Field of Dreams*. Despite all the opposing forces, he built a ball field, and the players and fans came. Wouldn't it be nice if we all had that kind of luck? Life is no movie set, but what you probably do have, similar to the character played by Costner, is *vision*. That vision, backed up with persistence, is crucial to the success of the entrepreneur.

Now you need to take that vision of your *ideal business*, and work backward. You know the outcome, right? You the successful entrepreneur heading up the world's fastest-growing widget company, with a staff full of loyal employees and plenty of free time to sail on your yacht. You just need the tools to build your dream. What are those tools? They are a combination of things, such as the business plan, which is a very valuable tool. But there are other business basics for starting up. These are the mechanical steps a new business owner must go through—raising capital, obtaining licenses, and hiring personnel. Not too sexy, but necessary. Then there are the intangible tools that are harder to grasp, but critical to success, such as a good business strategy, planning, and products.

neur voyaging into the new millennium, you have (at your fingertips) f new tools that business people before you could only wish for. The ced the world on your desktop, ready to answer research questions, siness tips, marketing tools, and real-time discussion groups. The running a business are a snap with user-friendly software packages ui online resources. It's easy to become fluent in modern-day business.

Battle Plan for a New Age

The past century rode in on horseback in 1900 and is streaming out on a digital wave. The way people work, live, and travel has changed dramatically in just 100 years, and many predict that the next hundred will move even faster. If there is any one strategy to keep in mind as a new business owner, it is to keep abreast of that change—move with it, anticipate it, plan for it, initiate it. Remember that old line circulating around Hollywood? "*Dahling*, never change, stay the way you are." Forget it, change or perish.

Everyone's trying to coin the best phrase for what is turning into the new business model of how to survive in the twenty-first century. It all hinges on the ability to stay lean and move fast. We can all see that the corporate giants, our heroes of yesteryear, no longer create new jobs; instead, they kill them with downsizing. So who's filling that role? Entrepreneurs are, with their fast growing companies. MIT economist David Birch calls these new companies "gazelles," much like the graceful animal of the African plains, these new startups move swiftly and shift direction the instant a new opportunity appears.

Of course, tracking and being part of change means placing yourself smack in the middle of the fray. The best place for managers to be is on the edge of chaos, according to authors Shona L. Brown and Kathleen M. Eisenhardt in their book *Competing on the Edge*. These authors spoke to the leaders of more than 100 top firms. They all emphasized that *on-the-edge* managers think of strategy as something to be changed. What works today probably won't work tomorrow, so your competitive advantage is fleeting.

Money Meaning

Time pacing is where you drive the rhythm of change inside your own company.

One recommendation is a process they call *time pacing*, where *you* drive the rhythm of change inside your own company. You can do that with the calendar, perhaps rolling out new products or stores at a steady pace. Time pacing is proven to work, but it goes against our natural tendency to wait and move more slowly. Watch out or you'll lose momentum.

Keeping pace in the new electronic economy and with technology's effect on the workplace is also a challenge, because it's changing so rapidly. But it's these very innovations and scientific advances that can catapult you into success. You can do the following:

➤ Form a niche market and easily target your audience.

➤ Cut the lag time between spotting an opportunity and putting it into action by selling a product or service.

➤ Work from home and do business with an international company half a world away.

But you have to keep pace; there is no standing still in this economy; there is only getting left behind.

As a business owner, you'll also want to watch regulatory changes and tax reform—as government adapts to the Internet (as mentioned earlier in this book)—and also to new growth of home-based and small business. Congress has introduced several bills to redefine the home office. With so many people working out of their homes, Congress had to address the issue. There are also bills to ease restrictions on S corporations, a common form of incorporation chosen by small business.

Bet You Didn't Know

In January 1999, the Chairman of the Senate Committee on Small Business, Senator "Kit" Bond outlined an aggressive agenda for the 106th Congress. The major components were: across-the-board tax relief, including 100 percent deductibility for health care; an easing of federal rules and regulations on small business; and a Y2K Relief bill unanimously approved by the Senate two months later.

Form It

How you form your company has a lot to do with how it can grow, and how it will be taxed and regulated. You have to decide which of the three basic forms your business will take: a sole proprietorship, a partnership, or a corporation.

If you go the route of sole proprietorship, you have the ease of flexibility. You own it, you run it, and you can change the direction of your company any time you wish. But along with that freedom comes the responsibility that can change your personal life forever. If the company makes money, it's your income. If the company incurs debt, you owe. If someone sues your company, he is suing you personally and you could lose the farm (so to speak). Not a risk you should take.

You could form a partnership, combining the expertise of two people for the good of your new firm. But a partnership has been described as marriage without the love. Doesn't sound very appealing, does it? Okay, maybe you're married and forming a business with your mate. It could work. It's a gamble, but it could work. Most people involved in partnerships will tell you it is difficult to get partners to agree 100 percent of the time. Just be sure to carefully map out the details and responsibilities in advance. This lessens the accusations and finger-pointing later on.

The third choice is to form a corporation. A corporation is an entirely separate entity from you, your partner, and your hard-earned belongings. It provides a shield between you and most legal problems or liability. Company debts are not your personal debts and as an added bonus, if you incorporate, you can have investors and raise money.

There are two main forms of corporations, the standard C corporation, such as all of those listed on the stock exchange—the big guys that sell shares of stock to raise money. Then there is the S corporation. The main difference between the two is in levels of taxation. C corporations pay a corporate tax, and then anyone drawing a salary from the company pays personal income tax. The money gets taxed twice, in other words.

Not so with the S corporation, which is why people in small business prefer it. S corporation income is just reported on the personal income statement of the shareholders, one-time taxation. But unlike C corps who have the option of going public and selling thousands of shares of their company as stock to raise money, you—the S corporation partner—are limited to 35 shareholders.

You can also choose to become an LLC, or a Limited Liability Corporation. LLC partners can still report on personal income tax returns, and are also offered liability protection without some of the restrictions applied to S corporations.

Take the time to research the differences in tax implications of the various forms of business before making your decision.

Click Here

You can incorporate your business or register trademarks by simply filling out an application online—**www.incorporate.com** and **www.corpcreations.com** are two Internet sites that allow you to apply in 10 minutes or less. The price and length of time until you are officially incorporated will vary, depending on the state in which you form your corporation.

You Name It

Naming your business is just as important and anxiety producing as naming your first baby, and maybe even worse! A child saddled with a monstrous moniker can be thrown a nickname, but your business name will be plastered all over your stationary, storefront, and advertising. A well-chosen name can also provide a real marketing advantage as customers spread the word.

Your name's legal availability is also important; so you'll want to protect it. A trademark can save lots of grief later on as your business grows and gains market acceptance. You can use the symbol ™ to alert the public to your claim, but the symbol ™ can only be used when the mark is registered in the PTO. A trademark is different from other forms of identity protection (such as a *copyright*, which protects an original artistic or literary work; and a *patent*, which protects an invention).

Why do you think companies such as Toys-R-Us and McDonalds aggressively pursue anyone who tries to put "R-Us" or "Mc" in their company names? They want to avoid any dilution of their identity and keep the market share to themselves. There may be plenty of different John Smith's in this world, but there is only one McDonald's, franchise or no franchise.

So how do you *trademark* a name? Check with the United States Patent and Trade Office. It's not as scary as it sounds. In fact, you don't ever have to set foot in that government office. The entire process can take place from your home computer—you can register your company name online at www.uspto.gov.

It can be expensive and time-consuming though. Application fees *start* at $245. And the whole process may take eight months to a year before you receive a final registration certificate, and that's if no one opposes the use of your name. If someone does file an opposition and you want to argue it, it's just like a federal court case, only it's held before the Trademark Trial and Appeal Board. Unfortunately, you will have to leave the comfort of your ergonomically correct computer chair for that life experience.

If you are good at generating business ideas, but having an identity crisis, call for help. You can have others put together the whole corporate identity package for you, from choosing a name to belting out a company jingle. But it will cost you. For $1,000 and up, Nameit.com will find you a creative, trademarkable name, which they claim you can build on without threat of infringement. The lowest fee is for a state trademark; federal and foreign trademarks for larger companies cost much more.

Money Meaning

Trademark is a word, phrase, symbol, or design—or combination of these—that identifies and distinguishes the source of the goods or services of one party from another. Trademark rights arise from either actual use of the mark or the filing with intent to use the mark with the Patent and Trademark Office (PTO).

Once you've decided on the company name, you need a logo for branding purposes. The logo becomes the symbol that triggers customers to think of your company and should be used liberally on all your stationary and advertising. Unless you are the artistic type or saw the logo in that dream, you should leave this job to the professional design services. One quick fix is to use a company that will do the whole enchilada, like 1-800-MyLogo.

This firm is based in Montreal, but you'd never know because the only office you'll ever see is their virtual one at www.1800mylogo.com. You can get help solving your identity crisis with the basic Ultra Identity package for $169. This bargain package includes a custom designed three-color digital logo you can use on your computer to create your own stationary, and they throw in a Web page for two years. When you're ready to do an advertising blitz, they also create interactive brochures and customized Web sites.

Finding the Dough

You have a name and an identity—you're somebody! You're very close to opening your doors to business, but what are you planning to do for startup capital? Most small business owners use their own savings to launch their companies. You may already have some capital saved up, good for you. If not, it's time to seek help from another source, such as the commercial banking system.

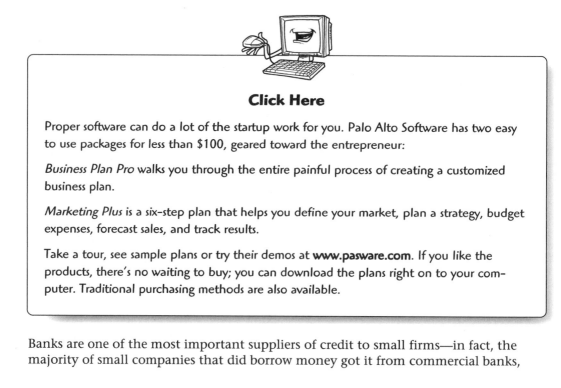

Click Here

Proper software can do a lot of the startup work for you. Palo Alto Software has two easy to use packages for less than $100, geared toward the entrepreneur:

Business Plan Pro walks you through the entire painful process of creating a customized business plan.

Marketing Plus is a six-step plan that helps you define your market, plan a strategy, budget expenses, forecast sales, and track results.

Take a tour, see sample plans or try their demos at **www.pasware.com**. If you like the products, there's no waiting to buy; you can download the plans right on to your computer. Traditional purchasing methods are also available.

Banks are one of the most important suppliers of credit to small firms—in fact, the majority of small companies that did borrow money got it from commercial banks, according to a National Survey of Small Business Finances. The banks realize that small business is the cornerstone of the U.S. economy. After all, small businesses employ nearly half of the country's workforce and account for over half of the sales receipts. The banks, of course, know a profitable venture when they see one. In fact from 1994–1996, the latest data available, small-business-friendly banks were more profitable than banks that made few small business loans. Take that data to your lender to bolster your proposal!

What Do I Have to Do to Get a Loan?

Don't even consider applying for a loan unless you have a very polished copy of that business plan discussed in Chapter 17. You will also have to supply financial statements projecting your future profits. Along with that comes the personal stuff—a description of your experience and management capabilities as well as the expertise of other key personnel. They want to know that you can run a company and make some money to pay them back.

Be prepared to answer these key questions from the lender:

➤ How will you use the loan?

➤ How will you repay the loan?

➤ How much do you need to borrow?

It is important to understand that you will be charged an interest rate on the money you borrow. You probably already know that. But did you know that interest rates often reflect the level of the risk the investor is undertaking? You shouldn't take it too personally when you realize that as a new business you are charged a higher rate of interest than some other well-established company. You represent a greater risk to the lender, despite the confidence you have in yourself and your ideas.

Money Meaning

An **angel** is a wealthy individual who provides startup capital to very young companies to help them grow, taking a large risk in exchange for a potentially large return on investment (also called an *angel investor*).

Although most lenders prefer to invest in proven businesses, there are banks that are truly small business friendly. The SBA Office of Advocacy realized how critical it is to small business to know which banks will help them out. It saves precious time and makes money shopping much more efficient. As part of ongoing study called Small Business Lending in the United States, they update an annual directory (www.sba.gov/ADV/lending/bk_int97.html) that ranks the small business lending performance of every commercial bank in each state.

A few things to remember when looking at the SBA online directory is that a small loan is defined as less than $250,000; micro loans are defined as less than $100,000. Also, bank consolidations continue to affect the small business loan market. From the SBA directory, we have compiled a condensed list of banks dubbed SBF, or small business friendly. Check out who the real friendly neighborhood banker is in your hometown in Appendix B.

Bet You Didn't Know

It may come as a surprise, but lots of companies fail because they get too big too fast. If you are a small dynamic company that's growing, you might consider selling shares of stock in your company in exchange for an infusion of capital and loss of some autonomy to investors. The Angel Capital Electronic Network (ACE-Net) is a nationwide Internet-based listing service that provides information to angel investors about growing businesses seeking $250,00 to $5 million in equity financing (**https://ace-net.sr.unh.edu/pub**).

Tax and Insurance

One of the drawbacks of being in business is the paperwork. If you are an organized person, you may enjoy setting up your accounting system. Sure, and you like filling out tax returns too, and questionnaires in doctors' offices, right? Sorry, not me. But it is important to start off with a good system right from the start. Your banker will approve, and it may even help you secure that loan. You will also be ready for all the forms that will inevitably come your way at tax season.

As a business owner, you basically become an agent of the government. You now have to collect sales tax and withhold income tax; you have to keep accounts of it and be ready to forward the government its share. The more you make, the more you pay—what a bittersweet pill to swallow. Before you give up in despair, take heart in the array of tax and accounting software available today. You can keep up the basic bookwork yourself with your mouse working with some of the following cutting-edge tax sites and software. Click on taxsites.com for a comprehensive resource of tax preparation, regulations, laws, associations, software and just plain helpful articles and tips.

A good tax program will help you avoid errors and find deductions. Here are some of the leading software packages:

➤ TurboTax Deluxe by Intuit—Many versions, from individual to sole proprietor to corporations and partnerships. www.taxcut.com.

➤ Kiplinger TaxCut—Tax preparation tools, tax advice, a good, usable interface. www.taxcut.com.

➤ TaxACT '98—A free standard version or the Deluxe edition for only $9.98. Download a copy at www.taxact.com.

But because tax laws are always changing, it really pays to have a professional accountant review your work. They can advise you on every possible deduction you can take to minimize the tax bite on your profits.

Don't forget to cover those profits and your assets with insurance. You will need to insure your business and any employees you may hire; so it pays to shop around. Explore the possibility of an umbrella policy that bundles together the different coverage such as home, fire, auto, and property, as well as business liability. You could end up with a lower-priced policy.

Human Resources

If you do need extra hands at work, your insurance needs hinge on whether you go with full-time help or temporary employees. A temp agency's hourly fees cost a bit more than if you hired directly. For example, you decide on a fair wage of $10 an hour for an entry-level office worker, but the agency charges you $16. That's because they cover all the tax and insurance issues for you, as well as conduct initial interviews. It's a pretty good way to solve your early staffing needs and allows you to screen people that you may want to take on full time.

Keep in mind that business owners are facing the worst labor shortage in 20 years. The baby boomers are coming of age and leaving the youthful market sparse. Of course that also means there may be a lot of boomers looking for part-time work to kill time.

Regardless of whom you hire, you want the right person, and that takes a lot of work. As usual, the amount of homework you do before you start hiring makes the whole process simpler and more effective. First conduct a thorough job analysis so that you know exactly what duties you want that person to perform. Then decide on a salary equal to the duties and the competition.

Practice your interview techniques and determine where you will recruit. A good place to start is to review the Electronic Recruiting News at interbiznet.com/ern/archives/recruitonline.html. Most high schools and colleges have career placement offices. Call and find out the best way to post your information. Once you hire the right people, make sure to offer challenges and incentives to keep them interested and loyal.

Turn the Key and Start It Up

You're anxious to launch your new business. Before you turn the key, however, it's time to go over that last-minute checklist. You may have a few more steps to go before opening day.

The Pre-Business Checklist—Are You Good to Go?

- ❏ Prepare a business and marketing plan (see Chapter 17). Include your action timetable.
- ❏ Choose a business name and check its availability.
- ❏ Register business name, copyrights, trademarks.
- ❏ File corporation papers (more on this in this chapter), if necessary.
- ❏ Acquire any licenses, permits, or zoning variations.
- ❏ Secure capital: bank loans, personal loans, savings.
- ❏ Find a location to set up your business.
- ❏ Secure furnishings, equipment, supplies, and stock.
- ❏ Determine business hours.
- ❏ Install phone lines, either business or extra residential.
- ❏ Check into business and health insurance needs.
- ❏ Apply for sales tax number with your state.
- ❏ Register for a federal tax number (Form SS-4).
- ❏ Get tax information on employee withholding from the IRS.
- ❏ Order the free IRS "Small Business Tax Kit," online at www.us.treas.irs.gov.
- ❏ Hire personnel. Set up job descriptions and training programs.
- ❏ Acquire business cards, stationery, and business forms.
- ❏ Open a business bank account, separate from your personal account.
- ❏ Find out about workers' compensation, if you are hiring personnel.
- ❏ Publicize your business: Send out press releases, tell everyone you know, advertise.

Click Here

The Small Business Association (SBA) has an online library reading room (**www.sba.gov/ library/sharewareroom.html**) that offers shareware files for small business operators. The downloadable files begin with Starting Your Business and go all the way through Financing, Managing, Marketing, and Running Your Business. They include the basics such as event planners and accounting forms as well as inventory-control programs and decision-analysis business tools. They even have the Zip application that allows you to open some of the larger compressed online files.

Taking It to the Street

Ah, that last step, publicizing your business. It's also known as *marketing*, and it's an important step for many reasons. It means that you've come a long way to even be considering a marketing plan, so congratulations. Now your primary job is to attract and keep customers.

Marketing concepts have changed pretty dramatically over the past several years. Instead of developing aggressive strategies to boost sales, the focus is now on the customer and creating solutions for their problems. Some call it *customer-centered* marketing. You'll also hear a lot about *one-to-one* marketing, where you customize for the individual rather than *one-to-many* where we scatter shoot at a mass market. We're getting personal with our customer.

In tough times, the marketing budget gets cut first; but if businesses continue to market effectively even in lean times, they grab more market share and come out ahead. Some of the best marketing methods are the cheapest, like those on our list:

➤ **Keep your customer happy**. Your best advertisement is a satisfied customer. Serve them well so they will brag about you.

➤ **Keep a list of client names and addresses**. The old rule of thumb is that it costs five times as much to get a new customer as to service an existing one. Use your database to communicate with your loyal customers often; send letters of upcoming sales, new merchandise, or a company event. Don't forget the email address. A recent poll by Ernst & Young and another by the American Management Association revealed that email is now preferred over the telephone, and is used more frequently that any other communication tool.

➤ **Ask for a response to your mailings and advertisements**. Offer an extra discount or a coupon or a free sample. This way you know if your advertisements are working, and potential customers get a close look at your product or service.

➤ **Build awareness through special events such as contests or sweepstakes**. This takes a bit of planning, but you have the opportunity to generate publicity through the contest and then by playing up the winners.

➤ **Post an electronic business card for free at U.S. Business Cards** (www.sba.gov/buscard). You can also search the cards for services you may need.

Marketing is the life-blood of your business and demands constant attention to your customers' needs. Besides the previously discussed ideas, you need to work to attract customers with every marketing vehicle appropriate (be it newspapers, brochures, direct mail, radio, or newsletters). With the digital age full upon us, you must also consider the advantages of a company Web site.

Click Here

The Smart Business Supersite, **www.smartbiz.com**, has a huge collection of business information in the form of news articles, careers, profiles, Web links, special services, events, and much more. For example, they have a fact sheet with detailed information on each state's requirements and licenses for small business. SBS is striving to be the Staples or Home Depot of business info, and they're pretty darned close!

Common Causes of Business Failure

We don't want to drop a wet blanket on your enthusiasm, but sometimes if you know where the potholes are in the road, you can avoid them while driving in a flood. The most common causes of business failure are usually internal. They are fairly easy to spot if you have your eyes open. Look out for trouble when any of the following happens:

➤ Expenses exceed revenues.

➤ You have inadequate financing.

➤ You fail to understand your market, your customers, and their buying habits.

➤ Your product or service is of poor quality.

➤ Management skills are poor.

➤ There is inadequate attention to marketing.

➤ You are overly dependent on a single customer.

➤ You have uncontrolled growth.

➤ You fail to react to competition, technology, or changes in the marketplace.

If you run into trouble in your business, only a good diagnosis can lead to a cure. You may be too close to see the real problem, but small business resources abound 24 hours a day—use them!

Finding Help Online

With Internet access, you're never alone. Check with your Internet service provider for a list of chats, discussions, and focus groups. Get out and search the Net.

The U.S. Small Business Administration (SBA) is an independent agency of the federal government. It is charged with providing four primary areas of assistance to American

Small Business: Advocacy, Management, Procurement, and Financial Assistance. Financing comes through SBA's Investment or Business Loan Programs.

Check out the SBA's Hotlist page at www.sbaonline.sba.gov/hotlist/. It has tremendous links to sites within the government, such as Business Information Centers (BICs), One-Stop Capital Shops (OSCSs), Service Corps of Retired Executives (SCORE), U.S. Export Assistance Centers (USEACs), and Women's Business Centers (WBCs).

They also have links outside the government, such as the CCH Business Owner's at www.toolkit.cch.com (offered by CCH INCORPORATED, a provider of business, legal, and tax information and software to the business community). The site has plenty of free downloads in the CCH Business Owner's Toolkit. There are also educational links such as the American Success Institute, a non-profit research, publishing, and educational organization in Massachusetts, media contact lists, and job listings. It's not to be missed as a one-stop resource center.

Here are some other places to search:

➤ The National Federation of Independent Business—www.nfibonline.com is the nation's largest advocacy organization representing small and independent businesses.

➤ Inc. Online: The Web Site for Growing Companies—www.inc.com. An electronic consultant to people starting and running businesses that provides resources and interactive networking opportunities on the Web.

➤ Idea Cafe: The Small Business Channel—www.ideacafe.com. The fast food section of small business resources. As they say on the sight, their information is fast, fresh, friendly and for real.

➤ Entrepreneurial Edge Online—www.edgeonline.com. With articles like, "Perk Up Your Staff," "Sharing the Wealth," "Trail-Blazing Women and Value-Added E-Commerce," need we say more? Yes, they also have extensive business resources and interactive tools and forums.

Finding Help Offline

Both current and potential small business owners have plenty of help in their own town or nearest city. Many are government sponsored and others are non-profit— guaranteeing, if not always free, at least affordable advice and direction.

Small Business Development Centers (SBDCs) provide assistance available to anyone interested in starting or expanding a small business but who cannot afford the services of a private consultant. The following are lead SBDCs:

➤ University of Alabama, Birmingham, AL 205-934-7260

➤ University of Alaska/Anchorage, Anchorage, AK 907-274-7232

➤ Maricopa County Community College, Tempe, AZ 602-731-8720

➤ University of Arkansas, Little Rock, AR 501-324-9043

➤ California Trade and Commerce Agency, Sacramento, CA 916-324-5068

➤ Colorado Office of Business Development, Denver, CO 303-892-3809

➤ University of Connecticut, Storrs, CT 203-486-4135

➤ University of Delaware, Newark, DE 302-831-2747

➤ Howard University, Washington, DC 202-806-1550

➤ University of West Florida, Pensacola, FL 904-444-2060

➤ University of Georgia, Athens, GA 706-542-6762

➤ University of Guam, Mangilao, GU 671-735-2590

➤ University of Hawaii at Hilo, Hilo, HI 808-933-3515

➤ Boise State University, Boise, ID 208-385-1640

➤ Department of Commerce and Community Affairs, Springfield, IL 217-524-5856

➤ Economic Development Council, Indianapolis, IN 317-264-6871

➤ Iowa State University, Ames, IA 515-292-6351

➤ Fort Hays State University, Hays, KS 913-296-6514

➤ University of Kentucky, Lexington, KY 606-257-7668

➤ Northeast Louisiana University, Monroe, LA 318-342-5506

➤ University of Southern Maine, Portland, ME 207-780-4420

➤ University of Maryland, College Park, MD 301-403-8300

➤ University of Massachusetts, Amherst, MA 413-545-6301

➤ Wayne State University, Detroit, MI 313-964-1798

➤ Department of Trade and Economic Development, St. Paul, MN 612-297-5770

➤ University of Mississippi, University, MS 601-232-5001

➤ University of Missouri, Columbia, MO 314-882-0344

➤ Department of Commerce, Helena, MT 406-444-4780

➤ University of Nebraska at Omaha, Omaha, NE 402-554-2521

➤ University of Nevada in Reno, Reno, NV 702-784-1717

➤ University of New Hampshire, Durham, NH 603-862-2200

➤ Rutgers University, Newark, NJ 201-648-5950

➤ Santa Fe Community College, Santa Fe, NM 505-438-1362

➤ State University of New York, Albany, NY 518-443-5398

➤ University of North Carolina, Raleigh, NC 919-715-7272

➤ University of North Dakota, Grand Forks, ND 701-777-3700

➤ Department of Development, Columbus, OH 614-466-2711

➤ Southeastern Oklahoma State University, Durant, OK 405-924-0277

➤ Lane Community College, Eugene, OR 503-726-2250

➤ University of Pennsylvania, Philadelphia, PA 215-898-1219

➤ Inter-American University of Puerto Rico, San Juan, PR 787-763-6811

➤ Bryant College, Smithfield, RI 401-232-6111

➤ University of South Carolina, Columbia, SC 803-777-4907

➤ University of South Dakota, Vermillion, SD 605-677-5498

➤ University of Memphis, Memphis, TN 901-678-2500

➤ Dallas County Community College, Dallas, TX 214-860-5833

➤ University of Houston, Houston, TX 713-752-8444

➤ Texas Tech University, Lubbock, TX 806-745-3973

➤ University of Texas at San Antonio, San Antonio, TX 210-458-2450

➤ Salt Lake City Community College, Sandy, UT 801-255-5878

➤ Vermont Technical College, Randolph Center, VT 802-728-9101

➤ University of the Virgin Islands, St. Thomas, VI 809-776-3206

➤ Department of Economic Development, Richmond, VA 804-371-8258

➤ Washington State University, Pullman, WA 509-335-1576

➤ West Virginia Development Office, Charleston, WV 304-558-2960

➤ University of Wisconsin, Madison, WI 608-263-7794

➤ University of Wyoming, Laramie, WY 307-766-3505

The SBA has offices located throughout the United States. For the one nearest you, look under U.S. Government in your telephone directory, or call the SBA Answer Desk at 800-8-ASK-SBA or 800-827-5722. For the hearing impaired, the TDD number is 704-344-6640.

The following are other sources of information:

➤ State economic development agencies

➤ Chambers of commerce

➤ Local colleges and universities

➤ Libraries

➤ Manufacturers and suppliers of small business products and services

➤ Small business or industry trade associations

Business Incubators also help to hatch young companies. Studies have shown that incubators increase a new company's chance of success by 80 percent or more.

They offer advice, facilities in which to work, and usually have access to capital. Both for-profit and non-profit incubators are growing around the nation. To find one near you, check with the National Business Incubator Association at www.nbia.org.

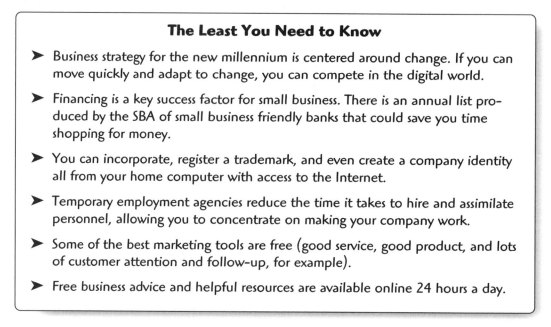

The Least You Need to Know

➤ Business strategy for the new millennium is centered around change. If you can move quickly and adapt to change, you can compete in the digital world.

➤ Financing is a key success factor for small business. There is an annual list produced by the SBA of small business friendly banks that could save you time shopping for money.

➤ You can incorporate, register a trademark, and even create a company identity all from your home computer with access to the Internet.

➤ Temporary employment agencies reduce the time it takes to hire and assimilate personnel, allowing you to concentrate on making your company work.

➤ Some of the best marketing tools are free (good service, good product, and lots of customer attention and follow-up, for example).

➤ Free business advice and helpful resources are available online 24 hours a day.

Chapter 19

Setting Up
Shop Online

In This Chapter

➤ Why you need a Web site

➤ Your Internet host

➤ Building basics—design, promote, maintain

➤ Telling the world

➤ Making the sale

People are logging on to the Net faster than ever before, and show no evidence of slowing down. As of June 1998, nearly 79 million people in the United States and Canada had become Netizens, or members of the Internet. If that's not reason enough for your company to have a billboard on this information superhighway, then get this. Of that 79 million, 20 million were there to buy products and services.

The Internet and the World Wide Web have burst into the scene like no other technology before, taking popular culture and the business world by storm. Pioneers can blaze their own trails now by leveraging this medium to reach customers and suppliers quicker and more efficiently.

Customers will order anything from wine to plane tickets to ostrich eggs; and if they haven't bought something, it's more likely that they just can't find what they want. The Internet is vast and unregulated; so it's easy to get lost. That's why it's important to avoid dumping your company and information on to the Net in a hurry to "get out there." Plan your Internet strategy as carefully as your overall business plan and reap the full benefits of this advertising and sales tool.

Benefits of Taking Your Business Online

Do you have to move on to the Internet to survive? No, but it's strongly recommended as a business tool. No matter what your business is, you can't ignore 100 million people. E-commerce is driving dollars into the hands of the merchant willing to take the step online.

Here are other advantages to an online presence:

➤ **Open 24 hours**. You may be sleeping, but your Web site is open for browsing around the clock. Sure beats paying overtime to sales clerks!

➤ **Global**. Making an international phone call can be frustrating, but global business on the Web is as easy as clicking the keyboard. Decide how your company will handle international business, however, because you're sure to get some transoceanic responses. Web research company International Data Corporation calls 1998 the year the Internet broke in Western Europe. By 2002, they predict that 34 million web users in Europe will spend over $200 billion online.

➤ **Improve method of doing business**. You can shorten sales cycle and completion, speed up transactions (including response time to orders, and make all your business information easy to find.

➤ **Reduce the cost of doing business**. You can save on marketing, print and mailing costs (build a catalog online and mail on request), shelf space (you can stock an item in 50 different places online, and you don't need physical space), and rent!

➤ **Build image and awareness**. The playing field is level on the Net. With a well-designed Web site, you can look as professional as the "big guys."

➤ **Increase productivity**. Make your employees more efficient and productive.

➤ **Sell more stuff**. If you register in the right search engines and drop your address in enough places, people will find you, and hopefully buy what you're selling.

➤ **Target a desirable market**. WWW demographics show a mass-market of college educated Web surfers with a high or growing salary. Think you can use customers like this?

➤ **Target a specific market**. The Net is an excellent place to create your niche business. Even the most specific interest group will have a large

Money Meaning

The **World Wide Web (WWW)** is the part of the Internet that is the most graphical and has become the most commercial. The Web allows you to view and interact with **HTML** (**Hypertext Markup Language**) files that can contain graphics, animation, sound, video, and interactive programs. You do this using a software program called a browser.

representation. With a keyword search, shoppers and browsers can find what they want. Make sure you show up in that search.

➤ **Get feedback**. Build an instant email response into your Web pages and find out what customers like or dislike about your business.

➤ **Test market new products or services**. Once you build a loyal customer base, you can ask them what they think of your new ideas faster and cheaper than traditional advertising methods.

No doubt you will find even more good reasons of your own once your Web site is up and running. If nothing else, you can think of it as passing out your business card to millions of people. Like good old-fashioned personal networking, you're bound to make some connections, and it's up to you to follow up.

Bet You Didn't Know

Virtual malls are just beginning to figure out niche marketing. If your ISP has a mall, find out who they target. If it's a scatter-shot, hitting every market around, forget it. But if it's a bulls-eye on your target, jump in. Otherwise, avoid malls; they tend to be overpriced and informal research shows that visitors don't seem to like malls much. Unlike real malls where people walk by your store to get to another and may be attracted by window displays, shoppers don't walk by windows in a virtual mall; they click right in to where they want to go.

A Web page is not your basic 8.5 × 11 paper page. Web pages are as wide as the viewer's computer screen and their length can go on indefinitely. But you will want to limit the length to about two scrolls and that's only if you've got something really good to say. People are more likely to click than scroll, so you should really keep your information confined to a full screen size and put the rest of the information on a new page.

Putting up a Web page and announcing your arrival is not really enough. If you have a real-life store or business with products and services attractively displayed, why not online too? You can build a full store, take orders, and track activity. You can also seek out customer traffic by registering with search engines, set up reciprocal links with like-minded businesses, and place ads on your page. Let's take a look at this process, one step at a time.

Welcome to the Internet, Let Me Be Your Host

As mentioned in Chapter 1, people and businesses gain access to the Internet by opening an account with an *Internet Service Provider* (ISP). You can sign up for anything from the basic personal account with email and limited online Internet time to commercial accounts with super storefronts, shopping carts, payment capabilities, and your private, dedicated information pipeline.

There are plenty of ISP's out there, close to 5,000 at the time of this writing. This bountiful supply is great for you, the shopkeeper, because they're hungry for your business. Whether it's one of the big guys like America Online and the AT&T Network, or some up-and-coming provider like Earthlink and MindSpring, they usually offer a hierarchy of services. This is the tricky part, deciding what features you'll need and who offers the optimum combination at the best price.

Money Meaning

An **Internet Service Provider (ISP)** is a company that provides individuals and enterprises access to the Internet. An ISP owns or rents the equipment required to have points of presence on the Internet for the geographical area served. Larger ISPs have their own high-speed leased lines so that they are less dependent on telecommunication providers and can provide better service to customers.

Money Meaning

File Transfer Protocol (FTP) is the process by which files are transferred to the Web server. You create and maintain your Web pages on your own computer, and then upload the files to your Web site at your leisure.

Types of Hosts

To succeed, you will need a combination of good technology, an appealing design, and a healthy serving of marketing. That means you'll need *Web space* and fairly sophisticated tools. So you have to look for a provider who is reliable, business-friendly, and who specializes in *virtual hosting*.

Let's take a look at your choices in service providers:

➤ **Dial-up**. Dial-up access providers are in the business of giving people *access* to the Internet. They sometimes offer Web hosting as well, but it's not usually their specialty. Ask your ISP about the access speed and bandwidth. Most ISPs have a bunch of users on their servers and divide up the bandwidth among them. Too many users, too little bandwidth; and that means slow access.

➤ **Web host**. This means your Web site will live on their computers and you simply carry the necessary software on your computer that allows you to access the site and make changes. Here's how it works. The host has a big connection to the Internet, whether it be ISDN or the T's, T1 or T3. You obtain dial-up access by your local ISP, and then send your Web page information via *FTP* to your Web host. Keeping your Web host and ISP separate makes good business sense, because you can then change providers without having to move your site.

Top-drawer Web hosts maintain dependable, high-speed connections designed to keep visitors and customers from getting frustrated with slow download times (you know, the ones that gave WWW the name World Wide Wait?). This is what you want.

What's the Real Price?

Ignore the free home page offers you see popping up on the Web. Although you do need to conserve resources as a startup business, those pages are really for personal introductions—like, "I am so-and-so and I like to sail, cook, and read the classics. Click here for a list of my favorite books and recipes." If you try to sneak your business into a personal account, the provider may get wise and dump you. Business accounts bring in more traffic and can tie up their service with busy signals. Check with your ISP about any restrictions on your account to avoid surprises.

Virtual hosting, also known as virtual domain, is when the ISP allows you to use your own domain name, www.yourcompany.com, rather than www.serviceprovider.com.yourcompany. You can have your provider check for availability and register your domain name or you can do it yourself.

Free storefront space is no bargain either. They are usually offered by startup companies that haven't worked out their own bugs yet. You have little freedom when it comes to changing or adding pages, and are also limited as to the number of items you can sell. It's also best to avoid the "instant sites," or Web pages that you create by typing in text and selecting options. Most of these sites email your completed pages to you, and you present the finished creation to a host service. It's an okay way to get out there fast, but they are fairly unprofessional looking.

For a good, business-friendly Web hosting service, expect to pay between $25 to $75 dollars a month. Remember all the hungry hosts out there? You can make deals, such as with design help or discounts for paying in advance and whatever else you can think up. You will probably be charged a onetime setup fee of $30 to $75, but that's negotiable too. Any other expenses come from the add-ons, such as design, management, retail tools, and upkeep of your site (if you don't want to do it yourself).

Click Here

To find an Internet service provider in your area, check out The List at (**www.thelist.com**), CNET's Ultimate ISP Guide (**www.cnet.com**), or Snap! (**www.snap.com**). Look for a provider that can offer you the access speed and computing services that fit your needs and budget. At the time of this writing, The List had 4,882 providers; CNET had 2,300.

Let's start by assuming that you will be doing the management, or updating of information, of the site yourself. It's cheaper, and gives you more flexibility and control. And it's fairly easy. You will need some very basic computing equipment and basic software, usually provided by your ISP or host. Here's what you need to get started:

➤ **The equipment.** A Pentium PC 90 MHz processor or higher or a Power Macintosh processor, 24MB of RAM, CD-ROM drive, 10 to 20MB of free hard disk space at the absolute minimum (memory gets gobbled up very quickly) 56K modem (28.8 will work, but it's slower on downloads).

➤ **Web pages.** You will design and upload your content and graphics to the Web site either with the software provided by the ISP or with your chosen authoring tool. Professional design and content developing will cost extra. Many services also have a design team or outsource to a consultant. You can always get help with the first phase and then add pages yourself.

➤ **Maintenance.** You will monitor your own site and update with any new articles, prices, or relevant changes to let visitors know that someone is there.

You probably have all the hardware, and the software should be part of the deal. Make sure you find out what kind of authoring tools the provider supports so that you don't have to switch formats after you've developed your pages.

Compare the Service

Whether a host is based next door or across the nation doesn't really matter, just make sure it's a local call for you to dial up. You can achieve that by obtaining a local access provider.

This section summarizes the range of services and business accounts a host may offer, based on an examination of six different Web host sites now online: AT&T, Bellsouth.net, WebCom, Digital Entertainment Network, CityOnline, Inc., and Zipwell.com.

The Standard Web Site Package

A good way to start an initial online presence for a simple low-volume site. Starting at $24.95 a month.

What they may provide:

➤ A service contract.

➤ Domain name registration.

➤ Email accounts, one or many to give to employees and others.

➤ Space to store your Web pages, from 8 to 20MB. Just like on your hard drive at home, more is better.

➤ Shared bandwidth on a high-speed line, about 500 to 2500MB, to allow for traffic on your site.

➤ Autoresponders, at least one. An auto-responder replies to incoming email automatically.

➤ Web-usage statistics to show the number of hits you get and the type of data being transferred. (Avoid counters, these look unprofessional.)

➤ Limited or no SSL, or space on a secure server for confidential customer information such as credit card numbers or home addresses.

➤ Any necessary software for file transfers to the host and content updating and editing.

➤ Technical support.

The type of technical support really varies, so be sure to ask what kind of assistance you can expect. It will cost more to have 24-hour technical support.

Money Meaning

Common gateway interface (CGI) is the standard way for a Web server (owned by your host) to pass data back and forth between the server and an application. If a customer fills out a form on your Web site, for example, it needs to be processed by an application program. The Web server passes the form information to the application program that processes the data and may send back a confirmation message. The process method is called CGI.

Basic Business

One step up from the standard, a basic business package offers more storage space and secure server space, as well as email accounts and bandwidth to accommodate moderate traffic. Starting at $59.95 a month.

What they may provide:

➤ A service contract.

➤ Domain name registration.

➤ Email accounts, a few more than the standard.

➤ More space to store your Web pages, from 20MB on up.

➤ More shared bandwidth on a high-speed line, 1000 on up, to allow for increasing network traffic.

➤ Several autoresponders, for incoming and outgoing automated emails.

➤ Web-usage statistics to show the number of hits you get and the type of data being transferred.

➤ RealAudio and RealVideo to allow for sound and video on your site.

➤ Password protection that requires passwords and usernames from your visitors to view specific information, files, or directories. Useful for pay-per-view or sites with secure information.

➤ SSL, or space on a secure server for confidential customer information.

➤ Any necessary software for file transfers to the host and content updating and editing.

➤ Technical support and service such as daily backups.

Some of these features are add-ons, but you get the idea of what to ask for.

Online Retail Stores

Online retail stores offer the same features as discussed in the business package, but includes a shopping-cart feature, payment capabilities, and a database server. More storage and bandwidth would also be included. This is a good bet for a high-traffic and animation-heavy site. From $100 a month and up, depending on the goodies you load on. These goodies might include the following:

➤ **Shopping carts**. Interactive programs that allow the customer to select products and services to order. They give a professional look and also improve sales speed.

➤ **Database server**. Most Web stores have both a product database and a customer database that include customer demographic information gathered from registered users. This helps you to track habits and background of your customers.

➤ **CGI-bin access**. Common gateway interface is the standard way for a Web server (owned by your host) to pass data back and forth between the server and an application. If you fill out a form online, for example, it needs to be processed by an application program. The Web server passes the form information to the application program that processes the data and may send back a confirmation message.

Of course, if you're running a store or any kind of business online, you'll need a way to collect the cash. Like everything else on the Web, you can go traditional or modern, but a combination works best.

How Do I Get Paid?

There are different ways to accept payment on the Web, and you should ask your ISP what types of payment transactions they support. What you can do will depend on what they can do, to a large degree.

If you are authorized to accept credit cards, this is the easiest way to handle payment. Customers give their credit card number over a secure connection (provided by the server), and the numbers are re-entered into your credit card terminal device or software (provided by your credit card processor).

Of course if you don't have an SSL, or secure server, there is always the telephone. No matter how sophisticated you get, you should probably always allow phone transactions, because some people are still a little Web-leery in terms of privacy. Place your telephone number prominently on the site and allow customers to call during business hours (put those up too!). A toll-free number is recommended because your audience will be national, even global, and you don't want to lose a sale over the matter of a phone call.

You may already have a merchant credit card account with your bank for phone/fax transactions. If not, you need to set one up with a bank that also handles Internet-based transactions with CyberCash or some other virtual pay system. Your bank will forward your Merchant ID and Terminal ID to CyberCash, who in turn will link those to your new CyberCash ID, and then you're in business!

It was hard work and a lot of research, but you chose an ISP, hammered out a service contract, and found a way to get paid. Now you have to build and transfer the Web pages themselves to your new host.

For Designing Websters

It used to be that if you needed help with a Web site design, you asked the 20-year-old next door with the tattoo and body piercing. It took a lot of time, computer graphics know-how, and just plain creativity. But Web site development has become the latest rage in marketing consultant firms, giving some indication that big business believes in the future of the Net.

For the little guy or gal just starting out, don't let big business scare you. We are not going to tell you how to create a site from scratch; we leave that to the computer geeks. There is plenty of software out there to help you get started, and what we can do is give you the do's and don'ts of Web design that are pretty much universal truths.

Brought down to the bare bones, a good Web site must have logical structure, a pleasing design, and relevant content.

Money Meaning

A **Web authoring tool** is software that allows you to develop and manage a Web site. Programs such as Microsoft's Front Page and Macromedia Backstage make it easy for the novice to work in a WYSIWYG (what you see is what you get) environment without having to learn HTML, the programming language of the Internet. You can edit content, make forms and tables, and create links to pages on your site and others. Make sure your ISP supports the software you chose.

Be Organized

You can start building your logical structure by drawing up an organizational chart such as in the figure below. Most Web pages begin at Home, and spread out from there to facts about the company, information on products and services, and so on.

This chart will also help you determine your *navigation system*—the series of electronic links that help people get around your site. Keep it clear and simple. Make it easy for visitors to find the information they want, especially if you have a complex product that can't be seen in one presentation. If there's no one around to help and customers can't find their way, it means frustration and good-bye site.

Basic company Web organization chart.

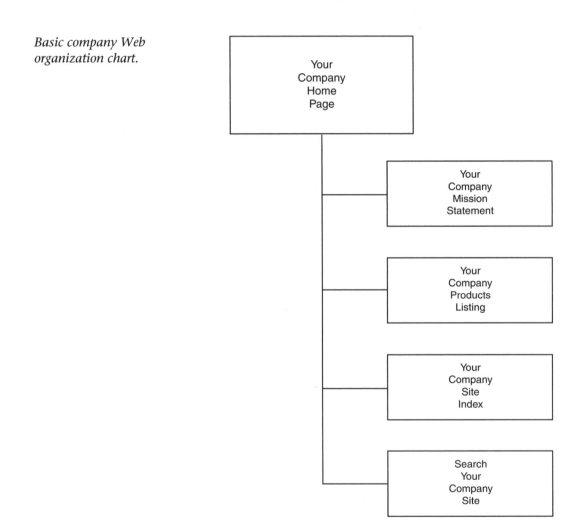

Pleasing Design

Think of one of your favorite shops. Is it clean, pleasant, and nicely lit? Why not give your visitors that same experience? You have basically two senses to work with: look and touch. Make sure your colors are clear, your graphics are quality, and your text is easy to read. Show a sense of unity with a common color scheme and font.

As for touch, remember that the Internet is interactive. Make sure to include ways that people can talk back to you, such as with an online contact form rather than an email link. You may want to include items such as a mortgage calculator for a real estate site.

Content

It's the information age, and you can take full advantage of it on your Web site. If you are not a writer, get someone who is to help you tell the world about your company, your products, and your services. Shorter is better; people are here for speed and convenience, remember? This type of content can be distributed over shorter pages, giving visitors the option to click on and read more or bypass what they have no interest in.

Make your product descriptions clear and compelling. Shoppers can't pick them up off the shelves, so they rely on you to replace that tactile experience with words.

Updating your content is essential for repeat visitors. No one wants to return to that same stale copy you posted on your site three months ago. A regular newsletter can help you stay organized and keep content fresh. You can reprint articles related to your industry, with the written permission of the owner or author. Or write your own, if you are an expert in your field.

Common Mistakes

It seems everybody has a theory on what makes good Web design, but not everyone agrees. What you will find assenting opinions on, however, are what makes for bad design. Here are a few mistakes you can avoid right from the start:

➤ **Too many animations**. Some designers say more than two constantly moving page elements is too many. They overpower and distract from the real content, your product or service.

➤ **Complex backgrounds**. Can confuse the eye and make the text hard to read. Make sure to use contrasting colors for background and text.

➤ **Too many fonts**. There are so many cool letter colors, sizes, and shapes. Use more than two and you show the world you're a newbie designer. Text needs to convey information, not complicate it!

➤ **Too little to say**. Don't copy what other sites say, and don't just create a site of links to other sites. Have something to say before you create your pages.

➤ **Too much to say**. Stick to your business. Don't try to dump your whole life philosophy on your Web site (unless your service is teaching philosophy). Focus on your topics, and make sure your site map and menu are organized and focused as well.

➤ **Outdated information**. This was briefly covered in the section titled "Content," but it should be repeated. No one wants to read old information, and they don't want to click on dead and broken links. Update!

➤ **Orphan pages**. Others may click to one of your pages directly from another Web site without going through your home page, so make sure every page is clearly identified. Also make sure there is a link back to the home page from every page for the same reason.

➤ **Long download times**. The World Wide Wait again. We've said it before and we'll say it again: Don't add bells and whistles just for effect; it slows customer access. They lose interest, get frustrated, go away, and never come back. Yikes!

➤ **Bad Netiquette**. Don't forget to use good manners on the Net. Don't publish copyrighted materials without permission, don't put up links to someone else's page unless the other person wants the exposure, and don't send unsolicited email even though it costs you nothing (it bogs down servers and wastes bandwidth).

Click Here

Who you gonna call? The Internet is an awesome place for research and retail, but it's also rife with scammers. Sites such as **www.scambusters.org** are trying to make the Web safe for surfers. They have articles detailing current scams and email hoaxes, called "urban legends." They also have a Check Station where you can scan a list of scams to protect yourself from being taken. Too late? They have ideas on where to find justice.

You should also do your best to learn as much as you can about the medium. You have a good start in these pages, but nothing beats hands-on experience. Log on and experiment with the tools available on the Internet. See what other sites use, and decide what will work for you. Get familiar with the medium and its potential. William Piniarski, owner of WEBster Computing Services and WEBCS.com, a hosting service, says that while it's important not to *underdo* your site, you also don't want to load up on the technology of the day and waste your money. He recommends reading a book on HTML to understand the processes going on underneath the codes.

The Job's Never Done

Consultants like Piniarski say a working Web site should take no more than a week to create from the designer end. Once it gets sent to the service provider, it can take another 72 hours. If they have to register the domain name for you, tack on another day or two. So all told, you could be live within two weeks. But, everyone on the Web is quick to emphasize that the site should never be completed. Updates (there, we said it again) and expansion should be your slogans once www.yourbusiness.com has a place on the Internet.

Are you ready to be the architect of your own success and build that site? If you're still not comfortable with the nitty gritty of Web design, you can have someone do it for you.

Let a Professional Do It

If you are technically or artistically challenged, you can get the whole package put together for you in one place. You can choose your host, have that host design your Web presence, register with search engines, promote your site, and help with maintenance. Sounds pretty easy, doesn't it? As usual, all that convenience will cost you, but it may be worth it for speed and professionalism.

How much, you say? Well, that depends on the complexity of your business; but sites such as Infopage (www.infopg.com) claim they can do all of this for as little as $1,000 for the first year. That includes a redesign of your site, periodic updates, mailing-list maintenance, monthly online newsletter publishing, and more.

If you don't need all that, you can have a basic home page designed for you for about $50. Designs for a complex page can run between $30 to $100 an hour. Startup companies such as Zipwell.com charge much less than the big firms and still provide all the pizzazz. Zipwell.com only charges $125 a page, and they also offer a $49.95 virtual hosting package that includes one month free hosting with 10MB of space (a $29.95 value). MindSpring charges range from $600 basic template page to their custom-designed page for $4,200.

Help Them Out and Save Money

The best way to take advantage of a good designer is to have all your company information ready and the organizational chart (see table earlier in chapter) of how you want the site to unfold before they begin the work. It will save you money.

Also, do some Web surfing and put together a list of sites you really like. Make sure to emphasize what you like about them. If you are impressed with the ease of ordering on www.ordering.com and the simple colorful beauty of www.beauty.com, for example, let your designer know.

Like most Internet businesses, you want to keep your site or online presence somewhat in-line with traditional shops. Online catalogs replace shelf space, and shopping carts hold wares while customers browse, all the familiar items. But Internet merchants also realize that imitating the brick-and-mortar business won't be enough to draw the Internet shopper. Value, selection, and entertainment are all factors to consider when building your Web site. That's why maintenance is an all-important feature.

Assign someone or schedule yourself to do routine maintenance of your site. Just like that garden outside your home, the weeds need to be pulled and the lawn trimmed. Check your links regularly within your site and to outside resources. And make sure you have current dates on your content. Nothing turns a visitor off faster than cobwebs and old dates.

Taking Your Site to the Public

Having a Web site itself is no guarantee of increased business. No one will know it's even there if you don't aggressively market it. According to a 1997 study by Viaweb Inc. of Massachusetts, 70 percent of online shoppers did a keyword search of the web before buying, contradicting an early theory that online purchases were impulse buys. So one of your first publicity moves is to register with the major search engines such as Yahoo!, Lycos, and Web Crawler.

Various sites search according to different criteria; so you need to find out their information before submitting your URL. This helps you to prepare your site as well to get the best possible results and rankings. Some sites ask for a description of the site, and others look for coded HTML information called meta tags. Here are some entries you may might to create for your site:

➤ **Description**. One paragraph with formatted links to your site.

➤ **Keywords**. A list of 25 or more keywords that you would expect people to use when searching for your site or your type of product or service.

You can do this registration yourself by visiting each search engine and submitting your site information one at a time. Boring and time consuming. Submission services can take the pain out of this crucial process for free; others require a small fee; and some offer free trials. The sites are also full of advice, tools, and other services, so be sure to visit:

➤ **DOOG!** (www.doog.com) will register your site with 500 search engines. They offer a six-month-free trial period. After that, each URL, or Web page is about $24.

➤ **123 Launch.com** (www.123launch.com) will submit to the top 30 search engines and directories for free.

➤ **Postmaster** (www.netcreations.com/postmaster/index.html) will submit to more than 300 search engines, directories, and cool sites for $249 per URL.

➤ **Register It!** (www.register-it.com) will register with 400 sites for $59.99 for two URLs.

➤ **Submit It!** (www.submit-it.com/services/webcomv.htm) will register with 400 sites for $60 for two URLs.

➤ **TheSubmitSite** (http://thesubmitsite.com/) offers a collection of sites, tools, books, and resources to help you bring the traffic you need to your site.

➤ **Atajog-Auto-Registralo** (www.enter.net.mx/xyz/atajos/autoregistralo.html) will register with all the Spanish-oriented catalogs on the Internet. For pages written in Spanish only. Free.

There are other ways to tell the world about your new Web site:

➤ **Linkexchange**. You can also gain exposure to your site by exchanging links with other successful sites that are related in subject to you.

➤ **Ad exchange**. You can swap banner ads with other sites as well, for free. Check out the Banner Ad Network at www.linkexchange.com/ for a list of sites willing to exchange ads.

➤ **Site promoters and monitors**. It's important to know how well your site ranks in the top search engines and what to do to improve your position. Sometimes you can pay your host to do this, or you can do it yourself by entering your keywords and phrases into 10 different search engines and scrolling until your company.com appears, or you can buy software like WebPosition (www.ariadesigns.com/webposition). Their standard edition for $99 can support up to 10 domain names, so you can track your site and nine competitors! They also give tips on how to improve your positioning. You can try a limited version for 30 days by going to site and downloading the software, but you won't get the "Secrets to Achieving a Top 10 Position," unless you buy the full version, also available by download.

Success at Making the Sale

Think like a shopkeeper. Learn how to attract customers online by wandering the shops offline. Look at merchandise arrangements and seasonal sales techniques and work them into your own marketing plan. For example, offer smart ways to search. If someone wants a book, for example, don't just offer a book title search. Let him or her enter keywords such as *mystery* or *romance*. When you walk into a bookstore, part of the fun is in browsing, not bee-lining to a particular book.

Offer very competitive pricing. One great feature of the Internet is the ability to search out rock-bottom prices. Web sites like PriceLine.com and BottomDollar.com have based their whole selling strategy on finding the best deals on the Internet. PriceLine even got a patent on their business model. The company lets shoppers name the terms and price for an airline ticket or new car, and then finds a seller to match the terms. The buyer backs up the request with a credit card, which guarantees the seller a sale.

Click Here

Do you need help with your web style? Yale University's Center for Advanced Instructional Media has published a Web Style Manual that's available online at **http://info.med.yale.edu/caim/manual/contents.html**.

People also shop online because it's convenient; so make the method of purchase easy to find. In real-life shops, people tend to ignore the first items they see when they enter the store, as they are adjusting to the new environment. Retail sales consultants call this the "decompression zone." The deeper into the store, the more likely the sale.

Bet You Didn't Know

What the heck's a "moof monster?" Confused by all the cyber-lingo, or futuristic techno words, spawning as quickly as Tribbles (space rabbits) on that old *Star Trek* episode? Check out **www.whatis.com** for enlightenment. They even have whole section on terms, tags, and steps for creating Web pages. Oh, and a moof monster is a vague and undefinable source of trouble for users of information technology. The term is used especially by people who frequent Internet relay chat (IRC) channels. If you suddenly get disconnected from your channel, it's usually blamed on the moof monster; you are said to have been moofed.

Not so on the Internet. Studies show that with each click it takes the customer to complete a sales transaction, your sales potential drops. Successful sites such as Amazon.com make buying a breeze. Your billing information can be programmed so that you can buy with one click. This automatic transaction requires no checkout or confirmation. Easy! Sold!

The Least You Need to Know

➤ As the 100 million online population continues to grow, Internet retail sales are expected to top $400 billion in the first two years of the new millennium, according to International Data Corporation's Global Market Forecast for Internet Usage and Commerce.

➤ You may not need a Web presence to survive in business, but it is one of today's most powerful tools for marketing, sales, and improving the way you do business.

➤ A Web site can be up and running within two weeks and can cost as little as $600 or as much as thousands of dollars. Start small and plan to grow.

➤ A combination of the traditional and cyber-age approach to shopkeeping will help attract and keep Internet shoppers.

Chapter 20

Tomorrow's Jobs

In This Chapter

➤ Tomorrow's labor force—who'll be out there doing what?

➤ Top-10 fastest-growing occupations

➤ Do I need a degree?

➤ Why the job search will never be the same

You will probably change careers at least seven times in your working life. Sound unrealistic? Well, if it's not true for you, it will be for your children. Forget that old rule about not changing jobs too often because it won't look good on a resume. Even resumes have changed! Gone is the icon of the lifetime company employee, signing on to the payroll post-college and signing off to retirement. *Flexibility* is now the work-place buzzword, and that means being flexible in both where you work and what you do there. Why, some of tomorrow's jobs aren't even *thought* of yet. Technology will generate new jobs in fascinating areas, offering untold opportunities. If you like stories of pioneers, whether they be in outer space, open ocean, or early America, now is your chance to forge a new path and become one yourself.

To take advantage of the opportunities, you'll need skills for the hunt *and* for the job. So how do you prepare for tomorrow's jobs? Two words: *career management*. Although you may not want to be self-employed just yet, it will pay to think of yourself as an independent business, a free agent. Have a business plan (where you want to go) and an inventory (job skills) and keep them up to date. Constant personal improvement, whether it be your "people" skills or your technical ones, will keep you in touch with trends in the workplace. With this constantly changing career landscape, one skill that is definitely required and hard to teach is...*imagination*. How about a job as a Web site service manager, email sorter, or robot technician? These positions are not unthinkable anymore.

Computer access and know-how are also "must-haves" on the road to finding the right job. Sure, the classifieds in the local paper can still be helpful, but chances are that the newspaper has an online classified ad section, and so does the town next door and the city on the coast where you've been longing to live. There are also countless career sites brimming with job postings and advice. After you've logged on and found the job you want, with a company you've researched online, you can fire your computer-savvy resume off into cyberspace.

Knowledge is power (as we are fond of repeating), and to manage your career effectively, you need to know which careers have a future and who will be your competition. Population growth limits the size of the ready workforce, and the types of jobs available are limited by consumer demand. By looking at the relationships between the population, its labor force, and the demand for products and services, you can create your own opportunities.

Who's Out There?

You and 149 million other people will be getting up and going to work in the new millennium, making products and providing the services that keep us moving forward. It's a good idea to know who your competition will be in the job market.

Although the labor force will continue to grow and add new laborers, it will be at a slower pace than in the previous 10 years when the baby boomers were first entering the world of work.

As boomers continue to age, they will tip the scales toward the older workforce. Not surprisingly, the 45 to 64-year-old set will grow faster than any other. As they have been doing with every stage along their life path, the boomers will now reshape the way the nation looks at their next step, retirement (or the postponement of it).

Retire at 65? No Thanks, Not for Me!

The number of workers over the age of 55 are projected to rocket to 22 million by 2005, compared to 15 million in the 1980s. Some experts think even that number is understated, and will actually be higher because a lot of boomers won't have enough cash stashed away for retirement.

In other words, many won't retire because they can't. A recent Retirement Confidence Survey revealed that three quarters of those interviewed believed they would have to work past age 65. Add this lack of confidence in retirement funds to longer life spans, throw in concerns over the availability of Social Security in 10 years, and you come up with a recipe for change in the workplace. Phased-out retirement plans and part-time consultant positions will likely evolve as the new way to approach retirement in the twenty-first century.

Other boomers may just want to keep on working for the excitement of it. The most ambitious in this group of the coffee generation over-achievers will no longer face the burden of providing for their young families. They'll want to reap the rewards of decades of job experience. This can affect the labor force in a couple of ways. While those seeking part-time work can help fill the gaps in labor shortages, the power players will have reached the top, and most financially rewarding, posts in government and business. What they should bring to these posts, however, is a greater understanding of the needs of tomorrow's workforce. The boomers were the first generation to experience the joys and heartaches of the two-career family, with its time restrictions and day-care dilemmas. Expect a change in the age-old corporate approach to on-site management and 40-plus workweeks.

Bet You Didn't Know

A survey of the chief executive officers of 76 of the nation's top–100 industrial companies in 1993 by the *Wall Street Journal* revealed that 95 percent had wives who stayed at home with the children. The CEOs were the first of the boomers, and childcare issues that caused family hardship were never experienced by more than 80 percent of them.

Hey, Kid, Need a Job?

What an exciting time to be on the job. We'll see such diversity in the faces going to work in the next 5 to 10 years. About one fourth of the labor force, those aged 35 to 45, should remain the same in terms of numbers. And while the 25 to 34-year-old group is expected to decline by about 3 million, the next group will increase by three million. That will make the 16 to 24-year-old gang the largest it has been in 25 years.

And ladies, it's your turn. Women in all age groups will enter the workforce at a faster rate than men. While we're at it, let's hear it for the cultural mix. The black labor force will increase five percent faster than the white. The Asian and Hispanic force will grow faster too, due to immigration and higher-than-average fertility, according the Bureau of Labor Statistics. What will we all be doing? Service, service, service. While manufacturing jobs are expected to dip, the service and retail trade industries are revving up for the future.

The Top–10 Job Opportunities

It's the future. Millions of new jobs will be created; others will disappear. But if you want to hop on the fastest-growing occupations bandwagon, look to the service-producing sectors such as business and computer services, healthcare, and social services.

The Fastest-Growing Job Markets

Of the 10 fastest-growing occupations, six are in the health services fields and four are computer related. So if you don't know your way around an operating room, but can kick-it-out on a keyboard, you're in luck. The table below shows that the computer industry will experience the largest percentage increase in new jobs; healthcare is a close runner-up.

Top Ten Fastest Growing Occupations, 1996–2006. (Numbers in thousands of jobs.)

Occupation	Employment change, 1996-2006	
	Number	Percent
Database administrators, computer support specialists, and all other computer scientists	249	118
Computer engineers	235	109
Systems analysts	520	103
Personal and home care aides	171	85
Physical and corrective therapy assistants and aides	66	79
Home health aides	378	76
Medical assistants	166	74
Desktop publishing specialists	22	74
Physical therapists	81	71
Occupational therapy assistants and aides	11	69

Source: Bureau of Labor Statistics

Business Bytes

You can't go wrong in the employment field if you keep updating your computer skills. The information explosion has brought us new careers and entire new languages with words such as *Java* and *applets*, *networks*, and *HTML*. All hot-track professions will require computer expertise because businesses rely on computers and the processing of information. The computer industry itself will bring on more than 1.3 million jobs—a 103 percent increase—due to technological advancements and the need for higher-skilled workers.

One thing to remember if you go to work in the computer industry is that job titles tend to evolve. So don't focus too much on what you're called; focus more on the job you'll need to perform. The most powerful combination is to have some technical background along with basic business or interpersonal skills. The business world still places a premium on the ability to communicate and work as a team member.

Bet You Didn't Know

Even though the United States led the world into the digital age, we face possible shortages of skilled labor in these fields. Without a strong effort to train workers to meet the new challenges of the digital economy, the United States will have to farm out high-skilled, high-wage jobs to other countries.

Hey Doc, I Want to Go Home

Healthcare will account for the largest increase of new jobs in any industry, about 3 million in the year 2000. Why? You guessed it, the boomers again. An aging population will demand and require more services. Also, patients will shift out of hospitals and into outpatient facilities, nursing homes, and home healthcare to try to contain costs. The country's move toward managed care will continue to generate a demand for primary-care physicians, the ones who practice a more generalized medicine.

Don't forget technology. Innovative medical equipment for intensive diagnosis and treatment will lead to growth in specialized healthcare fields.

Money for School

Education may finally get some of the recognition it deserves in the professions as it grows in bounds. The hottest jobs for teachers will be in special education and early childhood education. With some 11 million future children under the age of six with working mothers, forecast by the National Organization of Working Women, childcare and preschool workers will be in demand.

Click Here

The Bureau of Labor Statistics has an invaluable Web site at **www.bls.gov** for those deciding on a new or different career path. Click on the *1998-99 Occupational Outlook Handbook* for detailed descriptions of jobs available in the United States, the pay scale, and future outlook.

If I Had a Hammer

The construction industry will add more than 1 million new jobs by 2006, mostly in renovations and in replacing aging systems in our country. This growth will be slower than in past years, but still, it's growth. Industry experts expect a shortage of entry-level workers in the field in the next few years, due to past recessions and the concern for the environment, which slowed construction starts for the early 90s. So strap on your tool belts all you wanna-be Tim Taylors, the home improvement jobs await.

Where to Find the Most New Jobs

The fastest growing occupations are good to know about, but they don't always provide the *largest* number of jobs. If you look at the table below, you can see that a field with slower growth, such as a cashier, may produce more openings than a smaller-sized industry occupation with faster growth, such as computer engineer. So channel your search into an area where you think you'll have the most success. Making money is what matters here, after all. You may not want to be the world's coolest check-out guy or gal forever, but it does provide cash flow and an insider look at business management.

Occupations with the Largest Projected Job Growth, 1996–2006. (Numbers in thousands of jobs.)

| Occupation | Employment change, 1996–2006 | | Most significant source of training |
	Number	Percent	
Cashiers	530	17	Short-term on-the-job training
Systems analysts	520	103	Bachelor's degree
General managers and top executives	467	15	Work experience plus bachelor's and higher
Registered nurses	411	21	Associate's degree
Salespersons, retail	408	10	Short-term on-the-job training
Truckdrivers, light and heavy	404	15	Short-term on-the-job training
Home health aides	378	76	Short-term on-the-job training
Teacher aides and educational assistants	370	38	Short-term on-the-job training
Nursing aides, orderlies, and attendants	333	25	Short-term on-the-job training
Receptionists and information clerks	318	30	Short-term on-the-job training
Teachers, secondary school	312	22	Bachelor's degree

Occupation	Employment change, 1996–2006		Most significant source of training
	Number	Percent	
Child care workers	299	36	Short-term on-the-job training
Clerical supervisors	262	19	Work experience in a related occupation
Database administrators, computer support specialists, and all other computer scientists	249	118	Bachelor's degree
Marketing and sales	246	11	Work experience in a related occupation
Maintenance repairers, general utility	246	18	Long-term on-the-job training
Food counter, fountain, and related workers	243	14	Short-term on-the-job training
Teachers, special education	241	59	Bachelor's degree
Computer engineers	235	109	Bachelor's degree
Food preparation workers	234	19	Short-term on-the-job training
Hand packers and packagers	222	23	Short-term on-the-job training
Guards	221	23	Short-term on-the-job training
General office clerks	215	7	Short-term on-the-job training
Waiters and waitresses	206	11	Short-term on-the-job training
Social workers	188	32	Bachelor's degree
Adjustment clerks	183	46	Short-term on-the-job training
Cooks, short order and fast food	174	22	Short-term on-the-job training
Personal and home care aides	171	85	Short-term on-the-job training
Food service and lodging managers	168	28	Work experience in a related occupation
Medical assistants	166	74	Moderate-term on-the-job training

Source: Bureau of Labor Statistics 1998-99 Occupational Outlook Handbook

The deciding factor for someone trying to make money in the millennium is not only to keep up cash flow, but to keep on top of the fields with the most promise and the most pay. In 2000 and beyond, education is essential for a high-paying job.

What's in a Degree?

Here's an important equation to keep in mind when thinking about a career that makes money. High pay + low unemployment = education.

If you want a job with high pay and low unemployment, you'll most likely need a college degree. A bachelor's degree is almost elementary, followed by work experience. Here are the levels of education as defined in the previous table:

➤ **First professional degree.** To complete this academic program usually requires at least six years of full-time equivalent academic study, including college study prior to entering the professional degree program.

➤ **Doctoral degree.** Three years of full-time equivalent academic work beyond the bachelor's degree.

➤ **Master's degree.** One or two years of full-time equivalent study beyond the bachelor's degree.

➤ **Work experience, plus a bachelor's or higher degree.** Most occupations in this category are managerial occupations that require experience in a related non-managerial position.

➤ **Bachelor's degree.** At least four years, but not more than four years of full-time equivalent academic work.

➤ **Associate degree.** Two years of full-time equivalent academic study.

➤ **Postsecondary vocational training.** Some of these programs last only a few weeks, while others may last more than a year. If a license is required, you'll have to pass a course test.

➤ **Work experience in a related occupation.** Examples of occupations requiring work experience are supervisory or managerial occupations.

➤ **Long-term on-the-job training.** This category includes occupations that generally require more than 12 months of on-the-job training or combined work experience and formal classroom instruction. Formal and informal apprenticeships may last up to four years. Individuals undergoing training are generally considered to be employed in the occupation.

➤ **Moderate-term on-the-job training.** Workers are expected to develop the skills needed for average job performance after 1 to 12 months of combined on-the-job experience and informal training.

➤ **Short-term on-the-job training.** Most of us are familiar with type of training. We're expected to develop essential skills after a short demonstration or nearly a month of on-the-job experience or instruction.

Are there fields that offer higher-than-average earnings, without the diploma? Yes. Many occupations still do not require a college degree, such as registered nurses, blue-collar worker supervisors, electrical and electronic technicians/technologists, automotive mechanics—Had your car serviced lately? Seen that bill? Ouch!—and carpenters.

What You Can Expect to Earn

The Web has transformed the art of negotiating pay raises and even entry-level salaries. Thanks to the Internet, there are numerous job sites where you can check what you're worth, pay-wise. Because salary ranges are subject to change, check this list of sites regularly for updates on salary surveys, job listings with specific pay levels. You can even set up your own customized compensation analysis.

The following table lists Web sites with pay data.

Internet Address	What They Offer
Jobsmart.org	Links to more than 200 salary surveys on the Web.
Wageweb.com	Online salary service with free information on more than 150 benchmark positions. For detailed job specifications and locations, a $100 fee applies.
Execunet.com	Cruise their Career & Salary Watch free for the hot jobs and their salaries in the past two weeks. Job details and location information will cost you $125.

Armed with this information, you can march confidently into any recruiter's office and haggle for competitive pay. For the current starting salary range in the top-10 fastest-growing occupations, look at the following table. This starting salary chart from the Bureau of Labor Statistics and WageWeb can show you where to focus your energies for the best paid start in your career.

Starting Salary Range for the Fastest Growing Occupations, 1996–2006.

Occupation	Starting Salary Range (from '96 to '98)
Database administrators, computer support specialists, and all other computer scientists	$51,000 to $88,000
Computer engineers	$38,000 to $72,000
Systems analysts	$46,000 to $68,000
Personal and home care aides	$11,500 to $13,400
Physical and corrective therapy assistants and aides	$24,000 to $34,000
Home health aides	$11,500 to $16,000
Medical assistants	$20,000 to $24,000
Desktop publishing specialists	$24,000
Physical therapists	$42,000 to $57,000
Occupational therapy assistants and aides	$24,000

Source: BLS and WageWeb.com

What if you want to get a better job and know you need more education, but can't find the time? After all, you're already working full time just to pay the bills and treat yourself to a few luxuries. Here come a few more benefits of the digital age.

First, you can start on a cyber-degree from your home computer. Distance learning, as logging on to college courses is often called, is fast becoming a new-age education tool. You can live in Nebraska and earn a bachelor's degree from Virginia, driving little more than your mouse across the desk. Once you've completed that extra training, you can go on to do the entire job hunt right from home.

The Job Hunt in the Cyber-Age

Today's job search skills are very different from five years ago. Equipped with computer and modem, you have access to the World Wide Web and all its offerings. Not only can you read the daily classifieds online from the city or town newspaper of your choice, you can research the job types and salaries, even the companies offering them.

By learning all you can about an organization, you can pinpoint career opportunities that fit your skills, interests, and experience. Don't forget to learn the names of the people you need to talk to first at that company. It can save you a lot of time sifting through secretaries.

Click Here for Your Next Paycheck

Increase your chances of finding the right job by logging on and searching through professional associations and career-related sites such as Monster Board.com and Careerpath.com. A simple keyword search of the word *careers* will net you a wealth of job listings, postings, and information. If you're serious about finding a new job, or even just testing the surf, you can post your updated cyber-resume and wait for results.

Click Here

The **www.mediainfo.com** site has thousands of links to online newspapers and help-wanted ads. Increase your career opportunities by scanning these ads often. If nothing else, it will help you keep on top of industry trends.

Cyber-Friendly Resumes

Forget what you know about putting together a resume. Well, maybe the content can stay the same, but the paper you use and the way you submit them has changed with the digital age. Sixty percent of large companies now store resumes in a digital format. Just look on the shelves of your local computer store; *OCR* software is cheap and plentiful, so small businesses are not far behind in this practice. Human resource personnel use the software to scan the incoming flood of resumes and later do a keyword search when they want to fill a post.

A company's email address is often as prominent as their phone number in a want ad. Use it. Companies usually need to fill positions *yesterday*; so the sooner your resume arrives, the better your chances of an interview. Emails are instantaneous.

If the computer liked your resume, you're on the list of candidates. Otherwise it will spit your curriculum vitae out like so much digital waste. What do these computer systems like and dislike? You'll have to forget about presentation, and think information.

Money Meaning

Optical Character Recognition (OCR) software is used by many large corporations to read and store letters and numbers in a searchable text format. The human resources department uses this software to filter through hundreds of resumes with a keyword search for job candidates.

Here are some tips:

➤ Contact the company first and see if they scan incoming resumes. If they do, you may want to send in two copies, one for the humans and one for the scanner.

➤ Use only white 8 1/2 × 11 paper printed on one side.

➤ Do not fold your resume if you're mailing it. The text in the creases will warp, most likely at the point where you sing your highest praise.

➤ Use only sans-serif fonts, the ones with no jogs on the ends and make it 12 to 14 points in size. Both the humans and the system prefer to read large fonts.

➤ Use plain text only, no italics, bolding, or underlining. These make the letters run together, which translates into computer gibberish.

➤ No graphics. Those snazzy images you have peppered over your paper gives the computer indigestion.

➤ Increase the success of your email submission by restricting the width of your resume to 68 characters. Most email browsers display 70 characters across. This way your resume won't turn into a jumbled mess.

➤ Create a keyword section that will be sure to trigger the computer scanner. Use job specific words that would be recognized by a recruiter in your field. Make this a separate section and delete it from hard copies you mail in.

➤ Use a high-quality, high-resolution laser printer to print your scannable resume.

Tomorrow's Job Interview

What human resource specialists are saying about the job interview of the future is that people count. Although you'll be expected to have some of the required job skills, it's very important to have people skills. With the digital age firmly upon us, it's no wonder. We want good people around us to make up for the impersonal computer.

Here are a few tips on how you can prepare for an interview today and tomorrow:

➤ **Research the company.** Start with the Internet and learn some facts and names. Really impress the interviewer with your knowledge of their operations.

➤ **Role play.** Act out with your friends or family and get personal about it. You're going to be asked questions that deal less with the position and more with your work habits, your personality traits, how you interact with others, and the type of environment you need to be successful.

➤ **Dress conservatively.** Professional dress stands out, despite trends toward jeans in the workplace. Wear the denims once you get the job; we tend to act differently and are perceived differently when we dress professionally.

Bet You Didn't Know

The most common temporary jobs in 1997 were for secretaries at an average pay of $12.77 per hour and office clerks at $9.82 per hour. The highest paid temps were computer programmers at $39 an hour and engineers at $27.45 an hour, according to a 1997 survey of nationwide companies by Coopers & Lybrand.

It's Only Temporary...or Is It?

If you can't decide what you want to be when you grow up (and even us grown-ups still wrestle with that decision), one of the best ways to check out a potential field of employment is to do temp work. It's also a great way to check out a potential employer. According to a 1997 Coopers & Lybrand nationwide survey, 88 percent of the companies surveyed said they used temporary services in the past year. Those same companies hired an average of 22 percent of their temps as full-time employees. So it also proves to be an excellent way to become a permanent employee

Perhaps the best way to think of yourself in *any* job is as a temporary employee. In the words of the self-styled futurist Watts Wacker, if you're not an owner, you're a temp. So be ready to be mobile.

What Happened to Career Security?

Outsourcing, downsizing, rightsizing, and streamlining. Hearing those words from a supervisor can still the heart of the most upbeat employee. How can you take the fear out of employment in the age of the pink slip? There is only one way and we told you about it at the beginning of the chapter; it's called career management. Take charge of yourself and think like a free agent, even when you're collecting a paycheck from an employer, especially if you're working for an employer. Here are some tips to stay on your toes:

➤ **Inside**. Stay tuned in to the workplace. Information is power, and if you don't know what's going on in your own office, you could get left behind. This is really no time to mind your own business, but to mind the one you're in. Watch where your organization is headed, and hopefully you'll go there with them. If they're on the way down, it will be no surprise to you; your Abandon Ship bag will be already packed. Don't feel bad about looking out for yourself. There is no loyalty or justice in the age of the pink slip.

➤ **Outside**. Watch the world change, track societal trends, and think strategically. Is there anything you should be doing today to protect or propel your career into tomorrow? Do it.

➤ **Your Career**. Change means new opportunities. This is where your morphing skills and your detective tendencies need to be honed. Look for problems to solve as the company speeds through its rapid changes, or be ready to move on and take your carefully honed skills with you. Don't make deep sentimental attachments; find those at home or at church. And don't attach your photographs to the office walls too firmly—be ready to move like a gazelle at the chance for better grazing.

All these steps add up to good career planning, which means you cover more bases while expending less energy. That way you increase your chances of finding the company and job that matches your skills and allows you to grow professionally.

The Least You Need to Know

➤ The workforce will grow to a multicultural mix of 149 million in 2005, with many new jobs being created while others will disappear.

➤ The fastest-growing occupations for the future are in the health service and computer-related fields. An understanding of business and interpersonal communications will be welcome in all those fields.

➤ The highest paying jobs will go to those with an education, a bachelor's degree or higher.

➤ The computer is changing the way we look for jobs and submit resumes. If you're not computer-savvy yet, it's time to get wired.

➤ Career management is a personal project that everyone needs to undertake for the millennium. Corporate loyalty and workplace justice are notions of the past, if indeed they ever existed. Operate like a free agent, regardless of who you work for or where you work.

Chapter 21

Telecommuting into the Millennium

In This Chapter

➤ The changing corporate culture

➤ Forces that drive us from the workplace

➤ Why don't we all telecommute?

➤ Preparing yourself to beam to work

➤ Preparing your boss

Given the option from your employer of more spare time with your family or more money, which would you choose? If you're like most employees, you'd opt for time. Corporate America found that out in the early 1990s when to their surprise, employees revealed that money was not the greatest motivator. Although competitive pay and advancements are appreciated, it is the command of our everyday lives and an element of control in the work we do that keep us satisfied. Large organizations such as the Ford Foundation, AT&T, Dupont, and Johnson & Johnson learned that workplace flexibility and family-friendly policies were key to keeping good employees on the job.

They are also finding that it pays to be nice. By offering flex-time, telecommuting, job sharing, and compressed work weeks, business managers have seen a direct effect on the bottom line. Let's not forget to mention the increased efficiency, fewer sick days, and greater organizational commitment from employees.

So we see how the boss benefits by a more flexible approach, and we see how you reap personal rewards, but what about your financial gain? If you believe that money saved is money earned, you gain by paying less for transportation, food, and the clothing costs associated with the daily commute. And many telecommuters report a better rapport with the boss, which leads to a more prosperous career. One more thing, and don't use this to get the boss's approval for a new schedule, but it's been shown that successful telecommuting is one step away from successful business ownership.

Of course the information revolution is at the base of this change in the workplace. Modems, faxes, and computers make it just as easy for a manager to keep in contact with an employee down the hall as one down the highway. The technology exists, it's easy to use, and is getting cheaper every day. So as long as you do the job, who cares where it gets done?

From Disposable to Indispensable

Worn-out workers at the turn of the century were replaced as easily as we replace light bulbs today, and with just as much ceremony and sentiment. Anyone who's read Upton Sinclair's 1906 novel *The Jungle*, remembers how stockyard workers didn't miss a beat when one of the exhausted crew fainted and fell into a rendering tank. The substitute guy was just grateful to have a job.

One hundred years later, unfair labor practices still exist in the world, but the American workplace has changed. You could even say that it's moved closer to home. The focus is now on "quality of life" and choice. That shift in social thinking along with a tight labor market and the explosive growth of the Internet helped to boost the number of telecommuters in the United States to 11 million in 1997.

What Is Telecommuting, Anyway?

If you regularly work away from the office a few days a week, either at home or on the road, you are telecommuting. Often referred to as telework, this new method of organizing how the job gets done is being touted as the management tool for the 1990s, although it didn't really pick up speed until the late 1990s. By offering employees relief from long commutes and flexibility in their work hours, supervisors hope to increase productivity and morale.

Not necessarily a company benefit, telework is a cooperative arrangement between you and your boss. These arrangements are usually based on the needs of the job and your performance level. Here are some common options for a flexible workplace:

➤ **Telecommuting**. Working from home or a decentralized location one or more days a week during normal business hours. Telecommuting does not mean working from home full time.

➤ **Flextime**. A variable work schedule different from your department's normal work schedule, but using the same number of hours. Employees are often asked to be available during "core hours" of perhaps 10 a.m. to 3 p.m.

➤ **Compressed work week**. The same amount of hours worked in fewer days—for example, a 40/10/40 means a 40 hour week is compressed into 4, 10-hour days. Another example is the split week, where you work nine, nine-hour days over the course of 10 work days.

➤ **Job sharing**. Two or more employees share one job. Success depends on finding another employee at the same level who is interested in sharing or rotating job duties.

Naturally, some other office situations would have to adapt to these new flex schedules, such as the way the office is structured. We're all used to the traditional desk and chair for every employee (or one section of the prefabricated cube farm, as corporations started to pack more people into smaller spaces). The telecommute office setup doesn't need to be so rigid; in fact it doesn't need to be there at all! Here are some examples of current alternative office arrangements:

➤ **Virtual office.** With the proper communication tools and equipment, the employee can work from anywhere—the home, the office, even an airplane. Laptop computers fit easily into a briefcase, and bingo, you're self-sufficient.

➤ **Hoteling.** Shared work space. Fully equipped work stations are reserved by drop-in employees who spend most of their time in the field or at home.

➤ **Satellite office.** A secondary office location set up by the parent company, usually in suburban locations.

➤ **Telework center.** An independently owned satellite office where the parent company would secure space and pay rent.

Bet You Didn't Know

Working Mother magazine compiles an annual list of the 100 best companies that offer work–family programs. They don't rank them numerically, but do identify 10 as exceptionally progressive. For 1998, Citicorp/Citibank, Glaxo Wellcome Inc., IBM, Johnson & Johnson, Eli Lilly, MBNA America, Merck & Co., NationsBank, SAS Institute, and Xerox made the exceptional list.

Every one of these arrangements are in use now, by all sized firms. Look under "office space" in your local yellow pages, and you'll see more than one entry for offices to rent, already hard-wired for power, phones, and some even have ISDN computer lines. These are telecenters, and they're on the cutting edge of the millennium workplace.

Forces That Drive Us to Telework

By the year 2002, the Department of Transportation expects the numbers of teleworkers to swell to 15 million. Can you imagine a worldwide telecommuting force of well over a hundred million people? Those are the predictions. And the United States government plans for its workers to be among those ranks, thanks to their aggressive Flexiplace plan, started in June of 1990. Later, both the National Performance Review and President Clinton's Climate Change Action Plan of 1994 enforced and identified telecommuting as a way to enhance worker satisfaction.

The driving forces behind Flexiplace were threefold. First, there were the people to consider. Along with that quality of life factor, reports by the Departments of Energy and of Transportation (DOT) revealed what a huge impact telecommuting would have in economic terms and on the environment.

Bet You Didn't Know

By reducing the cars commuting to downtown areas, we limit the amount of roads, gas, and parking we need. The cost of an elevated parking-lot space ranges from $12,000 to $20,000 per spot. If five percent of Los Angeles commuters worked from home one day a week, they would save 9.5 million gallons of gasoline a year and generate 94 million tons less of air pollution, according to PS Enterprises.

Cut Back the Smog

You don't have to be employed by the DOT to recognize the toll that commuting has taken on the nation. Our over-dependence on the automobile is quickly depleting the earth's fossil-fuel reserves. We are also polluting the air so badly that few of the nation's metropolitan areas can meet the Clean Air Act requirements. Growth trends in places with moderate air quality pose future problems.

We can save energy, clean up the air, and avoid future problems by staying out of our cars and working from home a few days a week. AT&T claims that they reduced CO_2 emissions that cause greenhouse gas in 1997 by 80,000 tons with their telework program.

Bet You Didn't Know

In 1990, the transportation sector accounted for nearly 65 percent of all U.S. oil consumption. As a result, we face trouble in the areas of pollution (100 urban areas violate ozone air quality standards), balance of trade (because so much of our oil is imported), and greenhouse warming (because large quantities of CO_2 (the primary greenhouse gas) are emitted with oil combustion).

Buy Gifts, Not Gas

By creeping along bumper-to-bumper the commuter is not working, deliveries are late, meetings are delayed, and business comes to a halt. In the evening, traffic tie-ups mean time away from the shops and restaurants. Commercial activity is suspended while we sit in our cars on the freeways.

Employees spend money on fuel, transportation, wardrobe, and countless other details needed to get to the office. Business owners pay rent, buy supplies and install furniture and equipment to create a safe, effective work environment. That's the way the corporate culture has worked. But telecommuting is about change, and the greatest effect may be on company profits.

Quality of Life

Take a nine hour day of work, add a two hour minimum roundtrip commute, and you have little time left to socialize with family or friends. Dinner is a rush, kids' homework gets slapped together, and everyone gets up and does it again. Who has time to get involved in community projects?

By minimizing your time wasted commuting, you free up time to improve family relationships and increase social, spiritual, and community involvement. Society benefits from more civic participation, less-crowded roadways, and happier families.

On survey after survey, telecommuters report better relationships with their partners and children, and a better personal morale. Very few say they feel more isolated since they began working from home, and that's partly attributed to more family contact.

Telework arrangements also offer more opportunities for disabled or mobility-restricted people to do meaningful work. And temporary telecommuting can also be used when an employee has short-term special needs such as an injury, illness, or a new baby's arrival.

Telecommuting and Your Bottom Line

The cost benefits of telecommuting are worth looking at for any business owner, whether you have 10 employees or 10,000. Here are some examples of bottom-line savings and personal perks:

Reduce Real Estate Costs

In 1992, Ernst & Young started hoteling in their Chicago accounting and consulting operation. Employees frequently in the field with clients simply reserve in-house private workstations only when they need it. The firm trimmed space requirements by 7 percent the first year. Ernst & Young expects to save $40 million dollars a year by simply shrinking office space.

AT&T started a telework pilot program in Arizona in 1990. During that trial, teleworkers saved 3,705 hours of drive time and $10,372 in travel expenses. AT&T estimated they saved an average of $3,000 per teleworker annually in real estate and associated costs. By 1992, AT&T had adopted a corporate telework policy. Since then the number of U.S.-based AT&T managers who telework has grown to more than 50 percent.

IBM says it saved $70 million dollars in 1994 by eliminating 22 million square feet of office space in the Northeast and using the hoteling method in a converted warehouse in Cranford, New Jersey.

Call in Content, Not Sick

A typical employee misses 5 to 6 unscheduled work days a year, costing employers about $80 billion a year in lost productivity. Shaving that absentee rate by just one day could add a point to a company's profit margin.

You know those "mental health" days you and your coworkers joke about taking off? They're no joke. Low morale and stress-related illness have long been known as factors contributing to absenteeism. Does teleworking reduce stress? Yes. A Radcliffe College study showed that workers in a telecommuting situation experienced a significant reduction in sleep-related disorders. The majority also reported positive effects on their ability to balance life and work.

Convinced yet? Listen to this: Johnson & Johnson found that employees who used the company's family-supportive programs cut their sick days in half compared to other workers. And a study done for the Small Business Administration even found that telecommuters do not smoke, drink, or use drugs as much as people who do not work at home!

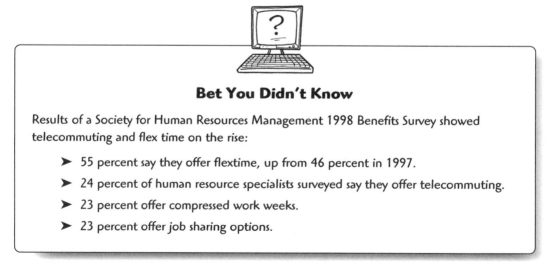

Bet You Didn't Know

Results of a Society for Human Resources Management 1998 Benefits Survey showed telecommuting and flex time on the rise:

➤ 55 percent say they offer flextime, up from 46 percent in 1997.

➤ 24 percent of human resource specialists surveyed say they offer telecommuting.

➤ 23 percent offer compressed work weeks.

➤ 23 percent offer job sharing options.

Lower Turnover Rate

It makes sense that a happy employee would stick around, right? Did you know that it costs less to keep an employee than to hire and train a new one? In the first three months on the job, a new hire can only accomplish a little over half of what an experienced worker can do. It's in the company's best interest to make work arrangements more attractive to keep key employees.

Increase Productivity

Telecommuters have more time, so they get more done. They don't drive to the office, socialize by the coffee machine, take a long lunch break or even shower if they don't feel like it on their *"at home"* days. AT&T teleworkers reported a *70 percent* increase in productivity due to a lack of interruptions and fewer meetings.

There is also the added benefit of uninterrupted work, especially for social-service sectors, during natural disasters such as flood, fires, or earthquakes if office site access is impossible.

The AT&T reports may not reflect the nation's averages, but telecommuting *can* increase employee productivity by roughly 20 percent, according to an annual National Work-at-Home study conducted by the marketing research firm, Link Resources.

Why Don't We All Do It?

Faced with such overwhelmingly positive evidence, you might be asking why don't we all do it? Well, there are several reasons why telecommuting is not yet a mainstream government and corporate practice.

The Culture

As mentioned earlier, telecommuting is about change and changing the way people think takes work. The corporate model relies on managing in the conventional office, face-to-face with employees. They measure results by the hours worked or activity levels, so just looking busy can suffice as work for some people. Conversely, telecommuting relies on performance management or managing by results. This requires an atmosphere of trust, and a whole new set of guidelines.

I'm sure you've heard the pep rally cries around your office; "Be a team player," they say. It's the fear of breaking up the team that can hinder the acceptance of the new telework model. But telecommuting teams do exist; they're just different. Telecommute teams need to be managed like a medical team or a band, where members practice on their own, but come together for the big events.

The Job

Job suitability is a major factor in determining who can and can't work from home. If you're a receptionist, obviously you can't work from home. Some positions just require more contact with a supervisor, other employees, or the public. Others require specialized equipment that would be too costly to move. Your dentist, for example, wouldn't be very productive working from home (of course, he could set up a home office).

Money Meaning

Information jobs are those that deal in the creating, processing, and storing of information. By the year 2002, approximately 59 percent of the workforce, or about 85 million people, are expected to be employed in information jobs according to the Congressional Office of Technology Assessment. These are the positions best suited for telecommuting.

Here are some types of jobs best suited to a flexible work arrangement:

➤ Thinking and writing jobs such as reporting, data analysis, and grants or case reviews

➤ Information processing such as accounting and bookkeeping

➤ Telephone-intensive positions such as setting up conferences and obtaining information

➤ Computer-related tasks such as programming, data entry, and word processing

These would be jobs for writers, editors, scientists, investigators, psychologists, environmental engineer, budget analysts, tax examiner, graphic designers, project managers and computer specialists. And if they've been doing work in their field for awhile, the situation works even better.

The Person

Obviously a new employee who needs to learn the ropes should stay near the office. Still others like the office camaraderie and would suffer from working alone. So personality makes a difference. But an organized, disciplined self-starter who requires little supervision who is interested in a flex arrangement should do well. Just make sure you don't get taken advantage of, and that all parties are comfortable with the arrangements at the start.

Bet You Didn't Know

The average telecommuter earns $51,000 a year, and is 40.2 years old. Seventy-six percent are married and 46 percent have children.

Labor Relations

With all the gains made in improving the workplace (remember *The Jungle*?), it would be a shame to take a step backward in labor relations.

If you're a long-term career employee, you may resent any efforts by management to move you toward what you may feel is a contract, or freelance arrangement. Keep your manager appraised of your concerns. And despite reports by people in flex arrangements that they feel more empowered, some fear a return to micro-management procedures, or the big brother approach where the boss is constantly checking up on every little thing you do.

If you belong to a union, you know that union leaders are always apprehensive about possible loss of employee freedoms. In this case, they fear that home inspections, electronic monitoring, and other invasions of privacy could become a standard part of the telecommute contract. Doesn't sound too appealing, does it?

It's been said that a problem identified is half solved. All these obstacles can be overcome by good communications. A detailed plan, a test run, and a great deal of open discussion are essential to success.

Am I Ready to Telecommute?

Even if your company has a flex-time policy, you're still going to have to convince your immediate boss that you're an ideal candidate. But let's take a step back. Are you convinced of this yourself? Your work environment will be a lot less structured and feedback won't be so readily available. No more popping your head up over the cube farm and getting a fellow prairie dog's opinion.

You have to decide if you're the type of person who can work outside the traditional office. Here are some personal-assessment exercises to help you find out your telework compatibility:

➤ Make sure you have a safe, quiet place to work at home. Don't set up office on the kitchen table and expect to achieve good results.

➤ Check with any family or friends living with you. Can they accept the new arrangement?

➤ Understand that you won't be able to care for elderly or very young dependents *and* telework. Although being at home in the afternoons may keep your older children from the latchkey life, you *cannot* baby-sit young ones and work efficiently.

➤ Finally, catalog a day's worth of work that can be done from home with a computer, fax, and phone. Is there enough? Good, let's move on.

If you have determined that your job can be done in a telecommuting situation, it's time to ask yourself some personal questions:

➤ Are you self-motivated?

➤ What are your professional strengths and weaknesses?

➤ Can you solve problems by yourself?

➤ Can you interact with office staff and clients effectively from home?

Did you answer Yes to all four? Okay, then it's time to convince the boss that telecommuting will benefit him or her, by establishing that it's critical to business. The best way to accomplish that is to outline a written proposal.

Click Here

The Mining Co. (**http://telecommuting.miningco.com/insub3.htm**) has a telecommuting guide that includes nearly two dozen links to teleworkers jobs and recruitment areas.

Hey Boss, I've Got a Plan

You need a plan, whether you are trying to convince your boss to let you telecommute or persuade your own employees to change their work habits. Before anyone can consider your request seriously, you've got some earnest work to do.

When you finally gather up the courage to approach the boss, you'll need a well-defined proposal in hand that the two of you can go over step by step. It will save you from instant rejection if he/she has something concrete to work with, make changes to, and show *her* boss.

If you're introducing telework for the first time, you'll have to touch on several complex topics. Ready? Here's your basic to-do list. Every job situation is different, but each telecommuting proposal should have these same elements included:

➤ Introduce telecommuting (Use this book!).

➤ Identify the benefits to your company.

➤ Identify telecommute workers and supervisors.

➤ Conduct formal training and provide reference materials.

➤ Identify the job, or the parts of the job that can be done by telecommuters.

➤ Establish work hours and attendance reporting.

➤ Establish equipment needs, ownership, maintenance, and use.

➤ Establish method of performance measurement.

➤ Address health, safety, and security issues.

➤ Develop agreements as shown in the following figure.

➤ Set deadline for a test pilot or prototype.

Once you've accomplished all that, you'll have to identify a person to monitor the new plan and submit reports. Maybe this could be your new position?

Sample Telecommuter Agreement

Both the manager and the telecommuter understand that home-based telecommuting is a voluntary option and can be discontinued at either one's request with no adverse repercussions.

The company will pay for the following expenses:

* Charges for business related telephone calls

* Maintenance and repairs to company-owned equipment

* _____

Claims will be submitted on a Travel Expense Claim along with receipt, bill or other verification of the expense.

The company will not pay for the following expenses:
* Maintenance or repairs of privately owned equipment
* Utility costs associated with the use of the computer or occupation of the home
* Equipment supplies (these should be requisitioned through the main office).
* Travel expenses (other than authorized transit subsidies) associated with commuting to the central office.

Telecommute days are scheduled and will not be substituted without advance approval of the manager.
* In office days will be _____.
* Home office days will be _____.
Telecommuters must be available by phone during the business hours of ____ to ____.

Telecommuting is not a substitute for dependent care, and telecommuters must make regular dependent care arrangements.

The telecommuter has read and understands the company's telecommuting policies and agree to abide by those policies.

The telecommuter is to carry out the steps needed for good information security in the home-office setting, and has a copy of the company's security requirements and procedures.

_____ (Supervisor) (Date)

_____ (Telecommuter) (Date)

This agreement expires _____ and must be renewed to continue participation in the company's telecommuting program.

A sample telecommuting agreement between employer and employee.

Making It Work

To be a success at virtual work, you'll need the following personal skills and home equipment. Don't worry if you don't have these now; they can be learned and acquired as you get closer to the day you launch your telecommuting schedule.

The following are self-management skills you need:

1. **Experience.** To be a success at virtual work, you've got to have experience at the job you'll be doing from home.

2. **Project management.** With no one looking over your shoulder, you are responsible to get the job done. Be results-oriented and set goals for yourself throughout the day.

3. **Time management.** Plan ahead, prioritize, create a "to-do" list, and stick with it. And hey, you workaholics out there? Take breaks! It's easy to get lost in your work when there are few interruptions.

4. **Self-discipline.** Make sure your family and friends know you are home to work. Develop a home schedule so you can begin and end your day at fairly regular times.

5. **Attitude.** You'll need to be enthusiastic about flex scheduling and also *be* flexible. Be open to change, and look for new ways to get the job done.

6. **Communication skills.** Share problems with your manager and coworkers and try to resolve them quickly. Encourage progress meetings and always attend staff meetings. Stay in touch!

Don't forget the following:

➤ **Business equipment.** A personal computer, company-compatible software, and a phone may be enough as far as equipment goes, but ideally you should have more. See how much of the following you can assemble with company support.

   ➤ **Remote access software.** If your company allows it, you can install a remote access package and swap files from the office network. About $150.

   ➤ **Printer/fax.** Sometimes both come in one machine, with a copier function too, but they run about $500 or more. A good laser-jet printer will do the trick for less than $200, and fax software often comes with your computer system.

   ➤ **VideoCam.** Miss that face-time with the boss? A cheap desktop camera costs about $200, or maybe you need the state-of-art videoconferencing gear (about $1,500). Just remember to hide the bunny slippers under the desk!

Bet You Didn't Know

Companies such as IBM and Sony are bringing the cyber-home to a neighborhood near you. IBM's HomeDirector ties appliances together (your air conditioner, coffeemaker, lights, and hot tub all on a computer server in your house). Sony has a digital set-top box designed to be the ultimate home entertainment system complete with digital camcorder plug-ins, DVD players, and high-speed Internet access.

➤ **Access.** How will you send your files to the office? This communication method will need to be reliable, or the whole plan is jeopardized. Here are some of the standard choices:

> ➤ **ISDN.** This digital phone line will supercharge your Web access and download times, but it can be pricey (up to $100 dollars a month). An ISDN modem costs extra too (between $200 and $600).

> ➤ **Internet Service provider (ISP).** Connects you to a world of information.

> ➤ **Email.** This is the easiest way to keep in touch with the office and send in written work. Your ISP will have a version. Use email to maintain contact and visibility by sending project updates and information.

Even with the proper attitude, equipment, and access, jump starting a telecommuting project can be a challenge. You will be a step ahead of the naysayers, however, if you have answers for their concerns.

Click Here

The International Telework Association (**www.telecommute.org**) is a nonprofit organization for telecommuting and telework professionals. Founded a decade ago, TAC provides education and information about telework as it pertains to business, environment, travel reduction, work/family balance, and telecommunications strategies within organizations.

Watching Out for Pitfalls

Half of all first time remote access pilot programs will fail, says John Girard, often called the father of telecommuting. Even so, he predicts that 137 million workers will be involved in telework worldwide by 2003. So what are the causes of failure? Fear, lack of information, decreased productivity, and increased equipment costs are some of the reasons. To succeed, be aware of the following pitfalls and concerns:

➤ Employee reticence due to fears of being overlooked for promotions, being seen as not highly committed to the organization, or losing out on plum assignments.

➤ Lack of formal training or manuals by companies for employees on how to telecommute productively.

➤ Employers don't always pay for essential tools needed to telecommute.

➤ Lack of technical support.

➤ Managers forget about the teleworker's schedule, and plan important meetings on "home" days.

➤ Coworkers don't want to call and "disturb" the teleworker at home.

➤ Work expectations are unclear between supervisor and employee.

➤ Missed deadlines and commitments.

➤ Reluctance to discuss problems for fear of jeopardizing the telework situation.

Everyone involved in a telecommuting pilot program needs to remember that program effectiveness can be difficult to measure. It really comes down to *performance*. Has the program effected performance at all, and in what way? Also, if you are finding that leave time, or overtime have been reduced, then your program is effective.

Finally, you must also look at the changes, if any, in morale. If your company has become an organization that others *want* to work for and stay with, then you have not only reduced the hassles and headaches of constant recruitment, but you've made a positive change in your corner of society.

The Least You Need to Know

➤ Technology is transforming the way the corporate culture looks at managing the workplace.

➤ The Department of Transportation predicts that 15 million people will be telecommuting by the year 2002.

➤ The positive impact of telecommuting is threefold: economic, environmental, and societal.

➤ If you are self-motivated and resourceful, you have what it takes to be a successful teleworker.

Y2K: How to Plan for the Year 2000

No one in America can make plans for New Year's Eve 1999 without thinking of, and possibly fearing, the predictions of modern civilization's end. Everyone is asking what the dawn of the new year and the new *millennium* will bring to the people of this earth. All religions have their doomsday prophecies, and it seems that the scientific realm of computing has one as well. It's called the *millennium bug*, a computer crisis forecast to stop us in our tracks on the stroke of midnight, December 31, 1999.

Will our homes be warm and cozy, still powered by electric heat? Will we be able to withdraw cash from the ATM to pay for food? Will we even be able to tap into our retirement portfolios, or will the bug have zapped it into oblivion?

This is not the time to panic. And although there is no magic repellent to wipe out the millennium bug, we do have one great advantage: We know the enemy and we have time to prepare.

With our daily lives already insanely complicated, no one wants to be told it's going to get tougher. But count on some real changes ahead, as a result of a seemingly innocent mistake made a few decades ago.

Where the Bug Found a Nest

You have heard of the millennium bug by now. We all have. Small problems began to surface as early as 1980, but few of us listened then. In 1997, some high-tech types were beginning get vocal about it. By the end of 1998, reference to the Year 2000 computer problem was shortened to "Y2K." It became a news story worthy of lots of follow-up by the daily papers and daily feed for the computer industry news.

By 1999, it was a countdown—who was more prepared than the next guy, who wasn't taking it seriously, and so on. A few more bugs began to pop out of the woodwork, such as some cases that have been reported where credit cards were rejected a few times not for overspending, but for that bank's inability to be Y2K-compliant with credit cards that had preprinted expiration dates ending in "00."

Overall, the predictions of what will happen in 2000 thanks to this computer glitch run from catastrophic global meltdowns, recessions, and depressions, to an uneventful new year—all depending on whom you talk to.

But the Year 2000 computer problem is real even if you don't own a computer. What remains to be seen is what damage it will do to your finances. For those of you who still aren't clear on the nature of the problem, we'll go back in history to trace the beginning of the end, as some would call it.

Making Every Byte Count

About 30 years ago, the early programmers were working with big, costly, mainframe computers. You know the ones; they filled up half a room doing the work of today's mini-microchips? At least you've seen pictures of them. Although these huge monoliths took up a lot of physical space, they held only a small amount of memory and disk storage space. You know how quickly your personal computer gobbles up hard disk space for storage? And how one CD-ROM game takes a huge amount of memory to run at top speed? Today it's no real big deal to add on an external hard drive for a few hundred bucks and get a few gigabytes, or billions more characters of storage space. And you can add on memory chips for less than $100 or even spend up to $1,000 to buy a new PC with several gigs already built in for storage and 32 megabytes of memory.

In the late 1960s and early 1970s, computer memory was very expensive. A company would spend a *million dollars* for a mainframe with only about 32,000 characters of memory and a mere two million characters of storage space—which was shared by the *whole company*, not just one personal computer. The solution? Programmers created a solution to please the cost-conscious management and shaved off a few digits here and there. All dates would be represented by only two digits. They saved valuable storage space and unintentionally built a self-destruct mechanism into the foundation of computer technology.

So here we were, happily chugging along in minimized memory format. The year 1959 reads as 59, the year 1998 is 98. This works great as long as the century doesn't change. Then someone realized that the Year 2000 will read as 00. Uh-oh. That translates into 1900 and, unless the problem is fixed, when the date changes to January 1, 2000 either the computer will spit out false data or it will shut down altogether.

Unfortunately the modern world, and in particular the financial services industry, such as banks, brokerage firms, and insurance companies, depends on data processing systems that rely heavily on dates and date processing. If the computer doesn't recognize that one date is greater than another, say that 00 is greater than 99, we're in for some pretty interesting results.

Here's an example of how the Y2K bug could affect your wallet. Let's say your 15-year mortgage loan has a start date of 1996 and a payoff date of 2011. The lender's program may subtract 96 from 11 and come up with a term of –85 years. Cool. Your house has been paid off for decades, but in reality the mortgage company's loan calculations are incorrect due to not being able to assess loan payment dates correctly.

So, why not do a *search and replace*, like you can do in your word processing software? Well, you must find every date in every line of code and change it. Fine, only in the 1960s and 1970s, programmers were writing programs in COBOL which is now an obsolete computer language and incompatible with today's programs.

To fix the problematic computer codes on these mainframes, a programmer has to sit at a keyboard and get through each line of code, adding the 19 in front of every two-digit date. This takes a lot of time, and time we don't have a lot of. It also costs a lot of money. Companies such as Walt Disney are spending more than $250 million to fix their Y2K problem, especially since their theme parks use computers to control rides and hotel reservations. Banks also are allocating incredible financial resources to this plight—to the tune of $300 million in some cases.

With the approaching Y2K dilemma, you can say that an awareness has surfaced among consumers, and in particular, financial services customers—definitely the first step to solving any problem. Thanks to the diligent bell-ringers and consciousness-raisers like programmer Peter de Jager, Senator Robert Bennett (R-Utah), chairman of the Senate Special Committee on the Year 2000 Technology Problem, economist Edward Yardeni of Deutsche, Morgan and Grenfell, and author/programmer Edward Yourdon, the problem is now well known.

Here, You Can Have My Chips

While everyone who knew anything at all about the problem was focused on fixing the older, mainframe computers, a less-visible aspect of the problem reared its digital head. The built-in preprogrammed chips called *embedded systems* that control every-thing from microwave ovens to automatic teller machines to bank vaults could end up being an enormous threat if not fixed.

Of course, your desktop computer is full of chips. Even relatively new PCs may not operate correctly because there is an embedded chip in the Real Time Clock on some computers that can't handle the century number.

It seems so silly, you may be thinking. It's just a date, for heaven's sake! We're much too smart to let a couple of numbers take down the *entire world* economy. Why, half the world's population doesn't even *own* a computer! But in case you were thinking it might not affect you, you better take a closer look.

How Will I Be Affected?

When looking at the overall Y2K problem, you have to consider the domino effect that could take place at the turn of the century even in your small corner of the world.

Ask your employer for a full Y2K disclosure, for example, to determine how they are handling the problem—if they haven't given you one already. You should find out things such as how they are handling direct deposit of your payroll and your 401(k) contributions. Plus, determine how they are working with their business partners, such as the bank and 401(k) plan administrators, to see if all relationships are seamless and compliant.

Exactly how much money is the financial services industry spending and what types of information should you gather from each? The following examples show what the computer bug can do to an industry.

Banking

In the banking industry, they will be spending billions of dollars to fix and test for Y2K compliance. Fortunately they are seen as ahead of the game, having foreseen the problems with calculations. According to Federal Reserve Board Chairman Alan Greenspan's testimony in February of 1999, the Federal Reserve System would complete remediation and testing of its 103 mission-critical applications by the end of the first quarter of 1999.

The Federal Reserve opened a test facility in June of 1998, at which more than 6000 depository institutions had conducted tests of their Y2K compliant systems. Also as a precautionary measure, the Reserve increased the national currency inventory by about one-third to about $200 billion in late 1998, and say they have other contingency plans available if needed.

Even if the millennium bug causes your bank to experience problems, all FDIC deposits will be covered up to $100,000 by FDIC insurance. That includes separate accounts of up to $100,000 each, such as checking, savings, and so on, by the same owner.

Securities

If an already distressed global market were suddenly plagued by computer problems, it could add up to the kind of uncertainty that gives world financial markets a bad case of the shakes. The millennium bug is expected to affect the global economy with some fallout that will even drop on Wall Street. The securities industry as a whole is estimated to be spending up to $6 billion to ensure computer systems will not crash, according to a March 1999 Reuters news report.

Basically, experts are saying that the extent of Y2K damage depends on how investors perceive the state of the American and foreign economies (including how well the economies planned for the Y2K problem). You are a driving force in the game of economics and finance, and your *consumer confidence* will play a large part in determining on which side of the fence the Dow Jones Industrial Average stands come the Year 2000.

Insurance Companies

The magazine *BestWeek* estimated that U.S. insurance companies will spend over $6 billion to repair Bug problems on their own computer systems. That's outside of any legal liabilites caused by the crash. And according to a report from consultants Conning & Company, insurers are doing a good job of fixing their own internal problems, with many large property and casualty insurers close to or already compliant.

Telecommunications

Telephones, faxes, mail, and email are the mainstays of modern trade. Just think of how many phone calls have you made in the past 24 hours—not just at home, but also at work. What if all mail and parcel post, including FedEx, UPS, and DHL, were suspended due to a breakdown in shipping? They all rely on planes, trains, and automobiles, and you know what can happen there. And the telephone line—it supports so much more than person-to-person calls. Deregulation has spawned an army of telecommunication vendors, from cell companies to Internet providers, and they're all connected, but not necessarily working together.

Government

They were the first real computer adopters and they're one of the most active users today. As you learned in Chapter 1, the federal government even started what is now known as the Internet (as a computer network primarily for the Defense Department).

You know how you tweak your software to perform the way you like it (preferences in your word processing application or the stuff on your computer desktop, for example)? Well, each government department has thrown in its own home-grown adaptations to programs to suit each department's needs. So some of those systems have been in place 20 years or more, and no one even knows who first set them up.

The chairman of the House Government Technology committee flunked the federal government in its Y2K preparations in mid-1998, so President Bill Clinton set a March 1999 deadline for the federal government to solve its share of the problem.

By the first quarter of 1999, the departments of Agriculture, Defense, and Health and Human Services were considered to be lagging in Year 2000 computer readiness, according to a report by the House Subcommittee on Government Management, Information, and Technology. The Defense Department received a "C," and the report flunked the Transportation Department, including the Federal Aviation Administration. Among the top performers were the Social Security Administration and the Nuclear Regulatory Commission. But overall, the report gave the federal government an unacceptable "C-plus," on a scale of "A," the highest mark, to "F" for failing.

The United States seems to be the country most aware of the Y2K problem. In fact, the information specialist for the Chamber of Commerce and Industry in France said in July 1998 that about two-thirds of that country's small businesses don't consider themselves affected by the bug and don't have the tools or technical support to repair the problems.

Bet You Didn't Know

The Office of Management and Budget reported that 21 of its 27 government agencies will implement their Y2K solutions during the last three months of 1999.

India's industry and government haven't done enough yet either according to top officials in the Federal Electronics Department. Many Indian programmers work abroad and are fixing the glitches for foreign companies.

Many other countries think that because their computer hardware is new, the millennium bug is not a problem. And to be sure, there are some villages in China where a telephone is a rarity and they wouldn't know what to do with a personal computer and probably don't care. The Information Ministry official in China has said that her country hasn't seriously considered the Year 2000 glitch. Some fear the country's problems are compounded by its reliance on foreign and pirated software.

Other countries are falling far behind the United States in terms of remediation—according to a study by the Gartner Group—and risk major disruptions. These countries include Argentina, Venezuela, and all the Middle East (except Israel). Even if all the governments of the world made Y2K compliance a priority, there are not enough computer-industry specialists to solve all the problems.

Zero Hour Is Already Here

What will happen on the dawn of the millennium? No one knows. Just like a few soldier termites signal deeper infestation, some computer problems started years ago; problems will surface throughout 1999 with frightening regularity. A Y2K bug affecting global-positioning satellites, which will timeout in August 1999, will potentially affect worldwide navigation according to reports by the Giga Information Group. Some people worry about September 9, 1999, because programmers have used 9/9/99 to indicate an invalid date field.

What's certain is that the number of failures will quickly accelerate as the Year 2000 enters the time horizon of millions of business processes. We won't really know what the final consequences will be until the actual date is here and all so-called *compliant* systems try to work with each other.

What Should I Do?

This bug will be remembered as the most terrifying pest in history. It is a most unusual pest, one that looms large in time rather than space. You can't see it crawling through the intricate computer systems that connect the world, but you now know it's there, and terrifyingly real.

Is it time to panic? You could, but it won't get you very far. Better to prepare yourself, your friends, and family for the great unknown adventure into the millennium. Let "Protect and Profit" be your battle cry during this war against the millennium bug. And consider us part of your defense to the bug (by providing a good offense—that is, important information).

Taking Care of Me

Gathering up important documents is even more important for Y2K than for any other potential disaster. If your documents were destroyed in a storm, you could get another copy. It might be tedious, but you could probably track down the right agency. But if you have no records of your birth, marriage, Social Security benefits, or investments, a global computer meltdown could wipe out your proof of existence. So make copies and file them in a safe place.

Assuming that your stash is in the bank, you most definitely want a hard copy of your bank account balance. If the bank's computers create errors on the accounts of every customer, you at least will have some record of what is yours. You may also want to keep sufficient cash on hand in the event that you can't get to the bank or can't access your account.

Just trying to prove you paid last month's telephone bill could be a nightmare if you can't get copies of cancelled checks or don't have a bill stamped "Paid." Get hard copies of everything important to you. Government and financial records top the list of must-have papers in your home safe. Here's a checklist of what you should have on hand:

➤ Family records (birth certificate, marriage licenses, death certificates, and so forth)

➤ Social Security card

➤ Immunization records

➤ Religious records (baptisms and so on)

➤ Passport (If you don't have one, get one as soon as possible.) It's the best form of identification and proof of citizenship you can have, and it's valid for ten years.

➤ Will and testament

➤ Insurance policies

➤ Deeds, titles, contracts, pensions, and proof of any other assets owned

➤ Loan agreements (mortgages, credit cards, and so forth)

➤ Inventory of valuable household goods and important telephone numbers

➤ Tax returns, W-2s, and IRS agreements (During their Y2K preparations, the IRS has already sent out mistaken notices to taxpayers saying that these shocked taxpayers owed $300 million.)

We've read enough history to know that war creates economic boom for the victors (and munitions suppliers). You can be a Y2K victor if you planning strategically— if you are financially stable and ready to take advantage of opportunities. First you have to be primed to minimize your damage, and then you must be ready to aid in reconstruction.

We will say it again: You cannot do nothing; otherwise, you put yourself in unnecessary danger. Some people do claim that the Year 2000 date change will be a non-event. Let's hope that's the case. Obviously, the more all of us prepare, the fewer people there will be who cry *unfair* when the bug strikes. Now let's get down to the survival strategies for your personal finances.

Covering Your Assets

What should you do personally to protect your financial life from Y2K fallout? The answer is simple: Make the same Y2K preparations as every other captain of industry. Find the problem areas, or Y2K weak links, in your life and fix them. Remediation experts have suggested using a five-step process to find, fix, and test for the bug. These steps work just as well in your personal life. These steps are referred to throughout this appendix because they can also pertain to your PC, whether you use it for personal or business use or both.

Step 1: Awareness—Educate and involve all levels of your *organization* in solving the problem. (This can be your family or your company.)

Step 2: Inventory—Create a checklist of Year 2000 readiness. You should identify and list all the different computer-based systems, components (such as purchased software, computers, and associated hardware), service providers (such as banks and utilities), and hardware that contain microchips that support your life (personal and business). Rank each entry on your list by how critical it is to operations.

Step 3: Assessment—Examine how severe and widespread the problem is in your life or business and determine what needs to be fixed.

Step 4: Correction and Testing—Implement the readiness strategy you have chosen, and then test the fix. This is the part that takes up the most time, correcting the problem. Testing is a critical aspect of any Year 2000 project. Testing verifies that the repaired or replaced system operates properly when the date changes and that existing business functions (such as accounting, inventory control, and order tracking) continue to operate in the same old way.

Step 5: Implementation—Move your repaired or replaced system into place. You'll also need a contingency, or backup, plan. List the problems that you can foresee and what steps you will take if these problems occur.

These five steps will go a long way toward helping you develop your personal finance plan. Because you are already aware of the problem—and hopefully your family is too—you have the first step covered.

Add More Toner, Make More Copies

By now you should have several copies of things such as family records, tax returns, Social Security card, deeds, and titles. These are fairly fixed documents (because they change infrequently). What you'll have to stay on top of now are all financial transactions. Keep a record of any monthly activity. If you manage your finances with computer software, make hard copies of your records and ask for hard-copy receipts for any bills you pay. Even if your computer and software are up-to-date, power interruptions can make it impossible for you to access your data. Tip: Notarize every copy of a brokerage account or bank account statement that you receive; this way, you have proof that your financial services representative knows of your assets.

Almost every type of transaction these days involves a database. They're used in accounting, inventory, shipping, appointment scheduling, email, and even Internet browsing. Because we don't know what, if any, systems will fail, here are the areas to track:

➤ **Automatic deposits**. It's the way to get paid today. There has been a huge push by the banking industry for companies to offer employees direct electronic paycheck deposits to their bank accounts. Why wouldn't they push for it? There are fewer opportunities for you to skip the bank and spend your pennies elsewhere. The banks get your cash first.

If your bank is not Y2K-compliant, however, don't count on any direct deposit or electronically transferred payments to be accurate. You may want to have cash on hand to cover expenses for a month or two.

➤ **Bill payments**. If you normally rely on automatic bill payments, consider another alternative for a while if you find that the recipients are not Y2K-compliant. Consider prepaying some of your fixed bills (such as mortgage or rent or car payments) in advance so that you can get hard copy receipts.

First find out whether you'll be charged any prepayment penalties, however, and negotiate to have them waived. Make sure the company that you're paying knows why you want to prepay. If they still insist on penalties for early payment, ask them to waive any possible late penalties should your paycheck not arrive or should your bank have trouble processing accounts.

➤ **Credit and debit cards**. Credit cards certainly ease the task of recordkeeping (especially with financial software that enables users to download transaction records right into computer files). These computer transactions may not be so easy to do come January 2000. Consider using cash for purchases as a backup.

Don't forget to protect all those hard-to-replace records. Important documents should be stored in a fireproof home safe (rated at least Class 350 for fire resistance by Underwriters Laboratories, Inc.). Plain metal filing boxes won't work. If there were a fire, papers would be burned to ashes. If you want to store computer disks with valuable information, get a Class 125 safe.

Diversify, Diversify, Diversify

As long as you keep your portfolio diversified, you'll be following an investment strategy that's sound year round, millennium or no millennium. Don't forget to consider the following investment sections when checking your asset allocation.

Your IRA and 401(k)

These investment vehicles should be considered for the long term, and will most likely ride out any deep valleys. If you're due to retire soon, by now you should have met with your financial advisor and tax professional to determine which types of asset classes (stocks and bonds) you should be invested in as your monetary needs change during retirement. Your tax advisor can also help you determine how any payouts, be they lump sum or in a steady stream, will affect your tax situation.

Stocks

It's a good idea to avoid speculative investments at this time with the majority of your investment portfolio. Due to possible worldwide financial market fluctuations, you should carefully monitor the remediation efforts of the companies you own shares in. In the summer of 1998, the Securities and Exchange Commission ratcheted up the standards of scrutiny and accountability of public companies for the disclosure of the risks of Y2K problems they face and their contingency plans. Those reports are available.

Real Estate

Having a portion of your investments tied to tangible assets is a good hedge, and land does have value (unless, of course, a major recession hits and property values tank as we saw in the Northeast in the early 1990s). Of course, if you can't afford to make the payments on an investment property—say, on a rental condo in a high-priced resort town that gets no visitors in a depressed market—meet with your financial professional to determine whether to hold on to that asset.

Will My PC Kick the Bucket?

A good question. It depends mostly on the age of your machine. All personal computers have an internal clock/calendar called the Real Time Clock (RTC) that maintains the date and time. And yes, in some computers the year is stored and processed in two rather than four digits. And yes, again, the Year 2000 will affect these computers just as it does other systems. Even a new state-of-the-art PC may not be ready; so all PCs should be tested.

The built-in software that controls your PC's main operations is called BIOS, or Basic Input Output System. BIOS gets its date information from the RTC when you first boot up. This is where PCs get into trouble; they won't recognize the Year 2000. Most *new* BIOS setups will automatically make the correction from *00* to *2000*; if it's misinterpreted as *1900*, however, incorrect data will go to the operating system and other applications. "Houston…we have a problem."

The underlying operating system in most PCs is called DOS. DOS does not even recognize the year 1900. So if the BIOS feeds it a date of 1900, it will reset the machine to some totally arbitrary date.

How Can I Test My PC?

The best way to determine whether your computer is ready for the Year 2000 is to test the system as if it were already the Year 2000. To do so, you just have to conduct a date-forward test. There are many free testing utilities on the Internet, or you can do it yourself with help from the Small Business Association's Y2K Checklist at www.sba.gov/y2k/indexcheck.html.

Click Here

Check out the health of your PC and compliance of your computer vendor online:

Microsoft Year 2000 Tools Guide in the MS Resource Center at **www.microsoft.com/ technet/topics/year2k/tools/tools.htm**.

NSTL, an independent information technology testing organization at **www.nstl.com/**.

Test 2000 for free PC test at **www.rightime.com/**.

Millennium Bug Fix Products at **www.computerexperts.co.uk/products/index.htm**.

Vendor compliance lists at **www.mitre.org/research/cots/PC_RESOLUTION.html**.

Of course, there are risks involved in rolling dates forward on computers. Some computer security systems keep track of the last time you accessed a system and will revoke your password if you haven't logged on for a long time. Rolling forward for a few months may be long enough to lose the password. And some items that should be retained may be marked as expired and could be written over. Be sure to make backups of any crucial data and applications before you run a test.

Oh yeah, don't forget to put the date back to the correct time after you've completed the test!

How Can I Fix My PC?

There are many ways to fix your PC, none of them too difficult. You can download software solutions from the Internet or you can purchase a new BIOS chip that's Year 2000 ready. If you're running a 386 or older, sorry; it that's the case, it's time to buy a whole new system anyway.

You could also go in and do it yourself by using the DOS command. Reset the date to include the four digit 2000. DOS will in turn tell BIOS what century it's in when we roll over into the new millennium. Just remember that anytime you reset the date on a PC, you run the risk of corruption. Once again, have a backup ready. That should be no problem if you made one for the test.

If you're still in the dark ages and using a Word version 5.0 for DOS, get new software. If you try to create a new file after 1999, you'll get a corrupted file that will eventually crash your computer.

If you're running on Windows 98, you don't have to do anything. Microsoft claims that Windows 98 and Windows NT will automatically detect and fix the Y2K problem.

Of course, if you use a Macintosh, you will have no date-related hardware problems. The time on every Macintosh ever made is designed to be accurate for the next 27,940 years.

It's Just a One-Man Show, but It's My Business

Today's personal computers are used in many businesses, too. If your hardware is more than five years old, chances are it's going to roll over with the new year and die. So whether you're a mom-and-pop shop or a multinational corporation, you should follow the same five steps outlined earlier in the section titled "Covering Your Assets": awareness, assessment, inventory, test, and implement.

As a business, you also have to prepare for any outside legal actions that might arise from possible Y2K foul-ups. Make sure to consult proper legal counsel. Keep in mind, however, that you'll have to address at a minimum the following concerns:

➤ **A Y2K plan.** A formal written plan of your Y2K preparations

➤ **Y2K disclosures.** To the public, owners or directors, lenders, and others

➤ **Insurance.** Coverage of policies for Y2K-related activities

➤ **Compliance.** Documentation of compliance with federal and state laws regarding Y2K issues

It's been estimated that 30 percent of organizations worldwide will experience failure of critical systems due to the date changes. Make sure it's not you, or one of your suppliers.

Bet You Didn't Know

The Year 2000 issue ranked number two on the top-10 list of critical technology issues for business in 1998. The number one issue was the Internet (according to the American Institute of Certified Public Accountants).

Profiting

About half of L.L. Bean's 200-person information services staff is assigned to combing lines of code. That's a lot of people-power focused on squashing a bug. But the mail order clothing company wants to be sure they can deliver those polar fleece caps and flannel shirts for Christmas 1999.

Click Here

Get your Y2K job search underway:

SBA's Business Cards (**www.sba.gov**) a search area for Y2K solution providers.

Jobs 2000: Finding Help (**www.year2000.com**). This site is owned by Peter de Jager, Y2K expert.

The National Bulletin Board for Computer jobs (**www.jobsbulletin.com**) drop off your resume.

ACS International Resources—Y2K Solutions (**www.acs-intl.com**) check job links.

EFG, Inc. (**www.efginc.com**) an information systems technology recruiting firm.

That's just good business. Compliant companies can capitalize on the Y2K problem and boost sales. The obviously victorious industries, like Information Technology, are looking at billions of dollars in opportunities. Despite the software developed to locate the bug, programmers still have to go in and replace code line by line.

If you're an IT programmer looking for work, you can write your own ticket. But do it fast; the offer expires on December 31, 1999 (or so they say). Don't believe it. That's the day when we find out what works and what implodes into a mass of computer gibberish. We also find out which fix is compatible with everybody else's. Who's going to pick up the shattered pieces on January 1, 2000? IT companies will be reaping Y2K benefits for years to come.

Small Business-
Friendly Banks

One of the biggest questions to plague small business is where to go for more cash? You've tapped out your savings and your in-laws savings. Knowing which banks meet the credit needs of small firms can be crucial to health and growth. We'd like to save you time when shopping for lenders. The following banks have been ranked among the top five in their state for small business lending activity. Give them a call before you need the money. Establishing early relationships with banks is key to getting the capital you need when you need it.

The following is the key to the table:

➤ **Bank name**
   Address
   Telephone number

➤ **Total Rank**. The total in the second column is the ranking of the bank in the state. The number is the aggregate measure of small business lending activity based on:

   ➤ Ratio of small business loans (less than $250,000) to total assets

   ➤ Ratio of small business loans to total business loans

   ➤ Dollar amount of small business loans

   ➤ Number of small business loans made (outstanding)

   The highest total score is 40. The lowest score of 0 indicates that there is no evidence of the bank's lending to small businesses.

➤ **Bank Asset Size ($)**. Bank asset size class is based on total domestic assets in dollars.

➤ **SBL ($)**. Small business loan amounts in thousands of dollars. Small business loans are defined as loans of less than $250,000.

➤ **SBL (#)**. Number of small business loans made (outstanding).

➤ **SSBL/TA Rank**. Decile rank based on ratio of micro-loans of less than $100,000 to total assets. A firm looking for a loan of $50,000 might be better served by a bank making more loans under $100,000 than by a bank concentrating on larger loans.

➤ **SBF**. Banks that continue to provide small business access to commercial credit.

Bank Name	Bank Total Rank	Asset Size	SBL ($)	SBL (#)	SSBL/TA Rank	SBF
First National Bank 101 W. 36th Ave. #216 Anchorage, AK 907-277-8602	23	1B–10B	137,194	3,230	4	Y
First Bank 2530 Tongass Ave. Ketchikan, AK 907-228-4235	23	100M–500M	29,962	727	7	Y
National Bank of Alaska 1351 Huffman Rd. Anchorage, AK 907-267-5700	22	1B–10B	232,075	4,773	2	
Denali State Bank 119 N. Cushman St. Fairbanks, AK 907-456-1400	17	100M–500M	16,090	238	9	
Northrim Bank 8730 Old Seward Hwy. Anchorage, AK 907-522-8886	15	100M–500M	30,771	590	5	
Peoples Bank & Trust Co. 1501 Highway 14 E. Selma, AL 334-418-8462	40	100M–500M	82,961	1,379	10	Y
First Bank & Trust Co. 131 Marion St. Grove Hill, AL 334-275-4111	40	100M–500M	47,619	1,344	10	Y
West Alabama Bank & Trust Co. 302 1st St. S. Reform, AL 205-375-6261	39	100M–500M	54,939	1,067	10	Y

Bank Name	Bank Total Rank	Asset Size	SBL ($)	SBL (#)	SSBL/TA Rank	SBF
County Bank & Trust Bank of Russell County 910 13th St. Phenix City, AL 334-297-7000	37	100M–500M	32,822	506	10	Y
First National Bank of Wetumpka 408 S. Main St. Wetumpka, AL 334-567-5141	37	100M–500M	43,281	856	8	Y
Caddo First National Bank Highway 8 & Fagan Glenwood, AR 870-356-3196	39	<100M	22,496	1,203	10	Y
Merchants & Planters Bank 915 Highway 67 N. Newport, AR 870-523-9831	38	<100M	19,660	586	10	Y
First National Bank in Mena 1 Financial Ctr. Mena, AR 501-394-3552	38	100M–500M	22,792	616	10	Y
Bank of Yellville Madison & Church St. Yellville, AR 870-449-4231	38	<100M	22,152	612	10	Y
Union Bank of Benton Military & Jameson St. Benton, AR 501-778-0411	38	100M–500M	27,899	1,024	8	Y

continues

309

Bank Name	Bank Total Rank	Asset Size	SBL ($)	SBL (#)	SSBL/TA Rank	SBF
County Bank 102 W. Gurley St. Prescott, AZ 520-771-8100	34	100M–500M	29,003	538	9	Y
Mohave State Bank 1771 McCulloch Blvd Lake Havasu City, AZ 520-855-0000	34	<100M	22,208	499	10	Y
Stockmens Bank 2611 Kingman Ave. Kingman, AZ 520-718-0660	34	100M–500M	35,309	810	9	Y
Community Bank of Arizona 2001 W. Wickenburg Way Wickenburg, AZ 520-684-5404	34	100M–500M	21,029	823	8	Y
Frontier State Bank 902 E. Deuce of Clubs Show Low, AZ 520-537-2933	34	<100M	15,468	345	10	Y
Bank of the Sierra 90 N. Main St. Porterville, CA 559-781-2525	39	100M–500M	71,747	790	10	Y
Six Rivers National Bank 402 F St. Eureka, CA 707-443-8400	38	100M–500M	29,448	561	10	Y

continued

continues

Bank Name	Bank Total Rank	Asset Size	SBL ($)	SBL (#)	SSBL/TA Rank	SBF
Scripps Bank 7817 Ivanhoe Ave., Ste. 100 La Jolla, CA 619-456-2265	38	100M–500M	58,057	1,076	9	Y
Nara Bank 3701 Wilshire Blvd., Ste. 220 Los Angeles, CA 213-639-1700	36	100M–500M	30,219	686	10	Y
Western Sierra National Bank Cameron Park Dr., Ste. 101 Cameron Park, CA 530-676-1010	36	<100M	31,679	290	9	Y
Independent Bank of Kersey 301 1st St. Kersey, CO 970-356-2265	39	100M–500M	27,745	645	10	Y
Bank of the Southwest NA 523 San Juan Pagosa Springs, CO 970-264-4111	39	<100M	27,541	568	9	Y
Community Banks of Colorado 101 E. Warren Cripple Cripple Creek, CO 719-689-2591	37	<100M	14,672	417	10	Y
Bank Of Grand Junction 326 Main St. Grand Junction, CO 970-241-9000	38	<100M	14,144	410	10	Y

Bank Name	Bank Total Rank	Asset Size	SBL ($)	SBL (#)	SSBL/TA Rank	SBF
First Community Industrial Bank 3600 E. Alameda Ave. Denver, CO 303-399-3400	37	100M–500M	42,322	565	7	Y
Bank of Southington 130 N. Main St. Southington, CT 860-620-5000	33	100M–500M	21,700	644	9	Y
Equity Bank 1160 Silas Deane Hwy. #101 Wethersfield, CT 860-571-7200	32	100M–500M	21,509	480	10	Y
Maritime Bank & Trust Co. 130 Westbrook Rd. Essex, CT 860-767-1166	30	<100M	13,347	306	9	Y
New Milford Bank & Trust Co. 5 Main St. New Milford, CT 860-355-1171	28	100M–500M	26,968	463	5	
North American Bank & Trust Co. 1151 Stratford Ave. Stratford, CT 203-377-8267	28	100M–500M	20,660	439	9	

continued

continues

Bank Name	Bank Total Rank	Asset Size	SBL ($)	SBL (#)	SSBL/TA Rank	SBF
Franklin National Bank of Washington DC 1722 I St. NW Washington, DC 202-429-9888	27	100M–500M	48,109	769	6	Y
Century National Bank 1275 Pennsylvania Ave. NW Washington, DC 202-496-4000	22	100M–500M	15,604	192	8	
First Liberty National Bank 1146 19th St. NW Washington, DC 202-331-7031	21	<100M	6,024	105	9	Y
First Union National Bank—DC 740 15th St. NW Washington, DC 202-637-7643	19	1B–10B	26,927	384	2	Y
Adams National Bank 50 Massachusetts Ave. NE Washington, DC 202-466-4090	18	100M–500M	11,724	202	5	
Nationsbank of Delaware Route 113 Dover, DE 302-741-1000	37	1B–10B	197,267	161,753	7	Y
PNC National Bank 103 Bellevue Pkwy. Wilmington, DE 302-791-1200	37	100M–500M	22,559	18,332	9	Y

313

continued

Bank Name	Bank Total Rank	Asset Size	SBL ($)	SBL (#)	SSBL/TA Rank	SBF
MBNA America Bank NA 11th & King Wilmington, DE 302-432-1251	34	>10B	108,835	41,139	6	Y
Chase Manhattan Bank 1201 N. Market St., 8th Fl. Wilmington, DE 302-428-3300	33	>10B	56,380	27,159	6	Y
Bank of Delmar 910 Norman Eskridge Hwy. Seaford, DE 302-629-2700	32	100M–500M	18,884	582	10	
Community Bank of Homestead 28801 SW. 157th Ave. Homestead, FL 305-245-2211	39	100M–500M	80,289	883	10	Y
First Community Bank 2240 S. Volusia Ave. Orange City, FL 904-775-3115	37	<100M	25,789	441	10	Y
United Southern Bank 750 N. Central Ave. Umatilla, FL 352-669-2121	37	100M–500M	40,059	807	9	Y
Ready Bank 71 Beal Pkwy. N.E. Fort Walton Beach, FL 850-243-7447	37	<100M	19,579	551	10	Y
Farmers & Merchants Bank 200 E. Washington St. Monticello, FL 850-997-2591	37	100M–500M	28,118	409	10	Y

continues

Bank Name	Bank Total Rank	Asset Size	SBL ($)	SBL (#)	SSBL/TA Rank	SBF
Community Bank & Trust Co. 400 Main St. N Cornelia, GA 706-778-2265	39	100M–500M	59,904	1,041	9	Y
Coastal Bank 101 W. Hendry St. Hinesville, GA 912-368-2265	38	<100M	26,780	660	10	Y
Bank of Dudley 1448 2nd St. Dudley, GA 912-676-3196	38	<100M	18,384	18,326	9	Y
McIntosh State Bank 210 S. Oak St. Jackson, GA 770-775-8300	38	100M–500M	40,158	880	9	Y
Bank of Toccoa 101 N. Alexander St. Toccoa, GA 706-886-9421	38	100M–500M	30,513	761	9	Y
City Bank 2301 Kuhio Ave. Honolulu, HI 808-971-4720	32	500M–1B	74,337	1,131	9	Y
Hawaii National Bank 1163 S. Beretania St. Ste. #A Honolulu, HI 808-536-3441	29	100M–500M	25,091	1,037	8	Y

continued

Bank Name	Bank Total Rank	Asset Size	SBL ($)	SBL (#)	SSBL/TA Rank	SBF
First Hawaiian Bank 765 Bishop St. Honolulu, HI 808-525-5380	27	1B–10B	173,291	5,936	5	Y
Bank of Hawaii 4634 Kilauea Ave. Honolulu, HI 808-733-7474	26	1B–10B	180,282	9,906	5	
Hardin County Savings Bank 1202 Edgington Ave. Eldora, IA 515-858-3407	40	100M–500M	18,309	506	10	Y
Pilot Grove Savings Bank 1341 Pilot Grove Rd. Pilot Grove, IA 319-469-3951	40	100M–500M	17,474	499	9	Y
Farmers State Bank 1310 6th St. Jesup, IA 319-827-1050	38	<100M	11,743	368	10	Y
Iowa State Bank 5 E. Call St. Algona, IA 515-295-3595	38	100M–500M	19,096	469	8	Y
Lincoln Savings Bank 508 Main St. Reinbeck, IA 319-345-6841	38	100M–500M	17,601	549	10	Y
Panhandle State Bank 231 N. 3rd Ave. Sandpoint, ID 208-263-0505	36	100M–500M	30,027	680	6	Y

continues

Bank Name	Bank Total Rank	Asset Size	SBL ($)	SBL (#)	SSBL/TA Rank	SBF
D L Evans Bank 124 E. 23 Dr. Burley, ID 208-678-6000	33	100M–500M	27,294	702	10	Y
Farmers & Merchants State Bank 703 E. 1st St. Meridian, ID 208-888-1416	29	<100M	25,902	546	7	Y
Pend Oreille Bank 3224 Hwy. 95 N Ponderay, ID 208-265-2232	27	<100M	15,203	212	9	
Bank of Eastern Idaho 399 N. Capital Ave. Idaho Falls, ID 208-524-5500	24	<100M	18,944	516	7	
Mercantile Trust & Savings Bank 440 Maine St. Quincy, IL 217-223-7300	40	100M–500M	88,692	1,000	10	Y
United Community Bank 301 N. Main St. Chatham, IL 217-483-2491	39	100M–500M	39,731	1,141	8	Y
Palmer-American National Bank 2 W. Main St. Danville, IL 217-446-6450	39	100M–500M	69,967	886	9	Y

continued

Bank Name	Bank Total Rank	Asset Size	SBL ($)	SBL (#)	SSBL/TA Rank	SBF
First Mid-Illinois Bank & Trust Mattoon, IL 217-258-0442	39	100M–500M	89,642	1,561	9	Y
Bank of Edwardsville 330 W. Vandalia St. Edwardsville, IL 618-656-0057	39	500M–1B	147,493	1,981	9	Y
Centier Bank 1500 119th St. Whiting, IN 219-659-0043	39	500M–1B	134,646	1,498	7	Y
Scott County State Bank 125 W. Mcclain Ave. Scottsburg, IN 812-752-4501	36	<100M	20,486	568	9	Y
Bank of Western Indiana 401 Washington St. Covington, IN 765-793-4846	36	100M–500M	25,029	545	10	Y
Community Bank, South Indiana 202 E. Spring St. New Albany, IN 812-944-2224	36	100M–500M	35,110	35,110	6	Y
Fowler State Bank 300 E. 5th St. Fowler, IN 765-884-1200	35	<100M	16,164	558	9	Y
First National Bank 124 W. Spring Ave. Conway Springs, KS 316-456-2255	40	<100M	16,593	393	10	Y

continues

Bank Name	Bank Total Rank	Asset Size	SBL ($)	SBL (#)	SSBL/TA Rank	SBF
Peoples Bank & Trust 101 S Main St. McPherson, KS 316-241-2100	39	<100M	25,677	504	9	Y
First National Bank & Trust Co. 225 State St. Phillipsburg, KS 785-543-6511	38	100M–500M	17,311	330	10	Y
Citizens State Bank 800 Broadway Marysville, KS 785-562-2186	38	100M–500M	24,875	393	9	Y
Farmers Bank & Trust 1017 Harrison St. Great Bend, KS 316-792-2411	38	100M–500M	32,507	1,046	8	Y
Bank of Columbia 144 Public Sq. Columbia, KY 502-384-6433	38	<100M	18,158	682	10	Y
South Central Bank 208 S. Broadway St. Glasgow, KY 502-651-7466	40	100M–500M	35,388	816	10	Y
Peoples Bank & Trust Co. 124 E. Main St. Hazard, KY 606-439-9243	39	100M–500M	43,723	1,097	9	Y
Farmers Bank & Trust 200 E. Main St. Georgetown, KY 502-863-2393	38	100M–500M	29,334	374	10	Y

319

Bank Name	Bank Total Rank	Asset Size	SBL ($)	SBL (#)	SSBL/TA Rank	SBF
First National Bank 120 Town Sq. Manchester, KY 606-598-6111	38	100M–500M	27,957	543	9	Y
First Republic Bank 107 Glenda St. Rayville, LA 318-728-4423	40	100M–500M	35,113	1,336	10	Y
Community Trust Bank 3921 Elm St. Choudrant, LA 318-768-2531	40	100M–500M	37,904	1,244	10	Y
Peoples State Bank 880 San Antonio Ave. Many, LA 318-256-2071	38	100M–500M	38,067	567	10	Y
American Security Bank 126 E. Main St. Ville Platte, LA 318-363-5602	38	100M–500M	47,867	2,325	9	Y
Central Progressive Bank 400 W. Oak St. Amite, LA 504-748-7157	38	100M–500M	29,410	627	10	Y
Bank of Western Massachusetts 29 State St. Springfield, MA 413-781-2265	36	100M–500M	75,359	1,233	10	Y
Enterprise Bank & Trust Co. 222 Merrimack St. Lowell, MA 978-459-9000	35	100M–500M	52,159	1,264	9	Y

continued

continues

Bank Name	Bank Total Rank	Asset Size	SBL ($)	SBL (#)	SSBL/TA Rank	SBF
Milford National Bank & Trust 300 Main St. Milford, MA 508-634-4100	33	100M–500M	25,898	604	10	Y
Slades Ferry Bank 100 Slades Ferry Ave. Somerset, MA 508-675-2121	32	100M–500M	48,803	884	9	Y
Park West Bank & Trust Co. 225 Park Ave. West Springfield, MA 413-747-1400	32	100M–500M	48,620	682	8	Y
Peninsula Bank 11732 Somerset Ave. Princess Anne, MD 410-651-2400	36	100M–500M	61,347	1,414	8	Y
Industrial Bank of North America 1900 John Hanson Ln. Oxon Hill, MD 301-839-4600	34	100M–500M	34,489	592	7	Y
First United National Bank & Trust Co. 19 S. 2nd St. Oakland, MD 301-334-9471	34	500M–1B	47,082	1,555	5	Y
Peoples Bank of Kent County 600 Washington Ave. Chestertown, MD 410-778-5500	33	100M–500M	22,301	525	10	Y

continued

Bank Name	Bank Total Rank	Asset Size	SBL ($)	SBL (#)	SSBL/TA Rank	SBF
Bank of the Eastern Shore 301 Crusader Rd. Cambridge, MD 410-228-5800	33	<100M	21,208	509	10	Y
Katahdin Trust Co. Main St. Patten, ME 207-528-2211	34	100M–500M	45,129	853	9	Y
United Bank 145 Exchange St. Bangor, ME 207-942-5263	33	<100M	33,183	736	10	Y
Union Trust Co. 66 Main St. Ellsworth, ME 207-667-2504	30	100M–500M	44,878	1,039	6	
Maine Bank & Trust Co. 467 Congress St. Portland, ME 207-828-3000	27	100M–500M	42,038	1,081	7	
First Citizens Bank 9 Dyer St. Presque Isle, ME 207-768-3222	26	100M–500M	20,855	722	8	
1st Bank 502 W. Houghton Ave. West Branch, MI 517-345-7900	40	100M–500M	49,756	1,142	10	Y
State Bank of Escanaba 112 N. 11th St. Escanaba, MI 906-786-1331	38	<100M	21,755	1,189	9	Y

continues

Bank Name	Bank Total Rank	Asset Size	SBL ($)	SBL (#)	SSBL/TA Rank	SBF
Signature Bank 833 N. Van Dyke Rd. Bad Axe, MI 517-269-9211	37	100M–500M	32,177	653	10	Y
MFC First National Bank 6615 U.S. Hwy. 2 & 41 Escanaba, MI 906-789-5266	37	100M–500M	43,373	612	10	Y
Community First National Bank 2015 College Way Fergus Falls, MN 218-739-0245	37	500M–1B	157,967	3,773	7	Y
First National Bank of Walker 600 Minnesota Ave. W. Walker, MN 218-547-1160	37	100M–500M	42,133	543	6	Y
Grand Marais State Bank 211 Hwy. 61 E. Grand Marais, MN 218-387-2441	37	<100M	14,947	482	7	Y
First Community Bank 214 5th Ave. Freeborn, MN 507-863-2371	37	<100M	12,149	406	9	Y
Security State Bank of Hibbing 701 E. Howard St. Hibbing, MN 218-263-8855	36	<100M	22,459	431	6	Y

continued

Bank Name	Bank Total Rank	Asset Size	SBL ($)	SBL (#)	SSBL/TA Rank	SBF
Nodaway Valley Bank 304 N. Main St. Maryville, MO 660-562-3232	40	100M–500M	51,401	819	10	Y
First MO State Bank 1902 Sunset Dr. Poplar Bluff, MO 573-785-6800	39	<100M	21,501	640	10	Y
First Midwest Bank 333 S. Westwood Blvd., #14 Poplar Bluff, MO 573-785-6288	39	<100M	34,210	538	10	Y
SAC River Valley Bank 312 Public Sq. Stockton, MO 417-276-3115	39	<100M	24,413	421	10	Y
Boonslick Bank 400 E. Spring St. Boonville, MO 660-882-7476	39	100M–500M	26,959	579	10	Y
Union Planters Bank of Central MS 329 E. Capitol St. Jackson, MS 601-969-6182	39	500M–1B	166,690	5,389	9	Y
Merchants & Marine Bank 1807 Market St. Pascagoula, MS 228-762-3311	38	100M–500M	66,369	2,303	9	Y

continues

Bank Name	Bank Total Rank	Asset Size	SBL ($)	SBL (#)	SSBL/TA Rank	SBF
Peoples Bank & Trust Co. 615 N. Gloster St. Tupelo, MS 601-680-1400	37	500M–1B	200,845	4,824	8	Y
First Bank 100 S. Broadway St. McComb, MS 601-684-2231	37	100M–500M	53,166	859	10	Y
Mountain West Bank of Helena 2021 N. Montana Ave. Helena, MT 406-442-4663	39	100M–500M	59,654	712	9	Y
Bitterroot Valley Bank P.O. Box 9 Lolo, MT 406-273-2400	38	<100M	29,501	481	9	Y
Rocky Mountain Bank 2615 King Ave. W. Billings, MT 406-656-3140	37	100M–500M	62,650	1,440	8	Y
First Security Bank of Missoula 3220 Great Northern Ave. Missoula, MT 406-542-8296	37	100M–500M	51,701	1,394	6	Y
Mountain West Bank of Great Falls 12 3rd St. NW. Great Falls, MT 406-727-2265	36	<100M	22,689	356	9	Y

Bank Name	Bank Total Rank	Asset Size	SBL ($)	SBL (#)	SSBL/TA Rank	SBF
Yadkin Valley Bank & Trust Co. 110 W. Market St. Elkin, NC 336-526-6300	36	100M–500M	88,266	1,798	10	Y
East Carolina Bank Hwy. 264 Engelhard, NC 252-925-9461	35	100M–500M	51,627	1,167	10	Y
Fidelity Bank 100 S. Main St. Fuquay-Varina, NC 919-552-2242	34	500M–1B	97,052	1,779	8	Y
Carolina Community Bank 300 Peachtree St. Murphy, NC 828-837-9291	34	100M–500M	51,354	2,011	7	Y
Triangle Bank 2127 Clark Ave. Raleigh, NC 919-836-8700	33	1B–10B	189,537	5,052	9	Y
Farmers & Merchants Bank of Valley City 240 3rd Ave. NW. Valley City, ND 701-845-2712	38	<100M	12,309	338	10	Y
First Western Bank & Trust Co. 2200 15th St. SW. Minot, ND 701-857-7150	36	100M–500M	50,875	792	5	Y

continued

326

Bank Name	Bank Total Rank	Asset Size	SBL ($)	SBL (#)	SSBL/TA Rank	SBF
Kirkwood Bank & Trust Co. 2911 N. 14th St. Bismarck, ND 701-221-9122	36	<100M	21,938	404	7	Y
Citizens State Bank 104 Main St. W. Mohall, ND 701-756-6364	35	<100M	7,271	147	10	Y
Stutsman County State Bank 401 1st Ave. S. Jamestown, ND 701-253-5600	34	100M–500M	22,294	908	4	Y
Commercial State Bank 519 E. Broadway Wausa, NE 402-586-2266	38	<100M	8,048	362	10	Y
Valley Bank & Trust Co. 1425 10th St. Scottsbluff, NE 308-436-2300	38	<100M	21,130	625	8	Y
Adams Bank & Trust Co. 315 N. Spruce St. Ogallala, NE 308-284-4071	38	100M–500M	26,443	677	9	Y
Hershey State Bank 100 S. Lincoln St. Hershey, NE 308-368-5555	38	<100M	9,047	369	10	Y
Gothenburg State Bank & Trust Co. 900 Lake Ave. Gothenburg, NE 308-537-7181	36	<100M	10,158	212	9	Y

continues

continued

Bank Name	Bank Total Rank	Asset Size	SBL ($)	SBL (#)	SSBL/TA Rank	SBF
Community Bank & Trust Co. 15 Varney Rd. Wolfeboro, NH 603-569-8400	38	100M–500M	45,089	723	10	Y
Village Bank & Trust Co. 1 Country Club Rd. Gilford, NH 603-528-3000	28	<100M	12,084	267	9	Y
Pemigewasset National Bank of Plymouth 287 Highland St. Plymouth, NH 603-536-3339	28	100M–500M	19,798	587	6	
First & Ocean National Bank 332 Lafayette Rd. Seabrook, NH 603-474-5552	27	100M–500M	24,683	542	7	
Minotola National Bank Landis & Union Rd. Vineland, NJ 609-696-8100	34	100M–500M	57,388	1,046	10	Y
Farmers & Merchants National Bank of Bridgeton 53 Laurel St. S. Bridgeton, NJ 609-451-2222	33	100M–500M	51,389	1,545	9	Y
Panasia Bank 183 Main St. Fort Lee, NJ 201-947-6666	32	<100M	12,662	513	10	Y
Centinel Bank of Taos 512 Paseo Del Pueblo Sur Taos, NM 505-758-6700	34	<100M	21,928	581	9	Y

continues

Bank Name	Bank Total Rank	Asset Size	SBL ($)	SBL (#)	SSBL/TA Rank	SBF
Citizens Bank 2200 Missouri Ave. Las Cruces, NM 505-522-1000	34	100M–500M	26,205	456	7	Y
Peoples Bank 1100 Paseo Del Pueblo Sur Taos, NM 505-758-5999	33	<100M	16,851	325	9	Y
First New Mexico Bank 300 S. Gold Ave. Deming, NM 505-546-2691	32	<100M	16,135	556	9	Y
Great Basin Bank 487 Railroad St. Elko, NV 775-753-3800	32	<100M	12,718	151	10	Y
Bankwest of Nevada 2700 W. Sahara Ave. Las Vegas, NV 702-248-4200	30	100M–500M	24,961	486	7	Y
First Security Bank of Nevada 530 Las Vegas Blvd. S. Las Vegas, NV 702-251-1100	27	500M–1B	64,733	1,257	4	Y
Heritage Bank of Nevada 1401 S. Virginia St. Reno, NV 775-348-1000	27	<100M	5,663	124	9	
Solvay Bank 1537 Milton Ave. Solvay, NY 315-468-1661	37	100M–500M	53,822	1,050	10	Y

Bank Name	Bank Total Rank	Asset Size	SBL ($)	SBL (#)	SSBL/TA Rank	SBF
First National Bank 300 Main St. Jeffersonville, NY 914-482-4000	35	100M–500M	30,566	562	9	Y
National Bank 2 Seneca St. Geneva, NY 315-789-2300	35	100M–500M	56,387	1,501	10	Y
Citizens Banking Co. 50 E. Main St. Salineville, OH 330-679-2311	40	1B–10B	263,658	2,821	10	Y
Croghan Colonial Bank 323 Croghan St. Fremont, OH 419-332-7301	37	100M–500M	61,067	1,229	9	Y
First National Bank of Shelby 60 W. Main St. Shelby, OH 419-342-4010	35	100M–500M	28,435	733	10	Y
Peoples Banking Corp. 1330 N. Main St. Findlay, OH 419-423-4741	35	<100M	26,873	385	10	Y
First National Bank of SW.Ohio 720 NW. Washington Blvd. Hamilton, OH 513-867-5571	34	500M–1B	138,366	2,764	6	Y

continued

Bank Name	Bank Total Rank	Asset Size	SBL ($)	SBL (#)	SSBL/TA Rank	SBF
Vinton County National Bank 112 W. Main St. McArthur, OH 740-596-2525	34	100M–500M	24,820	503	7	Y
Bank of Western OK 201 E. Broadway Ave. Elk City, OK 580-225-3434	39	<100M	14,956	581	10	Y
First United Bank & Trust Co. 102 E. Main St. Holdenville, OK 405-379-3307	38	100M–500M	37,981	951	8	Y
First Bank & Trust Corp. 923 W. Main St. Duncan, OK 580-255-1810	37	100M–500M	24,046	652	6	Y
Landmark Bank 128 Plaza Madill, OK 580-795-5503	37	<100M	21,114	423	8	Y
Security Bank 900 Hwy. 101 S. Coos Bay, OR 541-269-2311	34	100M–500M	31,398	1,767	6	Y
Bank of the Cascades 1100 NW. Wall St. Bend, OR 541-385-6200	33	100M–500M	39,555	1,089	6	Y

continues

continued

Bank Name	Bank Total Rank	Asset Size	SBL ($)	SBL (#)	SSBL/TA Rank	SBF
Columbia River Bank 520 Mount Hood St. The Dalles, OR 541-296-1157	31	100M–500M	32,596	1,006	9	Y
Pacific Continental Bank 255 Coburg Rd. Eugene, OR 541-686-8685	31	100M–500M	37,010	1,091	8	Y
Bank of Newport 506 SW. Coast Hwy. Newport, OR 541-265-6666	30	100M–500M	47,090	897	7	
Pioneer American 41 N. Main St., #1 Carbondale, PA 570-282-4121	40	100M–500M	75,168	1,642	10	Y
Jersey Shore State Bank 115 S. Main St. Jersey Shore, PA 570-398-2213	39	100M–500M	58,186	1,152	10	Y
Community Bank & Trust Corp. 347 Main St. Forest City, PA 570-282-4821	38	100M–500M	55,872	995	9	Y
Old Forge Bank 216 S. Main St. Old Forge, PA 570-457-8345	38	100M–500M	41,383	803	10	Y
Williamsport National Bank 1949 E. 3rd St. Williamsport, PA 570-326-2431	37	100M–500M	38,841	768	9	Y

Bank Name	Bank Total Rank	Asset Size	SBL ($)	SBL (#)	SSBL/TA Rank	SBF
Washington Trust Corp. 23 Broad St., #1 Westerly, RI 401-348-1200	31	500M–1B	111,650	1,323	6	Y
Citizens Bank of Rhode Island 1 Citizens Plaza #1 Providence, RI 401-456-7000	24	1B–10B	129,908	2,078	3	Y
Pier Bank 885 Boston Neck Rd. Narragansett, RI 401-782-4800	21	<100M	8,736	139	9	Y
First Bank & Trust Corp. 180 Washington St. Providence, RI 401-421-3600	20	100M–500M	19,148	260	8	Y
Bank Rhode Island 999 S. Broadway East Providence, RI 401-435-8600	20	100M–500M	23,349	329	5	Y
Anderson Bros. Bank 101 N. Main St. Mullins, SC 843-464-6271	34	<100M	23,940	643	10	Y
Palmetto State Bank 601 1st St. W. Hampton, SC 803-943-2671	34	100M–500M	35,915	585	9	Y

continues

333

Bank Name	Bank Total Rank	Asset Size	SBL ($)	SBL (#)	SSBL/TA Rank	SBF
Enterprise Bank of South Carolina 206 E. Broadway St. Ehrhardt, SC 803-267-3191	34	100M–500M	30,397	974	8	Y
F & M Bank 35 1st Ave. NE. Watertown, SD 605-886-8401	37	100M–500M	71,889	961	7	Y
Merchants State Bank 327 N. Main St. Freeman, SD 605-925-4222	37	<100M	9,792	445	10	Y
Bankwest 420 S. Pierre St. Pierre, SD 605-224-7391	35	100M–500M	31,928	789	8	Y
First State Bank of Miller 201 N. Broadway Ave. Miller, SD 605-853-2473	34	<100M	11,479	236	9	Y
Fulton State Bank 221 N. Main St. Fulton, SD 605-996-5731	33	<100M	4,102	324	8	Y
Farmers & Merchants Bank 3050 Wilma Rudolph Blvd. Clarksville, TN 931-503-2090	40	100M–500M	58,795	1,556	10	Y
First Bank 200 N. Main St. Lexington, TN 901-968-4211	40	100M–500M	73,517	1,837	10	Y

continues

Bank Name	Bank Total Rank	Asset Size	SBL ($)	SBL (#)	SSBL/TA Rank	SBF
Citizens Bank 406 Main St. N. Carthage, TN 615-735-1490	37	100M–500M	47,410	1,425	9	Y
Jackson Bank & Trust Co. 307 E. Hull Ave. Gainesboro, TN 931-268-2161	37	100M–500M	24,102	562	10	Y
First State Bank 1009 Hwy. 51 N. Covington, TN 901-475-5061	37	100M–500M	28,824	570	10	Y
First Bank of Conroe 1800 W. White Oak Ter. Conroe, TX 409-760-1888	40	<100M	34,005	831	10	Y
East Texas National Bank 501 S. Washington Ave. Marshall, TX 903-935-1331	40	100M–500M	40,645	774	10	Y
Midland American Bank 719 W. Louisiana Ave. Midland, TX 915-687-3030	40	100M–500M	83,402	1,326	10	Y
Navigation Bank 3801 Navigation Blvd. Houston, TX 713-223-3400	40	<100M	34,658	853	10	Y
First National Bank 418 E. 1st St. Hughes Springs, TX 903-639-2521	40	<100M	29,747	914	10	Y

continued

Bank Name	Bank Total Rank	Asset Size	SBL ($)	SBL (#)	SSBL/TA Rank	SBF
Advanta Finance Corp. 141 E. 5600 S. Murray, UT 801-263-6655	39	100M–500M	132,674	133,543	10	Y
Mountainwest Financial 855 E. 9400 S. Sandy, UT 801-566-4161	37	1B–10B	315,091	796,104	8	Y
First USA Financial Services 3995 S. 700 E., #400 Murray, UT 801-281-5800	36	<100M	20,183	5,884	10	Y
Highlands Union Bank 340 E. Main St. Abingdon, VA 540-628-9181	40	100M–500M	58,078	1,236	10	Y
Benchmark Community Bank 100 S. Broad St. Kenbridge, VA 804-676-8444	40	100M–500M	49,801	2,153	10	Y
Powell Valley National Bank 68 E. Main St. Jonesville, VA 540-346-1414	38	100M–500M	30,358	705	10	Y
Miners & Merchants Bank Corp. Route 460 E. Grundy, VA 540-935-8161	38	100M–500M	48,085	481	10	Y
Salem Bank & Trust 220 E. Main St. Salem, VA 540-387-0223	37	100M–500M	32,366	640	10	Y

Bank Name	Bank Total Rank	Asset Size	SBL ($)	SBL (#)	SSBL/TA Rank	SBF
Union Bank 20 Lower Main St. Morrisville, VT 802-888-6600	36	100M–500M	48,255	966	10	Y
Randolph National Bank 21 N. Main St. Randolph, VT 802-728-9611	31	<100M	19,194	857	9	Y
Chittenden Trust Co. 508 Shelburne Rd. Burlington, VT 802-658-3424	29	1B–10B	159,625	3,353	4	Y
Citizens Savings Bank & Trust Corp. A10 Green Mountain Mall Saint Johnsbury, VT 802-748-2454	28	<100M	18,867	692	8	
Community National Bank Derby Rd. Derby, VT 802-334-7915	27	100M–500M	26,856	733	5	
Bank Of The West 30 W. Main St. Walla Walla, WA 509-527-3800	35	100M–500M	24,591	590	10	Y
Towne Bank of Woodinville 17530 132nd Ave. NE. Woodinville, WA 425-486-2265	35	100M–500M	37,193	1,302	9	Y
First Heritage Bank 167 Lincoln Ave. Snohomish, WA 360-568-0536	34	<100M	22,407	472	9	Y

continues

337

continued

Bank Name	Bank Total Rank	Asset Size	SBL ($)	SBL (#)	SSBL/TA Rank	SBF
First National Bank 1488 Olney Ave. SE. Port Orchard, WA 360-895-2265	33	<100M	15,846	346	8	Y
Security State Bank 1231 Harrison Ave. Centralia, WA 360-736-2861	32	100M–500M	38,727	694	8	Y
Stephenson National Bank 1820 Hall Ave. Marinette, WI 715-732-1732	39	100M–500M	45,729	619	10	Y
F&M Bank of Winnebago County 124 E. Main St. Omro, WI 920-685-2771	38	<100M	28,091	600	10	Y
Farmers & Merchants Bank 1001 Superior Ave. Tomah, WI 608-372-2126	38	<100M	29,254	561	10	Y
F&M Bank–Lakeland Highway 51 & J Woodruff, WI 715-356-3214	37	100M–500M	44,474	805	7	Y
First National Bank of Fox Valley 161 Main St. Menasha, WI 920-729-6900	37	<100M	31,170	409	10	Y

Bank Name	Bank Total Rank	Asset Size	SBL ($)	SBL (#)	SSBL/TA Rank	SBF
Matewan National Bank 250 E. 2nd Ave. Williamson, WV 304-235-1544	38	100M–500M	59,722	1,548	8	Y
Greenbrier Valley National Bank 109 S. Jefferson St. Lewisburg, WV 304-645-2500	38	100M–500M	32,745	574	10	Y
Bank Of Raleigh Main & Kanawha St. Beckley, WV 304-255-7000	36	100M–500M	63,096	950	9	Y
First National Bank in Marlinton 300 8th St. Marlinton, WV 304-799-4640	36	<100M	15,521	428	10	Y
Bank Of Gassaway 700 Elk St. Gassaway, WV 304-364-5138	35	<100M	16,775	478	9	Y
First Interstate Bank 1613 Coffeen Ave. Sheridan, WY 307-672-1501	39	500M–1B	189,453	3,564	9	Y
First National Bank 141 S. Main St. Buffalo, WY 307-684-2211	36	<100M	14,475	426	10	Y

continues

continued

Bank Name	Bank Total Rank	Asset Size	SBL ($)	SBL (#)	SSBL/TA Rank	SBF
Riverton State Bank 616 N. Federal Blvd. Riverton, WY 307-856-2265	36	<100M	13,369	432	9	Y
First State Bank of Wheatland 1405 16th St. Wheatland, WY 307-322-5222	34	<100M	8,414	482	10	Y
Western Bank of Cheyenne 1525 E. Pershing Blvd. Cheyenne, WY 307-637-7333	32	<100M	10,617	288	8	Y

* *Small Business Lending in the United States, June 1997*

Online Discount Brokers

Ever wanted to know what online discount brokers are available to you? Now you can. We've compiled a list of popular online discount brokers that provides you with contact information, including their Web site address, what types of commissions they charge, and whether they use the Internet or software to execute trades.

Accutrade

4211 South 102nd Street
Omaha, NE 68127

Web site? www.accutrade.com

Web-based trading? Yes

Proprietary software? No

Email address? Info@accutrade.com

Toll-free number? 800-228-3011

AGS Financial Services

208 LaSalle Street, #2059
Chicago, IL 60604

Web site? http://ags-financial-services.com

Web-based trading? No

Proprietary software? No

Email address? Webmaster@ags-finanical-services.com

Toll-free number? 800-436-0705

American Express Financial Direct

P.O. Box 59196
Minneapolis, MN 55459-0196

Web site? www.americanexpress.com/direct

Web-based trading? Yes

Proprietary software? No

Email address? See Web site.

Toll-free number? 800-658-4677

Andrew Peck Associates

Web site? www.thehost.com/peck

Web-based trading? Yes

Proprietary software? No

Email address? apainc5@aol.com

Toll-free number? 800-221-5873

Aufhauser & Company

112 West 56th Street
New York, NY 10019

Web site? www.aufhauser.com

Web-based trading? Yes

Proprietary software? No

Email address? info@aufhauser.com

Toll-free number? 800-368-3668

Bull & Bear Securities

11 Hanover Square
New York, NY 10005

Web site? www.bullandbear.com

Web-based trading? Yes

Proprietary software? Yes

Email address? bulbear@aol.com

Toll-free number? 800-262-5800

Ceres Securities

P.O. Box 3288
Omaha, NE 68103-9964

Web site? www.ceres.com

Web-based trading? Yes

Proprietary software? No

Email address? info@ceres.com

Toll-free number? 800-669-3900

Charles Schwab

101 Montgomery Street
San Francisco, CA 94104

Web site? www.schwab.com

Web-based trading? Yes.
www.eschwab.com

Proprietary software? Yes. 800-435-4000

Email address? No

Toll-free number? Yes. 800-435-4000

Computel Securities

One Second Street, 5th Floor
San Francisco, CA 94105

Web site? www.rapidtrade.com

Web-based trading? Yes

Proprietary software? No

Email address? support@rapidtrade.com

Toll-free number? 800-432-0327

Datek Securities

50 Broad Street, 6th Floor
New York, NY 10004

Web site? www.datek.com

Web-based trading? Yes

Proprietary software? No

Email address? broker@datek.com

Toll-free number? 888-GODATEK

EBroker

P.O. Box 2226
Omaha, NE 68103-2226

Web site? www.ebroker.com

Web-based trading? Yes

Proprietary software? No

Email address? info@ebroker.com

Toll-free number? No

E*TRADE

Four Embarcadero Place
2400 Geng Road
Palo Alto, CA 94303

Web site? www.etrade.com

Web-based trading? Yes

Proprietary software? No

Email address? service@etrade.com

Toll-free number? 800-786-2575

Fidelity Investments

161 Devonshire Street
Boston, MA 02110

Web site? www.fid-inv.com

Web-based trading? No

Proprietary software? Yes

Email address? Yes, same as Web site.

Toll-free number? 800-544-8666

Freedom Investments

11422 Miracle Hills Drive, Suite 501
Omaha, NE 68154

Web site? www.tradeflash.com

Web-based trading? No

Proprietary software? Yes. 800-381-1481
or www.tradeflash.com

Email address? trdflash@ix.netcom.com

Toll-free number? 800-381-1481

Jack White & Company

9191 Towne Center Drive, Suite 220
San Diego, CA 92122

Web site? www.pawws.com/jwc

Web-based trading? Yes

Proprietary software? Yes

Email address? jwc@pawws.com

Toll-free number? 800-233-3411

J.B. Oxford & Company

9665 Wilshire Boulevard, Suite 300
Beverly Hills, CA 90212

Web site? www.jboxford.com

Web-based trading? Yes

Proprietary software? Yes.
sales@jboc.com or 800-500-5007

Email address? sales@jboc.com

Toll-free number? 800-500-5007

National Discount Brokers

50 Broadway, 18th Floor
New York, NY 10004

Web site? http://pawws.secapl.com/ndb

Web-based trading? Yes

Proprietary software? Yes. 800-888-3999

Email address? ndb@secapl.com

Toll-free number? 800-888-3999

Net Investor

Web site? http://pawws.secapl.com/
invest.html

Web-based trading? Yes

Proprietary software? No

Email address? invest@pawws.com

Toll-free number? 800-638-4250

Olde Discount Broker

751 Griswold Street
Detroit, MI 48226

Web site? www.oldediscount.com

Web-based trading? No

Proprietary software? No

Email address? No

Toll-free number? 800-872-6533

Pacific Brokerage Services

5757 Wilshire Boulevard, Suite 3
Los Angeles, CA 90036

Web site? www.tradepbs.com

Web-based trading? Yes

Proprietary software? No

Email address? tradepbs@interramp.com

Toll-free number? 800-421-8395

PC Financial Network

One Pershing Plaza
Jersey City, NJ 07399

Web site? www.pcfn.com or through
America Online (Keyword: PCFN)

Web-based trading? Yes

Proprietary software? No

Email address? Same as Web site.

Toll-free number? 800-825-5723

Quick & Reilly

26 Broadway
New York, NY 10004

Web site? www.quick-reilly.com or
through CompuServe (GO QWKI)

Web-based trading? No

Proprietary software? Yes. 800-837-7220

Email address? peter_t@ix.netcom.com

Toll-free number? 800-221-5220

Regal Discount Securities

209 West Jackson Boulevard, 4th Floor
Chicago, IL 60606

Web site? www.regaldiscount.com

Web-based trading? No

Proprietary software? Yes. 800-786-9000

Email address?
webmaster@regaldiscount.com

Toll-free number? 800-786-9000

Savoy Discount Brokerage

823 3rd Avenue, Suite 206
Seattle, WA 98104-1617

Web site? www.savoystocks.com

Web-based trading? No

Proprietary software? Yes. 800-961-1500

Email address? info@savoystocks.com

Toll-free number? 800-961-1500

T. Rowe Price Discount Brokerage

100 East Pratt Avenue
Baltimore, MD 21202

Web site? www.troweprice.com

Web-based trading? No

Proprietary software? Yes. 800-541-3036

Email address? info@troweprice.com

Toll-free number? 800-225-7720

The Vanguard Group

Vanguard Financial Center
Valley Forge, PA 19496-9906

Web site? www.vanguard.com

Web-based trading? No

Proprietary software? No

Email address? vgonline@aol.com

Toll-free number? 800-992-8327

The Wall Street Discount Corporation

100 Wall Street
New York, NY 10005

Web site? www.wsdc.com

Web-based trading? Yes

Proprietary software? No

Email address? info@wsdc.com

Toll-free number? 800-221-7870

Waterhouse Securities

100 Wall Street
New York, NY 10005

Web site? www.waterhouse.com

Web-based trading? No

Proprietary software? Yes. 800-934-4430

Email address? No

Toll-free number? 800-934-4430

Glossary of Terms

All or none   If you have a large order and want to be sure you'll sell all your shares, not just pieces of it, consider this type of order; but know that you may not get your trade executed.

Angel   A wealthy individual who provides startup capital to very young companies to help them grow, taking a large risk in exchange for a potentially large return on investment, also called *angel investor*.

Asked or offering price   The lowest price which any seller will accept for a security that you want to buy. You, as the buyer, would buy the investment at the asked or offering price.

Asset allocation   How you carve up your investment pie. Represented usually in percentages, such as the percentage amount you have in stocks, bonds, and mutual funds, which then makes up your investment portfolio.

Assets   What you own.

At the close   The final few seconds when the trading day stops. You can also put in an order to buy or sell a stock, for example, at the close. You would get the best price possible these last few trading seconds.

At the market   This is a market order.

At the opening   Opposite of the close. You would get the best price possible if you were to buy or sell a stock exactly when the market opened.

Averages   Also known as *indices*. The Dow Jones Industrial Average and Standard & Poor's 500 (S&P 500) are the most common. They represent a way of measuring the trend in security prices.

Balance sheet   Found in an annual report, it lists the pluses and minuses of a company.

Bear market   A market where prices drop rather sharply. Pessimism, growing unemployment, and sometimes a recession are common. Opposite of bull market.

Beta   A measurement of the sensitivity (risk tolerance) of a stock relative to current market activity.

Blue chip   The stock of a leading company that is known for superior management. Blue chip stocks are mostly listed on the Dow Jones Industrial Average.

Book value This is the historical value of the equity of a company.

Broker A person who handles your order to buy and sell securities.

Bull market An advancing market, where everything is on the upswing. Opposite of a bear market.

Buy order An order to buy a security that you specify.

Capital gain or loss Profit or loss from the sale of an investment.

CD-ROM CD stands for compact disc, and is a format for recording, storing, and retrieving electronic information. It can only be read using a special optical drive.

Closing costs All costs incurred before the loan is closed, and can sometimes be wrapped up in the loan itself. Many are negotiable, and they include the appraisal fee, credit report, attorney fee, survey, termite inspection, and the bank loan origination fee and/or discount points.

Closing price Represents the last price at which an investment security listed was either bought or sold.

Common gateway interface (CGI) The standard way for a Web server (owned by your host) to pass data back and forth between the server and an application. If a customer fills out a form on your Web site, for example, it needs to be processed by an application program. The Web server passes the form information to the application program that processes the data and may send back a confirmation message. The process method is called CGI.

Common stock An investment that represents ownership interest in a corporation.

COBOL Stands for Common Business Oriented Language. It was the first high-level programming language for business applications, and the most widely used. Although now thought of as out-of-date, many imbedded systems still rely on COBOL.

Compliant Webster says, submissive. In Y2K terms, it can mean anything from I promise not to have any problems after the year 2000 to, I have completed the minimum requirements.

Consumer Price Index It is one economic report that is looked upon as the best indicator of inflation.

Cyberspace Where humans and computers meet, disregarding earth's physical features. We get there by logging on to the Internet and can research all kinds of information, including financial information; we can also perform online transactions in cyberspace.

Cyberspeak The language of computer-savvy Net surfers. You too will be fluent in cyberspeak once you've read this book.

Cybersquatter Someone who buys up a domain name that is a well-known brand name, intending to resell it a company who has a trademark on the name.

Day order An order to buy (sell) an investment, which, if not executed, expires as the end of the trading day.

Deficit The money the government—or even a company—pays out in excess of what it takes in over a given period.

Delayed quotes Stock quotes that are provided online but the prices are delayed 15 to 20 minutes.

Digital footprints The information you leave behind when you post messages, stories, or items on the World Wide Web. Do a search sometime of your own name, and see what pops up. You may be surprised…or alarmed!

Digital IDs Also known as *digital certificates*, digital IDs are the electronic equivalent to a driver's license or membership card. With a digital ID, friends or online services can be assured that it is really you. Conversely, you can ask for someone else's digital ID before you do business.

Discount rate The interest rate the Federal Reserve charges to member banks for loans.

Diversification The spreading of investment funds among classes of securities and localities to distribute the risk.

Dividend The proportion of a company's net earnings paid to its stockholders.

Dividend reinvestment program A program that hundreds of publicly-traded companies offer that allow you to purchase additional shares of stock directly from the company without having to purchase them through a broker. Also known as DRIP.

Dividend yield Expressed as a percent. Divide the dividend payment by the market price of the stock.

Dollar cost averaging This is when a fixed dollar amount is invested on a periodic basis into one or more investments, thereby enabling the investor to average the purchase of shares (if it's a stock or mutual fund, for example) over the long haul.

Domain names Easy-to-remember names for Internet computers that map to IP numbers, which serve as routing addresses. Computers known as *Domain Name Servers* (DNS) translate Internet names into the numbers so that the information can be transmitted across the network.

Dow Jones Industrial Average Also referred to as DJIA. A popular gauge of the stock market on the average closing prices of 30 blue-chip stocks.

Earnings per share This is a company's net income minus preferred dividends divided by the outstanding shares of stock. Also known as *EPS*.

Electronic data interchange (EDI) A standard for compiling and transmitting information between computers, often over private communications networks called value-added networks (VANs).

Electronic signature An electronic or digital signature is the electronic equivalent to your written signature. As with digital IDs, it can be used by someone to verify identity. It can also guarantee that the original message content is unchanged.

Edutainment A nice word for computer games that make learning fun.

Electronic commerce More commonly known these days as e-commerce. It is basically the business of buying and selling goods and services on the Internet.

Embedded systems An imbedded system is one normally meant to be part of a larger operating system, or to be placed in a microprocessor to be part of a variety of hardware devices.

347

Encryption codes   Through encryption, your data—everything from your account numbers to account balances—is converted into a series of unrecognizable numbers before they are exchanged over the Internet. This series of numbers creates a mathematical lock—a lock that only your financial institution and browser have the key to. And, every time you create a new transaction, a new lock and key combination is randomly created.

Entrepreneur   One who organizes, manages, and assumes the risks of a business or enterprise.

Envelope accounting   Envelope accounting, or budgeting, is also referred to as "Bag" accounting, and is very simple. A certain amount of money is set aside on a regular basis in an envelope marked for a specific purpose or category. If you want to buy something in that category, you check to see if the funds are available. If yes, go ahead. If not, you don't buy.

Equities   Refers to ownership of property, such as having equity in your home or owning stocks.

Execute an order   To fulfill an order to buy or sell a security.

Federal Reserve System   The central banking system of the United States, made up of 12 Federal Reserve banks and supervised by the Federal Reserve Board.

Fill or kill   Sometimes confused with *all or none*, this means you want to sell all your stock at once or sell none of it *immediately*.

Financial statement   Another term for balance sheet.

Firewalls   A firewall is a set of related programs, located at one particular network server that protects them from users from other networks.

File Transfer Protocol (FTP)   The process by which files are transferred to the Web server. You create and maintain your Web pages on your own computer, and then upload the files to your Web site at your leisure.

Fluctuations   Variations in the market price of a security. Meaning, it goes up and down.

Gigabytes (gigs or GB)   A gigabyte (pronounced gig-a-bite) is a measure of computer data storage and is approximately a billion bytes.

Good 'Til Canceled (GTC)   You have a live stock bid or offer for the next 90 days or until you call and cancel the order.

Gross Domestic Product   The sum of all the goods and services bought and sold in the United States.

Growth stock   The stock issued by a corporation whose earnings have increased consistently over a number of years.

Hackers   Most commonly used to describe a clever programmer or geek that can break into other's computer systems.

Home-based business owners   Self-employed individuals who operate a business or profession primarily from, or in, a home office.

Hyperlink   A hyperlink is an electronic link providing direct access from one distinctively marked place in a document (Web page) to another in the same or different document, according to *Merriam-Webster Dictionary Online* at www.m-w.com. Hyperlinks are usually marked in blue and underlined.

Index funds   A fund comprised of securities that will produce a return that replicates a designated securities index.

Individual retirement account   Also known as an *IRA*. It is an account that allows you to save and invest money on a tax-deferred basis.

Inflation   A period of time in our economy characterized by changing economic conditions, including higher prices and a loss of purchasing power.

Information jobs   Jobs that deal in the creating, processing, and storing of information. By the year 2002, approximately 59 percent of the work force, or about 85 million people, are expected to be employed in information jobs according to the Congressional Office of Technology Assessment. These are the positions best suited for telecommuting.

Interest   The amount a borrower pays a lender for the use of the lender's money.

Internet service provider (ISP)   A company that provides individuals and enterprises access to the Internet. An ISP owns or rents the equipment required to have points of presence on the Internet for the geographical area served. Larger ISPs have their own high-speed leased lines so that they are less dependent on telecommunication providers and can provide better service to customers.

Investment objectives   These are long-term goals, usually, where you assess your risk tolerance and investment return expectations developed principally from consideration of what you want to do with your money and where you want to go.

Investment portfolio   A combined group of assets including, but not limited to, stocks, bonds, mutual funds, real estate, and collectibles.

Liabilities   The amount of money that you, a company, or the government owes others.

Limit order   Limit orders mean you want to limit your transaction to a certain price. If you're looking to buy a stock and it's trading at $25 a share, and that's as much as you want to pay for it, then enter a Buy Limit order with a price of $25. Use limit orders when you have plenty of patience and are willing to take the risk of not buying or selling your stock.

Leverage   The use of credit to enhance one's speculative capacity. If you make a down payment of 20 percent or less on your home, you still reap the 100 percent benefit of price appreciation when you sell. Basically, it's a condition where you get the maximum bang for your buck.

Liquidity   When you have sufficient cash available at the time you need it and the ability to get at your money quickly.

Margin   When you trade on margin, you are borrowing monies from the brokerage firm to buy additional securities. You are also charged an interest rate for borrowing this money, known as the *margin rate*. Low margin rates typically run less than seven percent.

Market order   This means you're willing to buy or sell a stock at whatever the market maker (the person in the trading pits) is willing to sell or buy the stock to or from you. When you want fast execution, this is the quickest way to buy and sell stock.

Market price   The last reported price at which an investment sold.

Megabytes   A million characters of storage space.

Mutual fund company   A company that uses its customers' deposits to invest in securities of other companies through their mutual funds and pools the money together into a fund that is based on specific criteria, such as investment objectives and risk tolerance.

NASD   Stands for the National Association of Securities Dealers. Organizes and enforces the rules of fair practice among the brokerage firms in the industry.

NASDAQ   Stands for the National Association of Securities Dealers Automated Quotations. A techno-geek automated information network that provides brokers with quotes on stocks.

Net asset value (NAV)   The value of one share in a mutual fund. When you buy shares, you pay the current NAV per share. When you sell shares, the fund will pay you the NAV less any other sales load (where applicable). A fund's NAV goes up and down daily as its holdings change in value.

Net worth   The total amount of assets you have after you calculate what you own against what you owe.

New York Stock Exchange   Known as the NYSE, this is an exchange where millions of shares of stocks trade during the business week.

Niche   Defined by Webster as a place, employment, status, or activity for which a person or thing is best fitted; a specialized market.

No-load fund   A mutual fund that does not carry any commissions or sales charges.

Offer   The price at which a person is willing to sell his or her stock.

Open order   An order to buy (sell) at a stipulated price that remains effective until it is executed.

Opening price   A security's price at the first trade of the day.

Optical character recognition (OCR)   Software used by many large corporations to read and store letters and numbers in a searchable text format. The human resources department uses this software to filter through hundreds of resumes with a keyword search for job candidates.

p/e ratio   Price-earnings ratio. This measures how much an investor is willing to pay per share given the stock's current level of earnings. You take the stock's market price and divide it by its current or estimated future earnings.

Price-to-book   This is the price per share divided by the book value per share.

PITI   Your total monthly principal and interest, taxes, and insurance payment for your home.

Point   In stock market trading, a point means $1. If XYZ company stock rises three points, it means it rises $3. In real estate, a point is equal to one percent of the mortgage loan.

Prime rate   The minimum rate on bank loans set by commercial banks and only given to its top business borrowers. A benchmark used by consumers to determine loan rates.

Principal   The dollar amount of your initial investment on which you earn interest, typically.

Profit   The money that you have remaining after all costs of either operating a business are paid or when you buy low and sell high.

Prospectus   A legal document that explains the complete history and current status of an investment security.

Purchasing power   The goods and services that you can buy given any amount of money. If there is inflation, you will have a loss in purchasing power of some goods.

Push technology   A technological feature that Web sites utilize to drive information directly to your computer screen without having you log onto their sites.

Quote   It is the highest bid to buy and the lowest offer to sell a security.

Rally   A quick rise following a decline in the general price level of the market.

Real GDP   An economic indicator that measures the sum of all the goods and services bought and sold in the U.S. and also takes into account inflation.

Real-time quotes   Stock quotes that are provided online as buy and sell transactions occur.

Reserve requirements   The amount of money that banks are required to keep in their vault per Federal Reserve bank rules.

Return   The amount of money that you receive annually from an investment, typically expressed as a percentage.

Risk   Any chance of loss.

Sales load   The amount of money charged to your initial investment on a mutual fund—and sometimes when you sell—by a mutual fund company to justify processing and execution costs by an investment professional.

Search engines   You can do so through the different types of indexing systems, much like a library uses a card catalog. These systems on the Web are known as search engines,

Shareholder   A person who has bought ownership, or shares, in a company that maintains a value of at least $1 per share. Also known as *par value*.

Smart card   Basically, plastic credit cards embedded with a computer chip that stores information right on the card. These card-sized computers are used everywhere, from business secure ID cards to paying for highway tolls and buying items on the Internet.

Small business   Basically, a small business has no more than 500 employees and generates no more than $500,000 in annual revenue.

Socially responsible mutual funds   These are mutual funds that invest in companies that have a greater social or moral quality.

Spread   The difference between the bid and ask (offer) price.

Standard & Poor's 500   Also known as the *S&P 500*. This is an index made up of a basket of 500 stocks that is considered to be one of the most well-known gauges of stock market movement.

Stock   A certificate of ownership.

Stock split   A division made of the stock, decided upon by the company's board of directors, to either create more shares or reduce the number of shares, which is known as a *reverse stock split*.

Stockholder   If you buy stock, you are a stockholder.

Stop orders   This type of order is when you own a stock and you want to be sure that you limit your loss on the stock. It is an order to buy (sell) at a price above (below) the current market price.

Techno-phobes   Computer 'fraidy-cats.

Time pacing   A philosophy of running a business where you drive the rhythm of change inside your own company.

Total return   The aggregate increase in the value of the portfolio resulting from calculating all of the pluses and minuses.

Trademark   A word, phrase, symbol, or design—or combination of these—that identifies and distinguishes the source of the goods or services of one party from another. Trademark rights arise from either actual use of the mark or the filing with intent to use the mark with the Patent and Trademark Office (PTO). You can use the symbol ™ to alert the public to your claim, but the symbol ∏ can only be used when the mark is registered in the PTO. A trademark is different from other forms of identity protection (such as a *copyright*, which protects an original artistic or literary work; and a *patent*, which protects an invention).

Typosquatter   Someone who buys up a domain name that is a simple misspelling of a well-known brand name.

Uniform Resource Locator (URL)   Much like your home address, a URL is the string of information that lets people locate specific sites on the Internet. It is unique—no two are the same.

Virtual hosting   Also known as virtual domain, virtual hosting is when the ISP allows you to use your own domain name, www.yourcompany.com, rather than their name followed by yours as in: www.yourserviceprovider.com.yourcompany.

Volume   The total number of shares traded during a given period.

Web authoring tools   Software that allows you to develop and manage a Web site. Programs such as Microsoft's Front Page and Macromedia Backstage make it easy for the novice to work in a WYSIWYG (what you see is what you get) environment without having to learn HTML, the programming language of the Internet. You can edit content, make forms and tables, and create links to pages on your site as well as to other sites. Make sure your ISP supports the software you choose.

Web crawlers, spiders, and robots   Programs that roam the Internet, searching all the available content. In addition to storing links to these Web sites, they also record information about each page that they visit. The information that comes from these searches is used to match your search query to particular Web pages and the link is used to give you the Internet address of the page.

Webzines   An electronic magazine

World Wide Web (WWW)   The part of the Internet that is the most graphical and has become the most commercial. The Web allows you to view and interact with HTML (Hypertext Markup Language) files that can contain graphics, animation, sound, video, and interactive programs. You do this using a software program called a browser.

Y2K   The year 2000.

Yield   The return of an investment, expressed as a percentage.

Index

Symbols

363